Foreign Travelers in America
1810–1935

Foreign Travelers in America
1810–1935

Advisory Editors:

Arthur M. Schlesinger, Jr.
Eugene P. Moehring

THROUGH

THE

LIGHT CONTINENT

WILLIAM SAUNDERS

ARNO PRESS
A New York Times Company
New York—1974

Reprint Edition 1974 by Arno Press Inc.

Reprinted from a copy in
The Newark Public Library

FOREIGN TRAVELERS IN AMERICA, 1810-1935
ISBN for complete set: 0-405-05440-8
See last pages of this volume for titles.

Manufactured in the United States of America

Library of Congress Cataloging in Publication Data

Saunders, William, 1823-1895.
    Through the light continent.

    (Foreign travelers in America, 1810-1935)
    Reprint of the 1879 ed. published by Cassell, Petter,
and Galpin, London.
    1. United States--Description and travel--1865-
1900. 2. United States--Economic conditions--1865-
1918. I. Title. II. Series.
E168.S25 1974   917.3'04'83   73-13148
ISBN 0-405-05472-6.

Second Edition.

THROUGH

THE

LIGHT CONTINENT;

OR,

THE UNITED STATES IN 1877-8.

By WILLIAM SAUNDERS.

"There is the marked peculiarity of the American people apparent almost from the first; the singular buoyancy and elasticity both of the national and individual character. It may be the product of their brilliant, exhilarating, invigorating climate; it may be the accompaniment of the vast horizon opened out by their boundless territory; it may be partly the youth of the nation, but its existence is unquestionable."

DEAN STANLEY.

"I do not think there is any subject to which leaders of working men can more usefully turn their attention than the supplying to those who want it here—accurate and trustworthy intelligence as to their chances beyond the Atlantic."

LORD DERBY, at Rochdale.

CASSELL, PETTER, AND GALPIN:
LONDON, PARIS, AND NEW YORK.

1879.

134189

PREFACE.

WITH a mind full of notes of interrogation, I landed at Boston in September, 1877. The information that I obtained proved to be more interesting and useful than I expected, and, withal, much more difficult of attainment.

Never was such a field for human energy offered to mankind as that which the United States presents—so vast, so free, and so fair. We see three million square miles of the earth's surface combined under one Government, and that Government freely offering inducements to labour and capital from all parts of the world. The efforts of politicians have been supplemented by those of engineers, who have intersected this vast space with railways; thus making the land accessible to all comers, and its produce available for all consumers.

We are surprised to find corn and beef pouring into this country, and Americans underselling our farmers at their own doors. Investigation will diminish the wonder, for the secret is an open one; in the States, land is free, and industry is stimulated by the reward of ownership.

The various aspects of political and social life in the United States afford topics of the highest interest; and I wish that an improved telephone could convey to our minds the tone and feeling of American life—not in all cases for adoption, but certainly for consideration.

A small portion of the following pages appeared in English newspapers during my visit to the States. More time than I anticipated has been occupied in the preparation of this volume, and thus its publication has been delayed; but I have availed myself of this extension of time to bring down some statistical information to the latest date.

Mount View, Streatham, S.W.,
May 27th, 1879.

TABLE OF CHAPTERS.

PREFACE TO THE SECOND EDITION.

THE welcome which has been accorded to this volume, in a most unexpected degree, arises perhaps in some measure from the increased attention which has been given to the United States as a field for agricultural enterprise.

The return of prosperity which I anticipated for the States has rapidly come about. I did not suppose that we should, at such an early date, find there a renewed demand for English iron. The present demand is apparently the result of speculative excitement, and it can scarcely be continued unless the American tariff is materially modified.

A friendly critic has expressed regret that I have not referred to religious parties in the States. The subject was necessarily omitted for want of time and space. The social and religious condition of the people in the United States would afford a most important, useful and interesting field of enquiry, upon which it will give me the greatest pleasure to enter, if future circumstances permit, and if in the meantime it was taken up by a more able writer.

The title of this book has met with almost universal objection. I still like it because it expresses what I felt. No one can travel in the States without feeling that they move over a light continent; light in every sense of the word, although not without shadows.

Streatham, S.W.,
December 1st, 1879.

INDEX.

Hull : Printed by the "Eastern Morning News" Company, 42, Whitefriargate.

THROUGH THE LIGHT CONTINENT.

"HAT parts have you seen?" I asked an American, who said he had just visited Europe. "Yorkshire," was the prompt and confident reply. "Did you go no further?" "No, I saw enough in Yorkshire; I should not like to stop there." It appears that he left that county thirty-six years ago, and he found that the same men who were small farmers then are small farmers now. "All they can make they pay away in rent; their children have not enough food, and the clothes they wear would not be put on by people in America. If they want a gate mended they must ask the agent, who asks the landlord, and then it's not done. The times are bad with us in America now, but not like they are in Yorkshire." So my friend comes back to the States and gives a bad account of Europe, because he has seen farmers in the West Riding who are not prosperous. I do not propose to follow his example, and describe the United States before

I have seen so much as would be covered by a three-penny piece on the map. It is clear that the country is one of almost inconceivable vastness and variety. Of its extent we get some faint notion by looking at a good map, but of the variety of men and manners, of soil and climate, we obtain but little idea. If, however, one parish cannot give a fair idea of a continent, a steamboat may convey some just notion of the character of a people; and on board a Cunard liner an Englishman gets much useful experience of American character. The steamship for Boston was crowded with New Englanders, who were returning to their native soil. Scarcely an Englishman was amongst them, and thus nothing interfered with the practice of American customs and the free expression of American opinions. The favourite subject of conversation was the examination of the detectives at Bow-street; the passengers seemed to have read every line of it. An elderly gentleman was energetic in his condolence with me upon the break down and exposure of our police system. I replied that in one respect the English were very much like the Americans—we thought a good deal more of other people's peccadilloes than our own. He took up my joke in a moment, and at once began to unburden himself as to the political troubles of his own country. He said " We have neglected politics and allowed adventurers to have their own way, and now we feel the want of honest public men. But we mean to get them. I wish we had an aristocracy like yours, we might get some help from such men at this juncture. Our great fault has been that we have not given sufficient attention to public affairs ; but we must neglect them no longer. We begin to see that the government of a country requires more attention than we have given to it ; the railway strike has opened our eyes. Our real difficulty is that the working classes have all the power, and they will never sanction the establishment of an army or a police force sufficient to control themselves." I said that I did not share his apprehensions ; the working classes were not less interested than other classes in the preservation of order, and would soon see the necessity of making sacrifices to maintain it. However, he would not be comforted, and went on to say that one of the difficulties in the way of a strong Government was the continued friction between the national Government and State rights. " We have thirty-seven Governments," said he, " and their interests are so opposed and divided that I do not see how to establish an efficient and permanent union." This conversation showed a character so

very different from the bumptious Yankee of whom
we so constantly read that I thought I must have
met with a very exceptional Conservative, but I
found that his views and apprehensions were shared
more or less by a number of our fellow-passengers ;
and I looked upon it as a hopeful sign that care and
caution had replaced that careless confidence which
is the real source of danger in public as in private
life.

It must be remembered that our company were
exclusively New Englanders. If I had gone in a
New York steamer I should have met with a very
different and much more varied assemblage, as it
was I had a good picture of New England life and
manners ; and the picture was one of which any
nation might have been proud. There was
scarcely a disagreeable person on the ship, and the
quiet, cheerful, friendly way in which they associated
was very pleasant to see. As usual with American
travellers, there were many children amongst them ;
but the only evidence of that precocity of which we
read so much was found in the early manifestation
of common sense and self-control. The most striking
contrast to English life was to be seen in the young
ladies. Here they are " persons " with independent
thought and action, which, under all circumstances,
is efficiently exercised ; they associated with whom-

soever they pleased, without forwardness and without hesitation. Throughout the voyage I did not notice a simper from a woman or a vulgar observation from a man ; even the boys and young men thought their family life the best thing in the world. I asked a lad of fifteen how he was getting on. He replied, " Oh, it is very jolly, but I should like it better if my mother were here ; my father tried to get her to come, but she would not leave the three younger ones." Generally speaking, the mother was travelling with the family group, and was always a great favourite.

As we approached Boston great anxiety was manifested to hear the news, and various speculations were indulged in as to what it would be. When the pilot tumbled on board the only question publicly asked was, " Are the Russians or Turks winning ? " The reply was, " Oh, the Turks are winning hand over hand ; " but when we got the newspapers we found that victories and defeats were awarded to both sides with great impartiality. Groups were immediately formed to read the papers. It was good to see the eagerness with which news was heard and commented upon. " By Jove ! The premium on gold down to 3 per cent. ! railway stock gone up to 10 per cent ! Gambetta sentenced to five years' deprivation of civil rights !" " That means a revolution," exclaimed several voices at once.

Then all was silence for a moment when the heading was read out, "Dreadful Collision in the Channel—100 lives lost;" but there was instant relief, and the subject was promptly dismissed, when the reader added, "'Tisn't an American liner, though." The topics which followed were so American that I was unable fully to comprehend them. But how cheerful we all were after the pilot came on board, and with what vigour we sang that evening—

> The land of the brave,
> And the home of the free.

Every evening we had some excellent singing, but it was much more energetic than usual on the last occasion.

Before landing we were boarded by a small army of custom house officers, who extorted an oath from each passenger as to the contents of his packages. The oaths and the contents were not found in all cases consistent, and, much to the amusement of some cynical persons, a very shabby-looking priest was made to pay 36 dollars for bales of silk and cotton. A liberal-minded cabman informed me that the legal charge for driving to the hotel, about two miles distant, was 20s., but he offered his services for 14s., which declining, I got upon an omnibus, the driver having assured me that it would leave in a quarter of an hour, but which remained for an hour and a half. During this time I visited the steerage passengers who, under a long shed, were patiently waiting the advent of the custom house officers to overhaul their small belongings. They declared that the voyage had been a pleasant one, and, be it said to the credit of the Cunard Company, I could not get a complaint out of them.

The day we landed at Boston was set apart for the dedication of a monument which has been erected to the memory of those who fell in the late war. I found all business and street traffic suspended for a grand procession, which was two hours late and three hours long, but the wonderful patience of the people knew no abatement; they waited and watched under a burning sun from early morning until late in the afternoon. There was not much enthusiasm, but Generals Hooker and Mc.Clellan were well received. The cheering was chiefly bestowed upon the tattered standards and wounded men. Oddly enough, there were a number of "Confederate prisoners" paraded under a big banner, and they marched along apparently rather proud of the proceeding. But I was most surprised on reading a paragraph in a Boston paper stating

that the number of Confederate officers taking part
in the procession would be fewer than was expected,
because it was found that they were too poor to pay
their travelling expenses and too proud to accept
assistance! I thought how remiss the Duke of
Wellington had been in not inviting French officers
to dine with him on the 18th of June and offering to
pay their travelling expenses. This monument
and demonstration do not meet with universal
approval in Boston; several people expressed a
very decided opinion that their "domestic quarrel"
should be allowed to sink into oblivion. In the
evening the whole of Boston was assembled
on the Common to witness the illumination of the
monument by electric-light. This illumination was
marvellously effective, and enabled the spectators to
see the smallest details of the monument much more
distinctly than by daylight.

While I was waiting for the display, I had a
good opportunity of conversing with working men
on the condition of the country. They complained
that wages had fallen thirty per cent., and that work
was very difficult to obtain. One of them, who
appeared to be of a convivial disposition, thought
that the worst thing in the country was the cost of
good fellowship. According to his view of the case,
you must treat a fellow when you meet him, "and

it costs a precious lot here, where you can't get a glass of beer under twopence-halfpenny." His companion considered that didn't signify, as a fellow could get on very well without the drink. He liked this country because a man was more independent. "In England you never see your master, but only the foreman, and if you don't bow to the shop foreman as if he were a lord you have little chance of keeping your place. In this country you see your master and you see your foreman, and both are as civil to you as you are to them." Nevertheless, this man was going back to Manchester for the winter, because work was so slack in Boston, but he expects to return to America in the spring. Our convivial friend was much scandalised because Wendell Phillips had been advocating Woman Suffrage. He said nobody can do anything in politics without attending caucuses, and if a woman left the house in the evening for a caucus, the man would have to stay at home and look after the children. This he seemed to regard as the horror of horrors. I suggested that perhaps it would be quite as fair if the man took his turn at stopping at home sometimes, but he declined to look at the matter in this light.

Boston is the home of New England capitalists. I was more than once informed that "Chicago is owned at Boston." Upon the fine buildings and wharves of that flourishing city Boston people have mortgages, and many of the railroads throughout the States are controlled by Boston shareholders. I afterwards discovered that Old England capitalists have investments at Chicago and elsewhere in the States to a much greater extènt than I had imagined.

Agriculture does not flourish in Massachusetts, of which State Boston is the capital, and while many of the farmers have gone West in search of better land the remaining inhabitants have devoted themselves largely to manufactures. We are beginning to find out in our own country how well they are succeeding. Even calicoes are now sent to England from the new country, and, as to watches, one company alone is sending to England 30,000 annually. There can be nothing in the circumstances of the two nations which gives one any natural advantage over the other in such a matter as the making of watches, and I determined to discover what it is that has turned the tables upon us, and not only deprived our watchmakers of the American market, which they used to supply, but actually taken from us a large portion of our home trade.

By the courtesy of Mr. Robbins, the manager

of the American Watch Company, I had an opportunity of inspecting the company's works at Waltham, which is situated a few miles from Boston. The establishment and the people connected with it present those appearances of comfort and prosperity, connected with superior intelligence, which have been so repeatedly noticed by writers who have described American manufactures and the people employed therein. It is clear that the American manufacturer commands the services of thoughtful, intelligent, and industrious workpeople. In the manufacture of watches this is a most important element; but as good and steady workmen are to be found not only in England but in Switzerland, formerly the centre of the watch business, we must look to other causes for the change which has come over the business of watchmaking. This change has been mainly brought about by the adoption of improved machinery. The delicate parts of a watch, which are so small that they cannot be examined without a microscope, are made much more correctly by machinery than by hand labour, and it is by perfecting the machines which cut and polish the delicate gearing of watches that so much excellence and accuracy have been obtained. Not only must the work of making watch wheels be done by a machine in order that they may be perfect, but the

machines themselves which do this work must be
made by machines, or they are not sufficiently exact
for the purpose. It is simply by the development
of suitable machinery that the American watchmakers have been enabled to distance all competitors. How completely they have done this is
obvious from the fact that the export of watches
from Switzerland to the United States has fallen
from 366,000 watches in 1872 to under 75,000 in
1876, while at the same time the English watch
trade has been seriously disturbed by the exportation from the United States to this country of 30,000
watches annually. So great has been the improvement in the business of watchmaking that in America
each workman produces on an average 150 watches
per annum, while in Switzerland only 40 watches
per annum are produced by each workman. If
in the space of seven years the Americans have
made such advances in one branch of industry, it
is clear that we must look out for our laurels. We
shall have, obviously, close competition in all parts
of the world. A few days before my visit the American
Watch Company had secured a contract from the
English Government for the supply of watches to
our own people in India, and this contract was
awarded to them in the face of a general competition.

Whatever the Americans were in former times it is certain that they are not now loquacious and inquisitive, as they have been so generally represented. Judging from my present experience, I should say that they are the quietest and most orderly people upon the face of the earth. Their silence is often oppressive. A party of Americans will often go through a meal without saying a word, and such a thing as a general buzz of conversation I have not heard since I left England. At Boston I entered a large shaving establishment, where there were a dozen operators, and several people waiting to be operated upon. When a chair became vacant the foreman pointed to the man whose turn came next, and he took the seat; but not a word was said. After being there some time I looked at the clock to see how long we should go on without speaking, and for the space of nine minutes the only sound was one sneeze and one enquiry as to the amount to be paid. I have since spent some weeks in this country, and have travelled through New York, Albany, Niagara, Buffalo, and Pittsburg; and although the people are not all so silent as in Boston, yet quietness and good order are universal. Americans will wait at a railway station without even kicking their heels. At a public meeting speakers will be patiently heard who would be shut

up in five minutes at a meeting in England. At
Gilmore's Gardens, in New York, a large company
assembled to hear a telephonic concert, which was
an entire failure; for two hours the patience of the
audience was tried, but not exhausted; several
hundreds of people had paid 2s. each for admission
to hear the telephone, and had heard nothing, but
no one complained. It is not difficult to ascertain
the origin of this quiet, patient order of behaviour.
On visiting the public schools you discover the
discipline which produces such results; if the
pupils go from one room to another, in doing so
they march to the sound of the piano, and the
slightest tendency to disorder, if it should arise, is
corrected not by words but by signs. From five
years old until fifteen or seventeen every American
is subjected to this constant drilling. Here the
school-master is the drill-sergeant, and his operations are universal.

To get a just idea of American men and manners
it is essential to visit small country towns and
villages, where all the merits and demerits of
practical Republicanism are to be seen in their
native vigour. The traveller on presenting himself
at the village hotel is regarded by the host with
unconcealed suspicion; if the scrutiny to which he
is subjected proves favourable, he is informed that

dinner will be ready about one o'clock, at which time the bell will be rung. About the appointed hour the bell rings ; you wander in the direction of the sound, and find yourself in a sort of kitchen, where several people have taken their seats. Silence prevails, and if you wish to break it you must be on your guard as to the manner of doing so. It will not do to begin upon the weather, which does not change here so frequently as in the old country, and to make an observation thereupon would at once indicate that you spoke mainly for the sake of talking ; it is necessary to think of something that you really want to know.

At the first village dinner which I attended I ventured to begin the conversation by asking about the geological formation of the neighbourhood. It was a hazardous experiment, but it proved entirely successful. One of the persons present, apparently a resident in the house, promptly gave me a clear and correct statement, which fully answered all the questions raised, beyond which he did not attempt to go. Other topics were discussed in a manner equally satisfactory. A quiet young man at table put in an occasional sentence with excellent judgment. After dinner I wished to visit a cheese factory, and arranged for a small carriage to be provided for the purpose ; on setting out I discovered that the intelligent young man at the dinner-table was the ostler, who took his seat to drive me to the factory. At a short distance we met a gentleman and lady driving a handsome pair of horses in a good carriage. They gave a familiar bow as we passed, but I did not remember having seen them before. We then met a young lady with blue spectacles, who seemed quite anxious for a recognition ; but I was sure that I had never seen her, and it then came to my slow mind that the gentleman and ladies were bowing to the ostler. The ostler proved to be as intelligent in the carriage as he had been at the dinner-table, and explained that the farms we were passing were generally of about 150 acres, with 35 cows on each ; that throughout the year the farmer, his wife, and one man would do all the work, except just at the haymaking, when an extra hand would be hired. Some potatoes, and a little corn, and probably fruit would be grown on each farm. The value of the land, including the house and farm buildings, was usually 100 dollars, or £20, per acre. The wages paid to the man-servant on the farm varied from 15 dollars to 20 dollars per month with board, or 30 to 35 dollars without board. The calves were usually killed at three days old, when the skin was worth a dollar. The milk was taken twice a day to the cheese factory, where it was sold for one cent (one half-penny) per pound, and the farmer might fill his cans with whey or butter-milk, free of cost, and bring it home for the pigs. At the cheese factory we found most convenient arrangements for receiving and weighing milk, which was poured into tinned receptacles about 15 feet long and 5 feet wide ; they were surrounded with running cold water when it was desired to cool the milk, and with steam when it had to be heated. Three men and a girl make all the milk from 800 cows into cheese and butter. These factories have proved to be of the greatest use to American farmers. They save them from all the trouble of making butter or cheese, and provide the merchant with a uniform quality which can be easily bought or sold, whereas the various small lots when made at each farm were irregular in quality, difficult to buy, and almost impossible to sell. On returning from the factory the intelligent ostler drove me round the village and explained its political institutions. The "township" was governed by a president and two trustees elected annually. One of the trustees was the path-master, and the other the poor-master—one repaired the roads, the other relieved the poor. It seemed that each administered his office very much in accordance with popular sentiment, and here, as

elsewhere throughout the States, public opinion was
in favour of low rates and unrepaired roads.   As to
the relief of the poor, it was administered much
more liberally in this district than it is in the old
country.

The houses were built of wood, as is the case
universally outside of cities.   They were clean,
roomy, and comfortable—there was not a sign of
squalor or poverty throughout the locality.   The
country was undulating and beautiful, abundance of
the original forest having been left untouched.
Children are certainly no burden here ; at sixteen
years of age both boys and girs usually leave the
parental roof, and return to it afterwards only as
visitors.   The boys seek their fortune in such ways
as suit them, and the girls get good wages at once
at factories or hotels not far off.

Into the midst of this Arcadia the demon of
speculative invention is now introducing a system
of which it will be well for the English Home
Secretary to take note.   English consumers of
American cheese are being made the victims of a
new and rapidly-developing system of American
ingenuity.   Not content with the ordinary profits
on cheese-making, some astute American has taken
out a patent for introducing refuse grease into these
rural cheese factories.   By this system the cheese

factors are enabled first to take the cream from the milk, and then introduce a villainous fatty substance which restores the cheese-making power, and thus turns the grease of New York into cheese for the English market.

Notwithstanding the obvious prosperity, comfort, and ease which surround the life of a New England farmer, numbers of them are now leaving the Eastern for the Western States, where land is cheaper, and can be much more profitably occupied. It is not that farmers here are badly off, as has been represented, but it is through the attractions of Western lands that they are tempted to leave their old homes in the East and follow the setting sun. On this account farms in the East may be had at very moderate prices, and the produce, although not equal to that of Western farms, is sufficient to enable a family to be supported in comfort.

During the last three years the people of America have been brought in contact with a great social difficulty. The spirit of rampant speculation and extravagant expenditure which have prevailed since the Civil War, and brought on the crisis of 1874, have paralysed industry, and thrown thousands of people out of employment. It is an odd thing to hear in this country the cry of " over-population," when the signs of a want of people to occupy and improve are manifest on every side; and yet many persons attribute the present difficulties to an excess of immigration, and believe that Europe is responsible for the troubles from which they are suffering. They think that if they could stop immigration, abolish the negro, and send back the Heathen Chinee, that then there would be abundance of work for everybody at the extravagant prices which became prevalent at the time of the war. The natural remedy for evils occasioned by fictitious prices and general extravagance would obviously be a return to natural prices and to the good old custom of living within your income; but this is not a pleasant process. Both tradesmen and workmen resist a reduction of prices and wages as long as it is possible to do so, and a multitude of workmen throughout the States find it much easier to become tramps than to continue work at such rates as are within the power of masters to pay. In course of time they become enamoured of a roving life; and by this obvious and simple process the Eastern States are overrun by a set of sturdy beggars. At Boston I saw scores of them every evening in the park. It is now dangerous to walk through the park and public gardens after nightfall, for fear of falling into the hands of these wild men. At New York a beggar is planted at every corner, and well-dressed men constantly bring themselves alongside of pedestrians, and make piteous appeals for alms. Throughout the country districts tramps walk into houses, sit down unceremoniously, and demand assistance, which is given, or refused at the risk of the barn and hay stacks being fired. Some of the States are waking up to the necessity for repressing this mendicancy, but it is contrary to public feeling and practice to punish anybody. If at length a man is sent to prison, he finds it a little paradise, where all his earthly wants are anticipated, and his intellectual and spiritual aspirations duly provided for. If he likes to work, he is carefully taught a trade ; if he feels indisposed, he remains in his well-warmed, well-ventilated, and well-lighted room. As for food, he gets the best the country can produce, served with such cleanliness and polite attention as would cause any hotel to be over-crowded. When a friend was driving me home, I remarked how many ladies you see driving in America. "Yes," he said, "you see a good many, especially on this road, which leads to the gaol, they are constantly going there to visit their friends."

There must be plenty of work to be done in a country which is 3,000 miles across, and which scarcely possesses a fully-cultivated farm, a well-paved street, or a sound road. Obtaining employment here is a question of price, but so extravagant are the ideas of the working classes that many of the conveniences and necessaries of life are run up to prohibitory prices. Some minor matters may, perhaps, best illustrate the excessive demands of labour. The usual charge for shaving is 10d. ; the lowest price I have seen marked up in places equivalent to the 1d. and 2d. shaving shops in London is 5d. For selling a newspaper a newsboy requires and obtains 1¼d. profit, whereas in London he is content with one-third of a penny. For cleaning boots the price usually charged is 5d., lowest price 2½d. The wholesale price of fruit here is very low. Apples are 8s. per barrel of 150lbs., and for 2s. you get half a bushel of peaches ; and yet these fruits cannot be bought in the street so cheaply as in London. The usual charge for washing a pocket-handkerchief is from 4d. to 6d. Cabmen appear to be idle nearly all their time ; and if you hire a cab to take one person and two small packages to the hotel the charge will be 14s. If you hire by the hour the charge will be 8s. ; and this in a land where the cost of horses and their keep is one half less than in London. I have asked working men if they can obtain washing or other services at less than these rates; they answer that they cannot. Thus they are obliged to do everything for themselves or leave it undone, and are the first to suffer from such excessive charges. When men prefer idleness and beggary to working for less than rates so extravagant as these, they deserve no sympathy; and public progress is paralysed by such charges. It seems a mystery how they can be maintained in the face of competition, but I believe the explanation to be this : If any man or boy did work for less than the usual charge he would probably get his head punched, whereas if he remains idle, and says that he is starving, he receives small presents, and he naturally prefers the latter. It is, however, scarcely fair to blame the workman and tradesman for keeping up prices when their Government maintain a Protective system for the special purpose of raising the price of certain manufactures for the benefit of individuals. The whole system of American life is founded on the great idea of Protection, which has taken so firm and fatal a hold of the American mind, and which has done so much to retard the national development.

The first view of autumnal tints on American foliage is a sight never to be forgotten, especially when seen under such favourable circumstances as steaming up the Hudson from New York on a bright fine day. I had intended going right on to Albany, but when I saw the beauty of the district I could not resist the temptation to stop at the Catskill Mountains. With a small hand-bag that will supply his wants for twenty-four hours, the traveller may stop whenever he pleases; the conductor will always fix your ticket, and as for baggage, that is represented by little pieces of brass, and if you have these in your pocket any experienced traveller in this country would think you an idiot if you felt any anxiety about it. Of course, the trunks will be at the place for which they are checked, and, as a matter of fact, they always are there. It is said that no American can read his Bible during October, because his wife has filled the book with pressed leaves, tempted so to do by the deep hues and beautiful forms which are seen in perfection at this period of the year, and especially so on the Catskill Mountains, near to the original abode of Rip Van Winkle. I spent a delightful day in gathering some specimens that were within reach, and brought back an armful to the hotel, it was useless to attempt to carry them further, but I left them with much regret.

With the first sight of Niagara I expected to be disappointed, but I was much more disappointed than I expected. I remained for three days, during which time it seemed to get bigger, and when the earth trembled with the force of the falling water the whole effect was impressive ; but beautiful or pleasing it is not. A waterfall may be spoiled by having too much water, just as an illumination is destroyed by too much light. It is only when the overflow is sufficiently thin to break and scatter as it falls that falling water is beautiful. This effect is seen with the American Fall, and at the end of the great Horseshoe Fall, where the overflow is comparatively slight; but the great bulk of the water goes over the centre of the Horseshoe in a straight determined manner which looks like business, but not like beauty. The surrounding country is as flat as a dining table, and a level district is not interesting even though nature has cut a big drain through it. The islands amongst the rapids above the falls are pretty and pleasant, and two or three days can be passed here very agreeably. After leaving the place the scene seems to grow and expand upon the memory, and certainly it is one which will never be forgotten. The water appears to be concentrating on the centre of the Horseshoe Fall, which is evidently breaking away, and the sides of the Horseshoe, which are now the most beautiful part, will be dry if this process is somewhat extended. Indeed, if it should be greatly developed the whole fall will become a mere rapid.

Near Niagara is an Indian reservation. About 7,000 acres of excellent land have been set apart for the use of the Indians, and this in many cases they are cultivating with satisfactory results. I found ten horses and a dozen men with a machine threshing excellent oats, and the whole was worked just as efficiently by these so-called Indians as it would have been by Germans or English. The tribe are increasing in numbers, and are upon the whole prosperous. They preserve their traditions and government, but they are by no means of pure Indian blood. Anyone may be received into the tribe by permission, and by marrying a squaw.

From Buffalo to Pittsburg the traveller passes through the district where oil has been struck so many times during the last eighteen years. Contrary to my expectations, the region is beautifully situated, forming a series of well-wooded hills and valleys, which are not disfigured by the process of getting oil. Wonderful indeed is the work which American energy and ingenuity have performed in the development of this industry. Generally speaking, the oil is reached by a boring 1,300 feet deep. For about five hundred feet the bore is made five inches in diameter, and lined with a five-inch wrought-iron pipe. The object of this is to keep

out water, which is found down to that depth.
Beyond 500 feet the bore is made two inches in
diameter. When oil is reached, if it does not flow
freely, a charge of dynamite is exploded at the
bottom of the bore, which often has the desired
effect ; a pump is then introduced, worked with
wooden rods $1\frac{1}{4}$ inch in diameter. There are
thousands of these pumps kept working at about
1,300 feet from the surface of the earth, and the
skill and perseverance necessary to carry on such
operations will be obvious to anyone. The holes are
generally bored by contract, and men who have
become efficient in such difficult work make large
profits. The cost of boring seems to be exceedingly
small when compared with the cost of similar work
in England. A boring will be carried down the
whole distance in about sixty days. Some of the
wells flow naturally to the surface, and from others
a vehement rush of gas takes place ; this gas is
now extensively utilised, and is effective in the
production of light and heat. Most of the neigh-
bouring towns are illuminated thereby, and at
Pittsburg I saw two ironworks in which fifty
puddling furnaces were kept going by the gas
brought a distance of twenty miles in a pipe not
exceeding six inches in diameter. The pressure is
so great that a pipe about an inch in diameter will

supply a puddling furnace, and keep up an intense
glow of the purest heat without a particle of smoke,
and, as a puddler said, without one quarter of the
trouble occasioned by the use of coal.

The industrial advantages of Pittsburg are
probably without a parallel in the world. I have
already described the flow of natural gas, which,
after the small outlay required for laying pipes has
been made, provides a fuel of unequalled value,
absolutely without cost. Coal is also found, of the
best quality, in the most convenient form. In other
coal fields the miners have to sink shafts and
expend much capital in arrangements for lifting the
coal and the water which penetrates the mine ;
but here no such difficulties present themselves. The
coal is found in a bed about five feet thick in the
centre of the adjoining hills. It crops out at a
considerable height above the level of the valley,
and is obtained at once by driving right into the
hill. As the bed of coal is nearly level, waggons
are easily drawn by mules to the mouth of the
mine, and then lowered on an incline. From this
point one small engine will take 400 or 500 tons
daily to the river, or the railway which runs along
the valley. I visited the mines of Messrs. H. B.
Hayes and Company, who are working three
thousand acres of this coal, about six miles from

Pittsburg. From the facilities afforded by nature it will be seen that very little ingenuity is required to mine the coal and put it on board; but these natural facilities are supplemented by excellent arrangements. At the delivery stage I noticed that eight waggons, each containing about a ton, were brought up, tipped, and the coal in each received and weighed, in ten minutes. Six men were employed at this work, and would put on board from 400 to 500 tons daily. The coal is received in flat-bottomed barges, each containing 500 tons, and at the proper season ten of these barges will be taken in tow by a small steamer and carried down the river as far as New Orleans, a distance of 2,000 miles, at a cost of transit, estimated at 2s. per ton for 600 miles, which is, probably, the cheapest in the world. The best hand-screened coal is put on board at the tip at five shillings ($1\frac{1}{4}$ dollars) per ton. This coal is of excellent quality for domestic purposes and for the manufacture of gas. We have thus a combination of the best coal with unequalled facilities for mining and transit; but so great is the depression of American trade at the present moment that even here the coal mines are but partially worked, and during the last few hours that I spent with the foreman of Messrs. Hayes' mines half a score miners applied to him for employment, which he was unable to give. The miners earn when at work about three dollars, or 12s., a day, and they have lately organised a successful strike, which has somewhat improved their position. It is a regular feature of American industry that, no matter how many men are wanting employment, those who are engaged often make a successful strike by boldly intimidating those who wish to take their places. The power which the men thus have is, however, of very questionable advantage ; it tends to retard industrial enterprise, and capitalists hesitate to enter upon undertakings which are subject to such violent interruptions. Trades unions are not organised in America on anything like the extensive scale which prevails in our own country, but local combinations seem to be often successful from the want of sufficient power on the part of the Government to prevent that violence which takes by force what the circumstances of the case do not by any means justify. In this respect the working classes merely follow the example set by capitalists : monopoly and restriction are the evil genii of American life. This is seen in the conduct of railroads. The great object of the railway directors is to secure a monopoly by combinations, in which the public interests are ruthlessly sacrificed. Such a combination has recently jeopardised the oil business ; big railway and oil men have lately combined to raise the rates for the conveyance of oil, and have thus rendered the existence of small oil producers impossible, as no chance is allowed to those who are not in the ring. Formerly the seat of the oil refining was at Pittsburg, but it suited the purpose of some railway magnates to remove it to a district in which they were personally interested, and this was accomplished by raising the rate of transit from Pittsburg, and giving more favourable terms to other places. How unjustly and ungenerously rates are arranged may be gathered from the fact that the charge for the carriage of ploughs from Pittsburg to New York in July last was 67 cents. per 100lb., whereas ploughs were conveyed from Chicago to New York, double the distance, for $22\frac{1}{2}$ cents. per 100lb. It was mainly through the bitter feeling occasioned by tariffs injurious to Pittsburg that the railway companies were subjected, during the late strike, to such a hostile expression of public opinion, which declared itself unmistakably on the side of the strikers, and which would have sustained them through the contest but for the riots which took place.

THE WESTERN STATES.

At Pittsburg are to be seen some of the rougher sides of American life, and these are further developed as the traveller advances towards the West. It was at Pittsburg that I first saw an American with his legs on the table. At Chicago the gentleman to whom you have a letter of introduction will throw back his chair, put his feet on the writing desk, and " guess there are many things in Chicago to astonish a Britisher." This was the first sign of brag which I discovered in travelling fifteen hundred miles. What chiefly astonished one Britisher at Chicago was the condition of the streets.   He arrived on a wet day, and unless a traveller sees Chicago on a wet day he loses one of the most wonderful experiences which the world affords.   To find your carriage rushing into a bog alongside of a pavement crowded with passengers, and in front of houses or buildings which appear to reach up to the very heavens, produces a new sensation. This danger may come upon you quite unexpectedly, or perhaps you may be saved from it by a notice such as is sometimes exhibited across the chief streets, which informs you that " there is no bottom here."   You then venture at your own peril, and when you begin to sink there is no knowing where you will stop. In, streets which are supposed to have a bottom the wheels go through almost to the axles, and the well accustomed horse puts himself to the work with a determination which shows that he has previously conquered similar difficulties. At brief intervals you come in contact with crossings, over which your carriage rises and falls again like a ship in a heavy sea. The foot passengers are kept out of the mud by means of a plank pavement raised on tressels, which is tolerably safe if you do not fall over the edge or allow your leg to go through any of the numerous holes, which would be regarded as dangerous in any other place.

The chief feature of Chicago is the cattle yards extending over 750 acres, where the cattle from a thousand hills and plains are assembled, and sold for death and transport to distant lands. Over a million cattle are sold annually in these yards, and the number of pigs exceeds four millions. The value of the live stock passing through annually is now about twenty-five millions sterling. A large proportion of the cattle are slaughtered and packed up in tins or tierces for export, chiefly to Britain. The extent of business carried on here is indicated by the fact that one firm kill and pack over one thousand head of cattle a day during the season. Another concern slaughter and cure 3,000 pigs daily. I did not visit the slaughter houses or pig killing establishments, and therefore I will not venture to describe them.

Chicago is the birthplace of Reaping Machines. Mr. Mc.Cormick, the grandfather of the present manager of the firm, founded the business and made these machines common in America almost before they were known in England. At the last great fire this huge factory for reaping machines was burnt to the ground, and it was determined to rebuild it at a distance of five or six miles from the city. Many of the workmen continue to live in Chicago, and a train of omnibuses takes them to and fro morning and evening. It was expected that the men would have obtained houses near the factory, and some have done so, but many of the wives of the artisans are fond of gossip, and object to remove their residence from the centre of intelligence.

If you ascend a tower at Chicago, the horizon presents the same perfect circle which is seen from a ship at sea ; the land is so level that no difference in the elevation can be discovered by the most experienced eye. For more than a thousand miles to the south-west it rises just enough to allow of drainage. A good deal of this distance is necessarily travelled at night, but, as far as it is visible, the whole country, from Chicago to Cheyenne, seems to be good land, most of it free from timber and at once available for the agriculturist.

"Go West, young man," was Horace Greeley's advice, and West I went accordingly. I was determined, if possible, to find out what the West really is, and I concluded that to do this most effectively it would be desirable to stop at some small station on the Western Railways and visit the farms in the locality. I chose Grand Island, on the Union Pacific Railway, as my first stopping-place, partly because it is as nearly as possible the centre between the Atlantic and Pacific Oceans, *i.e.*, just half-way across the continent. It turned out, however, to be a larger place than I expected. A capital hotel has been erected by the railway companies, and placed under excellent management. At a charge of 8s. per day the traveller can live at this hotel in cleanliness and comfort. I hired a pair of horses and drove out about fifteen miles, and a more delightful drive it would be difficult to imagine; the bracing air of the plains gives an enjoyment to life which is never felt in more relaxing atmospheres. Everywhere in America the horses are cheerful and good tempered,

and ours bounded along over the springy road as if
they enjoyed it.   I first noticed a herd of about 150
cows, which I found was the town herd.   Any one
who can get a cow may have it kept with the town
herd on paying his share of the cost of looking
after.   As at most other places in the West, a large
proportion of the ground near Grand Island,
although owned, is not occupied, and is, therefore,
available for grazing purposes.   Thus any family
who can buy a cow, at a cost of about four pounds,
and a few boards to make a shed, can get it grazed
from April to November for the payment of a few
shillings, and for the remainder of the year it may
be kept on excellent hay from the prairie, which is
obtainable at 12s. per ton.   It is no wonder that you
never see any people in America who look as if they
wanted food when the necessaries of life are so
cheaply and easily provided.   We drove through
several farms ; on most of them the wheat had been
already threshed, but the Indian corn was still un-
gathered.   There were, however, sufficient threshing
machines at work to enable me to see that the wheat
was of good quality, though the quantity is not large,
from the fact that no pains are taken with cultivation ;
everything is done in the roughest manner, and the
use of manure often entirely ignored.   A Western
farmer looks upon manure as an incumbrance which

he has to get out of his way. Mr. Macdonald, who has written some excellent letters to the *Scotsman*, which have recently been published under the title of "Food from the Far West," says "It sounds strange to a Scotsman to hear a farmer assert that his land, for so many years farmed for wheat, will no longer produce paying crops of this variety, and in the next breath complain that he does not know where to put his farmyard manure to be out of the way—all the hollows around the sheds having already been levelled up." What is called ploughing is merely a scratching of the ground to an irregular depth of two or three inches, and not even by accident does a furrow ever form a straight line. With the exception of Indian corn, the crops are usually so hidden by weeds that you can only guess what they are; the Indian corn towers above the weeds, and becomes prosperous from its own native strength, and in spite of all neglect. At each farmstead fifty or sixty pigs are usually to be seen enjoying themselves on the corn, which is given to them in the husk; they seem so perfectly satisfied while they are munching, and sleep so soundly afterwards, all in a large heap, that animal enjoyment can scarcely be more fully developed. It is said of some of the immigrants from the north of Europe who settle in the Western States that they give the best of their produce to their cattle, the next best to their pigs, and what the pigs won't eat they eat themselves. This description may give a true idea of the hardships endured by those who take land with insufficient means, but it is not of general application. So far as food is concerned, the condition of the Western farmer is usually that of wholesome abundance. The farm houses and buildings vary with the tastes and means of the owner. Many persons go there without money to provide themselves with the ordinary necessaries of life, and in their passion to become landowners endure privations to which, under other circumstances, they would never submit. The Government will grant 80 acres of land within twenty miles of a railway, or 160 beyond that limit, to any one who lives for five years on the land. To a working man this is a great object for which to struggle ; but unless he can command two or three hundred pounds to buy farming implements, build a small house, and get the necessaries of life until his first crops come in he will be subjected to severe hardships, and a struggle which it will be difficult to bring to a successful issue.

After driving five miles through land slightly cultivated, or not cultivated at all, we come to a school-house, which looked like a solitary barn. On entering, I found five children under the tuition of a young lady, who seemed to be devoted to her work. She said that twenty children in the neighbourhood ought to attend the school, but the average attendance was three only; most of the farmers in the locality were Germans, and kept their children at home. Here, therefore, was a case in which a school-house was erected and an able mistress maintained for the education of three children, while six times that number were allowed to go without these advantages through the cupidity of their parents. The State was evidently doing too much or too little. To build a school-house and maintain a teacher for three children was an extravagance, and it will obviously be necessary to make the attendance of the children compulsory in order to secure for them the benefits provided for their use.

As several flocks of wild geese made their appearance in the distance, our coachman begged permission to drive to the Platte River, where he said we should probably find lots of geese. On approaching the river he took the carriage through a field of Indian corn, the stalks of which were about ten feet high, and completely sheltered the horses, carriage, and ourselves from observation. When I called the attention of the driver to the fact

that we were trespassing, and by crushing down
the corn stalks we were doing damage that would
have to be paid for in England, he laughed and said
that in his country people did what they liked, and
if anybody put Indian corn in the way they must
take the consequences. After travelling about half
a mile in this way we came suddenly upon the
river, which was literally crowded with geese, many
of which were well within gun shot. Three of
them had their heads just in the right line, and
might have been taken off at one shot, but we
had no gun. As a rule there are no game laws
in America, but in this State (Nebraska) the shoot-
ing of prairie hens has been forbidden for three
years on the ground that they are getting scarce.
In the States any laws may be made which are
supposed to be for the public advantage, but none
to give special privileges to individuals. One man,
whether rich or poor, is as good as another, and if
one shoots all may shoot.

The land near the banks of the river was
uncommonly good, and the farmers in the neighbourhood looked prosperous. They were certainly
securing good crops with very little trouble. As
compared with the United Kingdom, this district is
a paradise for *small* farmers. What can a farmer
with three or four hundred pounds do in our own

country ? He may go down on his knees to a landlord for the privilege of paying him every year two
or three times as much as would enable him to buy
good land in the States, where he may become a
landowner, reaping thenceforth all the advantages
of his own industry and taking his position
in public affairs as the equal of men who surround
him.

We came back to the town in time to see the
schools before they broke up. Of these there were
four — three under mistresses and one under a
master. One hundred and twenty-three children
were in attendance, and their education was carried
on in the same cheerful, bright, intelligent manner
which is so obvious in all American schools. The
chief business of the place seemed to be providing
for the teams of horses which brought in produce
from the surrounding farms. It was not an unusual
thing for a farmer to bring a four horse team loaded
with corn a distance of seventy or eighty miles,
and as he takes back his winter supplies there is
considerable business done in the place. Some
of the shops or stores were of great extent, and
appeared to be doing a good trade. A Western
farmer likes to be a " whole man to one thing." He
and his wife devote themselves to the work of the
farm, and make or grow nothing but farm produce.

Even vegetables for their own table they will buy, if possible, rather than potter away their valuable time in sowing small seeds or planting out little cabbages. Hence the demands which they make on shopkeepers are much greater than would be made by a population of equal number in the United Kingdom.

Most of the available Government land in the locality had been taken up, and settlers who wish to be within reach of any sort of civilisation and business would have to purchase land at a cost, probably, of four or five dollars per acre, or more if determined to have a choice spot. So far as I can discover, there is no opening at present in this country for labourers. Any person coming without means would have a hard time of it; but a man with three or four hundred pounds and a strong pair of arms would be able to purchase a good property at the present depreciated rates, and be comfortably independent for the remainder of life. There never was a better opportunity than is now offered for such small capitalists to settle in America. A newly-married couple might go there with the certainty of doing well, provided they had suitable means to make a good beginning; the wife would everywhere be treated with the greatest respect, and with moderately good management need never be

subjected to any special discomforts. They could
buy a farm quite in the country, and grow corn
and wheat, or purchase a few acres of land
near a town and cultivate it as a garden. Either
would be a comparative certainty to those who had
suitable means, good health, and some little knowledge of agriculture.

Cheyenne is the centre of an enormous grazing
district, where the whole talk is of oxen. Young
men desirous of becoming prosperous patriarchs
might go to Cheyenne, where flocks and herds
are counted by tens of thousands, and land is
spoken of by the hundred square miles. Cattle
keeping is done in the same rough and ready bt
incomplete manner in which all agricultural operations are carried on in America. The herds have
to take care of themselves in winter as well as in
summer. During the storms of winter they have a
rough time of it, and lose much of the flesh which
they put on during the summer, while many die
outright ; but a farmer would rather keep a thousand
cattle in this rough and barbarous manner than five
hundred on the plan of giving them corn and
shelter during the winter storms. As the best beef
cannot be produced in this way, it is to be hoped
that competition and the increased value of land
will lead to the general adoption of a better and a

more humane system, which has been already commenced by some of the best graziers, who give their cattle some corn and shelter during the winter season. The profits on grazing appear to be very large, as cattle improve in value at about the rate of five or eight dollars per annum per head, while the cost of looking after them does not exceed one dollar per annum. Two-year-old steers can be purchased at Cheyenne in the spring at twelve to fourteen dollars per head, and when five years old should be worth thirty to forty-five dollars each; after allowing for losses and cost of looking after, the improved value should be at least five dollars per head per annum. Twenty-four thousand head of cattle, weighing from ten to fourteen cwt. each, had been sent from Cheyenne to Chicago between July 1st and October 1st of 1877. If a young man went out to Cheyenne he could become acquainted with the cattle business by living on one of the ranches and assisting the drovers; if he had a little capital he could buy a few cattle and put them in the drove with which he was connected. He would have horses to ride and plenty of space to ride over, with the prospect of becoming as wealthy as Job, if he studied his business and persevered with it. Sheep as well as cattle are kept in large numbers on the plains surrounding Cheyenne. Sheep require much more care than cattle, it being necessary to bring them to the stock-yards every night; this is a more certain mode of doing business, as every morning a man knows how many sheep he has, whereas cattle are collected and counted only twice a year. Wool brings a much higher price in America than it realises in New Zealand or the Cape, and therefore its production ought to be more profitable. Many men have risen from small beginnings to become the owners of enormous flocks, and, as is usual in all human undertakings, this result has been obtained by close personal attention; but no special hardship is involved in this, as most of the men engaged in the work like it above all other employments, and would on no account change their mode of life.

GOLD AND SILVER.

The Rocky Mountains extend from the north to the south of the North American Continent, and in these mountains, and the hills between them and the Pacific Ocean are found deposits of gold and silver. Within the last twenty-five years the precious metals have been discovered at intervals over an area 1,500 miles long and 750 broad. It is impossible to say to what extent these discoveries may continue, but it is probable that what has hitherto been found is the mere fringe of the great bulk of the deposits. The most important of the latest discoveries have been made at the Black Hills.

Mr. Post, of Messrs. Stebbing and Post, bankers, at Cheyenne, described the chief deposits of gold at the Black Hills as being found in a vein of hæmatite ore, which is nearly horizontal, and varies from ten to twenty feet in thickness. Above this bed are porphyry rocks, below it slate. A ton of ore contains from half an ounce to an ounce of fine gold, which is separated from the ore by stamps, of which about 600 are now working at the Black Hills. The cost of stamping this ore is about 1 dol. 75 cents per ton ; the cost of mining is 1 dol., and hauling 50 cents per ton. The ore is conveniently situated at a short distance above the bottom of the watercourse, and is obtained by tunnelling. It is a matter of great importance to the public to know the extent of these gold deposits. The mineral belt, to which reference has been made, is about three miles wide and six miles long, and has been opened by the working of nearly 100 claims; it has thus been thoroughly tested. This little spot of ground, six miles long and three miles broad, probably contains gold to the value of £200,000,000 ; and it can be obtained with great ease, at a cost not exceeding one-third of its value.

It is very unusual to discover gold deposits in horizontal beds ; the gold bearing veins are usually perpendicular, and in a hill opposite to the one described there is a perpendicular vein of quartz containing gold, which has been worked, and produces about one ounce to the ton of ore. Miners in this district are paid from 3 dol. to 5 dol. a day. At present the cost of transit for all goods from Cheyenne costs from 2d. to 2½d. per pound. The road is good, and the distance about 250 miles. Road agents, or robbers, are not uncommon, but will probably soon be hunted down or starved out by improved arrangements for the transport of

gold. Surveys for a railway are being made by
the Union Pacific Company, and as the country
presents but few difficulties, this railway ought to
be constructed in a few months after it is commenced. It should be mentioned that ore containing
a large percentage of silver has been found in the
Black Hills, about twelve miles from the gold mines.

As evidence of the energy with which new
districts are developed in this country, it may be
mentioned that three daily papers are already published at the Black Hills. Although the production
of gold did not commence until June, 1876, before
the end of the year gold to the value of three
million dollars had been produced; the total production during 1877 was expected to reach ten
millions of dollars. The district to which reference
has been made embraces Deadwood, Carter City,
Rapid City, Negro Gulch, and Iron Creek, distant
from Deadwood from 20 to 50 miles, throughout
which gold mines are being profitably worked,
this affords evidence of the extent of the deposits
which have so recently been opened up.

As another instance of the energy with which
operations connected with mining are carried on, I
may refer to the creation of Garland City. This
" city " is the present south-western terminus of the
Denver and Rio Grande Railway, and is the base of

supplies for a mining and agricultural county about
the size of Great Britain. Four months ago Garland
City was not. It was created in four weeks, partly,
like Adam, from the dust of the ground, and partly,
like Eve, from ribs (of timber). It contains several
hotels, two of which are quite imposing in appearance, each of them presenting a street frontage
with twenty-eight windows, and affording excellent
accommodation at a charge of three dollars a day.
Besides these hotels there are twenty - three
restaurants for supplying the wants of hungry and
thirsty miners who flock to the city. Other shops
number about twenty-five, and are mostly handsome
" stores " for groceries, drapery, hardware, and
" notions," including a splendid hair - dressing
saloon, which is much patronised. The total number of houses is 120, and the resident population is
supposed to be about 800 ; but the place is filled
with visitors, some for trade, and others for such
" pleasure " as the place affords. The attendant
who shewed me to my room was good enough to
inform me that a fortune-teller had occupied the
place the previous night. Two lawyers and a
justice of the peace have already favoured the city
with their presence. I looked in (through the
window) at one of the lawyers' offices. This office
contained two handsome rows of books, upon

D

which the lawyer was bringing his understanding to bear by placing his heels upon the shelves, his head resting upon a sofa about three feet below. This position is considered favourable for reflection; the information no doubt flowed downwards from the book-shelves to his cranium.

But the place most frequented, and in fact the only crowded spot, was a restaurant where dancing girls were kept. A notice over the bar informed the visitor that the charge for a dance and drinks was one dollar (four shillings). The walls were covered with outrageously indecent pictures, and some of the wretched girls were not more than twelve years of age. Most of the men and boys present were in rough mining dresses. This is the way in which, for want of knowing better, they take their "pleasure" in Garland City and other border places. The question arises as to what is the use of national education or religious teachers when one man is allowed, for the sake of a few dollars, to bring wholesale degradation and ruin upon men and women. I was glad, however, to see that several respectable women, the wives of the miners in the neighbourhood, were daily coming up by train to join their husbands, which will, no doubt, lead to an improvement. Places like Garland City seem to be quite overlooked by the religious and missionary associations in the States, and for some weeks or months the devil and his angels are allowed to have everything their own way in new localities.

At Greely I first became acquainted with the Colorado system of irrigation. The climate in this district is so dry that only fifteen inches of rain falls annually, and without irrigation agricultural operations would be impossible. Nature has provided an abundant supply of water in the snows which accumulate in the Rocky Mountains and swell the streams in the plains below during the summer, when irrigation is necessary. Irrigation companies have been formed, which bring the water over the plains and supply it to farmers at very moderate prices ; for 20 dol. (about £4) per annum a farmer can obtain water for 160 acres, and the land is so level that it is distributed with little difficulty. The irrigation secures a crop, and the dry climate affords a certainty of saving it, and as the soil is good the crops are generally large and profitable. When the land is manured and pains taken in its cultivation the produce is truly enormous. At the garden of Mr. J. Leavy, I saw celery the white part of which was 30 inches long, cabbages each 10lb. to 16lb., and he assured me that his strawberries, the second year after planting,

produce a quart to each plant; he obtains an
unlimited sale for strawberries, at an average price
of 1s. a quart, for sending to Cheyenne and
Denver. Vegetables sell largely even in Greely,
for neither tradesmen nor farmers take the trouble
to grow them, and, therefore, have to purchase.
Cabbages are a profitable crop, at a halfpenny a
pound; these vegetables are kept in pits until
the spring, when they will bring double that price.
Here, as in many other places in the States,
gardeners might find very profitable occupation by
purchasing a few acres of land and cultivating it as
a market garden.

Greely was established about seven years since
as a co-operative colony. A large extent of land
was purchased by about 700 shareholders, each of
whom paid 155 dollars, and obtained a town lot of
about 30 feet by 150 feet, a suburban lot of 5 acres,
and a farm lot of 40 acres. A supply of water for
irrigation was secured, and the whole seems to have
been judiciously planned and successfully carried
out. The soil is of excellent quality, and the effects
of irrigation are now seen in fine rows of trees and
ornamental gardens. Fruit trees prosper wonderfully; one gentleman shewed me an apple tree which
was started last spring, and had grown a bush six
feet high during the summer. Greely is a Tem-

perance town, where no intoxicating liquors are
allowed to be sold; the regulation appears to be completely observed, and the results are regarded as
quite satisfactory by the inhabitants. It presents a
striking contrast to Omaha and Cheyenne, where
drinking saloons, and the vices which accompany
them, are more rampant than in Eastern Cities.

COLORADO.

I reached Denver late in the evening on a very light night, and taking a stroll I came suddenly and unexpectedly upon a full view of the Rocky Mountains. There they stood, reaching up to the very heavens, and stretching right and left as far as eye could reach. In their rugged calmness, the white moonlight mingling with the pure snow, they looked as if time and eternity were nothing to them. There they stood, the back-bone of the North American continent. They have waited thousands of years for civilisation to reach them, and they are in no hurry now; to them it is all the same whether ants make their nests at their base or miners drive tunnels to reach gold and silver. The splendid resources they provide for mankind are, however, to be wasted no longer. Towns are rising at their bases with people determined to penetrate their fastnesses, and bring forth their treasures. The streams which flow from their snow-clad sides, chiefly in the summer, are being utilised to water the millions of acres of fertile plains by which they are surrounded. Colorado is becoming the El Dorado of the miner, the most promising field for the agriculturist, the greatest attraction to the tourist, and the safest resort for the invalid.

Mining towns are not often pleasant to reside in, and all that can be said for Denver is that this place is one of the best of its kind.

There are, however, localities in Colorado which offer many attractions to settlers. Colorado Springs is one of these. Here the new comer would find himself in the midst of a quiet, orderly, and intelligent population, surrounded with natural beauties and with a climate which affords a panacea for many kinds of disease. Consumptive patients brought here in a dying state not unfrequently recover, and many persons whose life in other localities would not be worth six months' purchase live here in perfect health and security. With an elevation of six thousand feet above the sea, and the peculiar climate which can be found only in the centre of a great continent, the lungs throw off disease and perform their duties in a manner which seems almost miraculous. To the ordinary visitor the air of Colorado is most invigorating, and it enables even the dyspeptic to forget that he has internal organs. I sought in vain for an explanation of the circumstance that cold and heat are not felt here as in other localities.

If in Europe you ascend 6,000 feet you have to beg, borrow, or steal every imaginable wrapper, but here you do not want an overcoat; I enjoyed the open window, although the temperature at half-past six a.m. was only 32 degrees. With this temperature in Europe I could not have endured the rush of outer air which would have entered the room, but in Colorado it was balmy and pleasant. Going over the La Veta Pass, the railway ascends to a height of 10,400 feet, and yet, even in the night air in November, it is quite pleasant to sit on the outside of the car, and peer down the tremendous ravines along which you are carried; at this elevation you are surrounded with snow, and yet there is no feeling of cold. As I have said, I could get no explanation of the fact that cold and heat seemed alike unable to produce any unpleasant effect; in other dry climates, such as Egypt, I found both cold and heat particularly penetrating, and the dryness produced a roughness of the skin which made shaving impossible; but here the effect was to make the skin hard and smooth, so that I never shaved so easily in my life. I use these personal and homely illustrations, as I know not in what other way to convey an idea of the salubrious and agreeable character of the climate.

A settler going to Colorado for business would

be compelled to fix his residence in accordance with his occupation; but anyone retiring from active engagements might choose a delightful residence in Colorado, and lend his capital with perfect security to farmers in the State at 12 to 15 per cent. The system of land registration enables loans to be made with perfect security, and at an expense to the borrower not exceeding 1 per cent It is often greatly to the advantage of a farmer to borrow money, even at the high rate of interest named, as it enables him to purchase cattle for grazing on the unoccupied land adjoining his own, by doing which he obtains a profit two or three times greater than the interest he would have to pay. In default of payment the lender can at once advertise and sell the property on which he has a mortgage, so that if he takes care not to advance too large a proportion of the value of the property he is perfectly safe. To men of business Colorado affords abundant room for mining, corn growing, cattle raising, and gardening. The ravages of the beetle, about which we have heard so much in connection with Colorado, seems to be a thing of the past, and many persons who sold their lands on the appearance of this pest now bitterly repent the haste with which they parted with their property. Grasshoppers are easily destroyed on irrigated

lands by the simple expedient of dropping petroleum oil on the waters used for irrigation ; directly
a grasshopper touches this oil he dies.

   One of the most interesting features of Colorado
is the construction of narrow gauge railways
throughout some of the mountain passes. These
railways are constructed for the purpose of opening
up the mining districts. The Denver and Rio
Grande Railway Company are constructing a line
from Denver to the town of Mamoosa, on the Rio
Grande River. The gauge of this railway is three
feet, and throughout the plains it has been constructed at the low cost of from 4,000 to 7,000
dollars (£800 to £1,400) per mile, including the
cost of plant for working. Throughout the
mountains the cost is necessarily much greater,
amounting to 20,000 dollars, or £4,000, per mile.
Some of the gradients on this line are as steep as 4
feet in 100, or 216 feet per mile ; the smallest
curves have a radius of 197 feet. An engine will
take two passenger cars, with 41 passengers in
each, and a baggage car, over the steep mountain
inclines at a speed of seven miles an hour ; on the
plains the speed is $22\frac{1}{2}$ miles an hour. This railway is well adapted for districts on which the
ordinary railways could not be constructed, or
would be too costly for the traffic they could obtain.

When we see what enormous sums have been wasted on some American lines it is quite refreshing to discover a railway which is being constructed at such a moderate cost, and with so much practical attention to the circumstances of the case ; under equally sensible management, no part of the United States need be left without railways. The times are favourable for economical construction ; the Denver and Rio Grande Railways are buying steel rails at 40 dollars (£10) per ton, and they find a rail 30lbs. to the yard sufficient for the purpose. A large number of tourists are brought over this line by the attraction of the mountain scenery. I never left any place with more regret than that with which I turned my back upon the invigorating plains and refreshing beauties of Colorado ; but it was time to move towards the south and east.

Over the Aitchinson, Topeka, and Santa Fé Railway I travelled from Pueblo to Kansas City, through a district which is but slightly occupied ; for hours and hours you bound over plains without seeing a sign of cultivation, and you feel that millions and millions of immigrants might find abundant room. May they be drawn thither by the prosperity of the United States, and not driven across the water by European distress.

Kansas City is a thriving and ambitious place.

The inhabitants have recently started a corn exchange, and Chicago, being jealous, sent some of her merchants to the first meeting of the exchange, who, in five minutes, bought more corn of the Kansas merchants than they could manage to deliver, and thus "busted" some of their competitors. The Kansas Exchange is, however, going on ; but, as compared to Chicago, it is a slow and solemn affair. On perambulating the city after dark my progress was somewhat impeded by the number of rats which were holding their orgies on the pavement, and seemed to have entrenched themselves in the various recesses between the timbers of which the pavement is composed. The land about Kansas City is undulating ; much of it is of good quality, and abounding timber gives the neighbourhood a pleasant appearance.

Hearing of a farm for sale about six miles from the city, I drove out to see it. The farm consisted of 160 acres, beautifully situated, with a farm-house and buildings, orchards and gardens, the whole being well formed ; the land was very rich, and such as in any part of England would be worth £75 per acre. The price asked was 25 dollars, or £5 per acre, including the buildings. Near to the farm-house was the district school, and as I approached, about four o'clock in the afternoon

—the children were just leaving—I saw three little girls on one horse riding off merrily, and followed by another horse, on which were two much older girls, who, with more propriety, but scarcely less humour, were making for their home. I was told that these girls came daily a distance of four or five miles in this manner. The circumstance afforded another illustration of the all-pervading influence of the American school system.

THE SOUTHERN STATES.

I travelled from St. Louis to New Orleans *via*
Texarkana and Galveston, which gave me an
opportunity of passing through the wonderful iron
region known as the Iron Mountains. Ore is still
being raised here and shipped to Pittsburg and
other places ; but the iron furnaces are shut up, and
several acres of the companies' property are covered
with pig-iron, made from charcoal, for which they
cannot find a market at remunerative prices. We
fell in with the stream of emigration which is now
flowing strongly towards Texas ; sixty or seventy
emigrants went down in our train, and the conductor
said that he had as many every day. These people
were not foreigners, but families from other States
who hoped to do better in Texas. One man told
me that he made up his mind to leave Illinois on
Monday ; he sold all his things on Monday afternoon, and set off with his wife and three children
on Tuesday morning. Under these circumstances,
it is obvious that his belongings must have been
sold at a great disadvantage, and the cost of his
railway fares could not have been less than £15.
It appears quite common for Americans to rush

about in this way; but I fear that here, as elsewhere, such rolling stones do not gather much moss. If a oad harvest, or a drought, or a severe storm, or caterpillars, or potato beetles, make their appearance they rush off to some other spot, thus selling in the cheapest market and buying in the dearest; and much suffering is the result. I heard of some cases in which people overtaken by misfortune were compelled to remain, from their utter inability to obtain the means for removal; and this circumstance had proved the foundation of their prosperity, as they held on until the turn of the tide which led them on to fortune. Here, as in older States, perseverance is the precursor of success.

Texas is at present the chief favourite with emigrants. The eastern part of this State is a swamp, and the western remains in unsettled lawlessness; but the centre is declared to be a Paradise, with excellent soil, and a climate which brings visitors, for profit, pleasure, and health, from all parts of the world. At San Antonio it is declared that people never die; very old persons sometimes dry up and are blown away, but cemeteries are unnecessary. To make a more practical observation I will quote Mr. Macdonald, who writes, "That stock-raising in Texas has been, and is, a profitable line of business there can be no doubt. Almost every one who has entered into it with even a fair amount of care and earnestness, and had any knowledge of the work, has made money; while a great many have raised themselves from the humble position of a herd boy to the possession of great wealth. A gentleman who had been engaged in the stock trade for many years in the south of Texas assured me that, though he had seen a few reckless Americans go to the wall at cattle-raising, he had never known a Scotchman or an Irishman fail; they all make money." He relates a case of a firm which four years since began to buy and fence in cheap lands. They have now 230,000 acres of pasture and their "stock cattle" account shows a profit of 770,000 and they have not used over 35,000 dollars cash on these purchases.

The cattle and sheep of Texas are of very inferior quality, but improvements are now being made.

When entering the Union the State of Texas stipulated for retaining all the land under her own control, and splendid estates can be bought for 2s. an acre or less.

In travelling from St. Louis to the Northern part of Texas, I passed through forest for about 800 miles. I used often to wonder what was the difference between the appearance of an American forest and an English wood. In America the trees are much closer and taller. The opening cut for the railway looks as if it were walled in 100 feet high; the forest is so thick that you can see only a few feet into it. There are occasional small clearings made by the owners of saw-mills, and at such spots one sees a number of dead trees which have been barked near the root, so as to kill them; this also is frequently seen on lands partially cleared for farming purposes. Most of the forests on the railway line through Arkansas and Eastern Texas are swamps, and the change from the invigorating atmosphere of the north-western plains is by no means agreeable. But nothing stands in the way of American enterprise; and men, white and black, will build houses and saw-mills on miasmatic marshes where they may truly say— "Let us work, for to-morrow we die." I saw scores of houses so placed that if anything fell through the floor it would drop into water. I was assured that on such spots negroes die as rapidly as the whites; but still they are occupied, because the timber trade is profitable. As the south coast is approached the trees are covered with moss in a manner which in this country would be destructive to their existence. This moss depends in tassels many feet in length, and is supposed to be beautiful,

E

but it looked to me so much like destruction and decay that I could not admire it. The freaks of nature when she is left to her own devices are not a little interesting. The traveller through a forest is sometimes surprised to find a line of trees standing on stilts so that he can walk right under them, the roots being like forked branches growing downwards. If he is of a contemplative turn of mind he will be puzzled to account for this phenomenon. How could trees have grown with their roots raised several feet in the air? Further on the traveller will probably find a former monarch of the forest prostrate on the ground, and as the timber begins to decay the seeds of other trees vegetate thereon; the roots of these small trees will run down the sides of the decaying timber and reach the ground. In time the trunk of the old tree becomes entirely rotten and disappears, thus leaving the roots of the new trees exposed in the manner which has created interest and surprise.

On arriving at New Orleans the traveller at once discovers the great difference in the social atmosphere, which is manifest at every turn. At the railway station I asked, "Is this the ticket office? and not only received a civil reply, but the persons waiting stood aside to give precedence to a stranger. The first man of whom I asked a

question in the streets raised his hat as he replied.
As I descended from the omnibus in front of the
St. Charles Hotel, a news boy said " Permit me to
sell you a paper, sir, published on the eve of your
arrival."   A Northern boy would have bawled out,
" *Re-pub-lie-can.*   Five Cents.   Last Chance."   On
entering a church the next morning I asked a little
girl at what time the service commenced.   She
said, " When the Sunday school is over."   " When
will the Sunday school be over?"   " When the
bell rings."   " When will the bell ring?"   " When
we have done singing."   No Northern girl, however tiny, could have given such poetical and
unpractical answers.

Judging from the manner in which the congregation was dressed, and the prosperous appearance of the numerous young gentlemen who were
waiting for the young ladies as they came out of
church, I should think that prosperity was returning
to New Orleans.   Of course the slavery revolution
was felt here to its fullest extent.   Thousands of
persons then in affluence are now in poverty and
at work; it is no longer an idle community, everyone sees that usefulness is his only resource.   Much
pains have been successfully taken to introduce
various industries, such as brush making, ice
making, &c.   The people are determined as far as

possible to render themselves independent of the Northern States and to make all the articles they want. The chief ice factory is well worth a visit. The water flows down a series of perpendicular iron pipes cooled by ether, and ice forms on these pipes about a foot thick in two days. The factory is capable of producing seventy tons daily, employing only ten men. The ice is sold at £2 per ton.

The government of New Orleans is peculiar. All authority is vested in the mayor and four assistants, each of whom is paid a suitable salary, and is expected to devote his time exclusively to public business. These gentlemen are subject to election, but between the elections they appear to be under no control. The system gives great satisfaction at present, and I was assured that it had led to improved administration and a reduction of taxation.

In New Orleans, as in many other places in the United States, there is no coin in circulation of a lower value than five cents, or $2\frac{1}{2}$d., so that this sum is the lowest that can be paid for any article. This leads to mcuh extravagance, and I never felt so much respect for the English penny as since I have placed the comforts and advantages it will bring in comparison with coins of higher value elsewhere. Compare an English newspaper, for instance, with the miserable sheet for which you have to pay 2½d. or 5d. in the United States. In mining districts the lowest circulating coin is often a quarter-dollar, or one shilling; nothing less is ever seen or charged. The smallest drink of any kind would be charged a shilling, and the same amount would be paid for any service, however trivial. In mining districts money is easily earned and freely spent, but in ordinary towns and cities the want of a coin of a small denomination is a great inconvenience to the poor.

Labourers are well paid in New Orleans. Negro porters are receiving 70dols. per month, and a strike for higher wages is imminent, but at slack seasons of the year the same men get only 30dols.; some of them are very fine stalwart fellows, who looked as if they could do a good day's work. Tramways in this city are laid down in every direction, and must be very profitable, as they are conducted with great economy; one mule draws the car, and one man acts as driver and conductor. A glass box is placed at the driver's side, and every one who enters the car goes to this box, and drops the exact fare therein. Five cents, or two-pence halfpenny, is the fare for any distance, and so general is the use of these cars that no one walks. I have seen children of apparently poor parents enter the car, pay the five cents., and leave it after riding only two or three hundred yards, a distance which they might have walked with advantage, but the languid habits adopted in hot weather continue after the heat has ceased.

My next stopping place was Montgomery, the capital of Alabama. The city contains 15,000 inhabitants, of whom 8,000 are whites and 7,000 negroes. It is pleasantly situated, and favourably placed for the development both of trade and agriculture. Upon this devoted city a shower of carpet-baggers descended at the close of the war. They came claiming for themselves that they had delivered the slaves, and were now their natural protectors. The whites who had taken part in the war were disfranchised, and the negro vote, therefore, carried the election; but, to make doubly sure, batches of negroes were organised to vote over and over again, and thus an overwhelming majority was obtained for the unscrupulous men who claimed to represent the power and prestige of the Northern States. No sooner were these men installed in office than they began to advance their personal aims by expending or appropriating the public money, and pledging the public credit for the advantage of themselves and their friends. The city had to endure this infliction until 1875, but in December of that year carpet-baggers were ignominiously expelled, and local gentlemen, in whom their fellow citizens had confidence, were installed in their places. The condition to which they had reduced the city is described in a report recently presented by the Mayor. On entering upon their duties the Mayor and his fellow officers found an empty treasury, the City Building advertised for sale to satisfy an execution of a judgment obtained in the United States court, and a large floating debt of unknown amount, as no proper accounts had been kept. This debt, it has since been ascertained, amounted to 167,000dol., on 51,000dol. of which interest was being paid at the rate of twenty-three per cent. per annum. The credit of the city had been pledged to the extent of 500,000dol. for worthless railway bonds, bearing interest at eight per cent. No proper accounts had been kept, so that it was difficult to tell what was owing to or by the city. The absence of accounts was part of the plan under which it was hoped to cover the personal appropriations of the former officers, but subsequent investigations have fixed upon them defalcations to the extent of 11,785dol., which it is hoped may be recovered.

Such were the difficulties which had to be met by the newly-elected Mayor of Montgomery and his

officers.   In sixteen months from entering on their
duties they were enabled to report that the sale of
the City Building had been averted by an arrangement with the judgment creditor, and that under
the terms arranged three-fourths of the debt for
which the building had been mortgaged was paid,
and the remainder in course of liquidation.
Respecting the railway bonds for 500,000dol. a
mandamus had been served on the Mayor commanding him to levy a sufficient tax to pay judgments
obtained for 15,000dol., due for interest.   The
Mayor was wisely obedient, he duly levied the
required tax, thus satisfying the *mandamus*, and the
judicious citizens declined to pay it.   The holders of
the bonds were dismayed at the prospect of having
to take proceedings against 3,000 taxpayers, and
thought it better to make a compromise. The creditors agreed to receive twenty-five per cent. of their
amount in stock of the railway, and take three per
cent. interest instead of eight on the balance for five
years, four per cent. for five years, and five per
cent. for twenty years, the bonds then to be
paid, this arrangement reduces the present interest
from 49,600dol. per annum to 14,850dol.   Of course
this is repudiation. but where fraud and violence
have created unjust claims from which the city de-
rives no advantage, it is but just and right that a

compromise should be made. But more substantial
reforms were effected. The salaries of the city
officers, which had been unduly raised, were
reduced by the amount of 6,040dol. per annum,
and the general expenses of the city from
92,343dol. to 63,142dol., shewing a reduction of over
28,000dol. per annum. The inhabitants now feel a
degree of confidence in the future to which they
have long been strangers. It is not a little singular
that the Mayor and his brother, to whom the city
are so much indebted for these prompt and judicious
measures, are German Jews. It is creditable to
the good feeling of all concerned that they should
have been entrusted with such important duties, and
and that these duties have been so ably fulfilled.
What has occurred at Montgomery is the counterpart of what has taken place throughout the
Southern States. In every city, county, and State,
you hear the same story of fraud and violence, and,
in most cases, the people have at last succeeded, by
peaceable means, in expelling the intruders, and re-
storing order and local government.

Not a single person in the Southern States, so
far as I could discover, is now an advocate of
slavery. Old planters and old slave dealers, men
who had no sort of scruples as to breeding slaves,
or selling, or flogging them—ladies who had charge

of household affairs, and overseers who had to manage estates, one and all admit that in a social and industrial sense freedom is better than slavery. Even those who take the most desponding view of the negro character, and look with apprehension as to the consequences of having such a race in their midst, admit that the evils and dangers are less under freedom than under slavery. It would, indeed, be difficult to maintain the contrary in face of facts which are patent to everybody. Under the former dispensation the man who required labour had to buy negroes at a cost of 800 to 1,000 dollars each, or hire them at 150 dollars per annum. First-class negroes can now be hired at from 100 to 120 dollars per annum. Under the old system you had to keep your negro in sickness or health, whether he suited or not. Now, if one man does not suit he can be changed for another. The power of flogging is gone ; but it does not seem to have been a great privilege to the masters, as the temper and capacity of a negro were not easily adjusted by such a process. Housekeepers rejoice greatly in a change which has relieved them of much trouble and responsibility. Between the wilfulness of young negroes, the cunning of old ones, and the frequent sickness of both old and young, they often had a hard time of it. It was no joke to keep house for

your own family and the families of all your
servants. If the master of the house, having a heart
or a conscience, objected to selling the children
of his servants, the difficulties were much increased,
as the estate did not extend while the number of
slaves multiplied, and thus there were more mouths
to feed without more to give them.

Of course, there were difficulties with freedom
at the commencement. Some of the negroes thought
it a good joke to manifest their independence by
changing their places every month, and some short-
sighted and selfish masters refused to give wages to
the negroes upon which they could live. But such
difficulties have now been got over. When the war
ceased the owners of land were in many cases
destitute of the means for working it, and therefore
employment was scarce. The negroes often went
to work on the promise of receiving half of the
crops, and this led to much misunderstanding, as
the negroes were generally cheated, or thought they
were. At that time they could not read or write,
but now many of them can keep accounts and thus
protect their own interests. The negro, as a
labourer, succeeds as well in manufactures as in
agriculture. At Greensboro', a small town in North
Carolina, many of them are employed in making
handles. Here wood is cheap, the best kinds, in-

cluding the celebrated hickory, being obtainable at
6d. per cubic foot. By very simple machinery
timber is sawn and shaped into handles, which are
sent all over the world. Negroes work in these
factories at wages varying from 2s. to 3s. per day,
with the abundance and cheapness of negro labour
in the Southern States, various manufactures may
be advantageously established there.

At Richmond I visited a large flour mill and
found many negroes engaged therein. The proprietor stated that they were more regular in their
attendance than white men, and therefore he gave
them the preference. In all kinds of offices, both
in the Northern and Southern States, negroes are
employed as attendants, for which purpose they are
much preferred to white men, as being naturally
more civil and attentive. I saw many fine old
black men in such situations, who bore on their
countenances the stamp of fidelity. Some of the
negroes are becoming small contractors, which is a
point of great importance, as it enables them to
teach the coloured boys the trade in which they are
engaged. They are also becoming owners of
property to a very respectable extent in the state
of Alabama. The property held by negroes at
the last assessment amounted to seven millions
of dollars. If you ask intelligent negroes how

they are getting on as compared with former times they usually reply, "Well, sir, most of us are doing better, but some are doing worse. Those who can't take care of themselves are going to the bad faster than before ; but if a man can take care of himself, he now has the chance."

Not only are negro children educated in schools apart from the whites, but the two races do not meet for religious observances ; you rarely see a negro in a white congregation, or a white, except the preacher, in a negro chapel. At the first congregation of negroes which I visited I found myself the object of marked attention. The congregation appeared to be in doubt as to whether I was a preacher or a detective. Two deputations of deacons came and asked me to preach, which, not being in my line, I declined. In each case where I attended a negro service a white man preached, and in these congregations were delivered some of the best sermons I heard in America. A white preacher seems to have no hesitation in speaking plainly to a coloured congregation, as he appears to have no doubt that they may be sinners. There is a good deal of philanthropic effort amongst the negroes, supported by themselves, and their votes will usually be given on the side of social order, even when their conduct may not be of the same high standard as their votes. At Richmond the negroes publish a weekly paper, called the *Virginia Star*, which is entirely edited, composed, and printed by coloured persons, and is a very creditable publication. In consequence of an objection on the part of whites to meet coloured persons in Good Templar Lodges, as they formerly did, the negroes are now carrying out these organizations by themselves, and have several lodges in a flourishing condition.

So strong are the imitative propensities of the negro that in all cases the race will be greatly influenced by the example which the whites place before them. It is quite amusing to notice in hotels and factories how exactly the coloured waiters or artisans imitate the style of the foreman. They are a people evidently born to be led, and it will be the fault of the whites if they are not led in the right way.

The manifest influence which the whites have over the coloured race is the more surprising, as there is no social intercourse between the two. I never saw white and coloured men in friendly conversation, and so great is the separation that not in a single instance did I find white and coloured children playing together. As fellow workmen, and as master and servant, the two races get on well, but socially there seems to be an impassable barrier between them.

And yet there are symptoms that cannot be over-looked which indicate that the coloured race will ere long become amalgamated with the white. If you suggest the possibility of this to an American, whether he belongs to the North or to the South, he will lift up his hands in pious horror, and exclaim, " Is thy servant a dog that he should do this thing?" But evidence thereof is seen in every congregation of coloured persons. In their schools I found that three-fourths of the children are more or less white, many of them are quite fair, and some have red or golden hair, which would prevent them from being regarded as mulattoes in any place where their parentage was unknown. The nearer the mulattoes are to white the brighter, as children, they seem to be, but as they grow up they appear to become sensible of their position, and to chafe against the social ban under which they are placed.

There are no people in America so happy as the genuine blacks—if you hear a cheerful laugh in a railway carriage you may be sure that it comes from a party of negroes ; and if a light and pleasant melody meets your ear you may be certain that it comes from negro voices. Some of the blacks are becoming quite proud of their pure descent. They are, in fact, almost the only unmixed race in America. As there are but few of them, and they marry with mulattoes their purity will soon disappear. Many persons think that the presence of the negro race is an unmixed curse to the American people, and that it tends inevitably to their degradation. But, while I cannot venture to give a definite opinion on such a complicated question, I may say that from my own limited experience I should not have taken such a view. It is obvious that in an industrial sense the negro is a great convenience. In social character, the worst of the blacks are not worse than the worst of the whites. What their general standard will be after a few years of improved influences we cannot yet tell, but certain it is that some of the qualities conspicuous in the negro might, with advantage, be grafted on to the American character. So great is the revolution which has taken place in the Southern States, that it is surprising to find the people who have gone through such sufferings and humiliation can display so much energy and good sense as they now manifest, but it is not the only instance in which adversity has borne wholesome fruit.

There are two nations in the world suffering from the effects of wars undertaken in error, in which they have been soundly beaten, and each nation is enjoying the sweet uses of adversity, while the victors are suffering the consequences of unhallowed success. France at the present moment is a happier and more prosperous country than Germany, and the Southern States of America are in a better condition than the Northern. The difference between personal economy and extravagance has a far greater influence on national prosperity than any amount of revenue or taxation. In the Northern States extravagance has led to very general fraud and very widespread ruin. In the Southern States economy has made the people comparatively wealthy, *i.e.*, in proportion to their wants, and generally honest. A Northern merchant will boast of giving £500 a year rent for his house. A Southern banker will tell you that a good house and garden, with coach-house, can be had in his neighbourhood for £50 per annum, that a first-rate man-servant can be got for £2 per month, and, that in order to economise the household expenses, the gentlemen of the place do their own marketing before they sit down to breakfast, and find themselves the better for it. There are many reasons which would lead an immigrant at the present moment to choose his residence in the South. He would find himself in the midst of a refined and intelligent people, who would give him a hearty welcome. Excellent land may be had at extremely low prices, and labour can be obtained on moderate terms.

F

If confession is good for the soul, it is a pity that we have so little of it. No one in the Southern States will admit that they were wrong on the question of slavery. It is true that it has been shown that slavery was a mistake, but the surprising part of the business is that they always knew it to be so. They went to war to uphold it, not because they believed it to be a good thing, but because they wished to postpone the revolution for another generation. Now, they are all glad that the unpleasant process has been completed, and they find the coloured people alongside of them free and friendly.

EDUCATION IN ATLANTA.

On reaching Atlanta I had a good opportunity of investigating the question of negro education. Professor Mallon, who superintends the schools of that city, very kindly took me to several of them. The Professor is an Americanised Irishman. Like many Irish gentlemen in the States, he has become as grave as a German without losing his Irish humour and enthusiasm. On passing from class to class, and from school to school, the professor entered quietly, and the work in hand was continued without interruption, unless he saw fit to interpose a question, which was always introduced in a telling and practical manner. A girl was explaining the properties of gold, and stated that a piece was beaten out to a length of 15 feet. "How long is 15 feet?" asked the professor. "Is this room 15 feet long?" "Yes, more." "Is it 15 feet wide?" "Yes, more." "Is it 15 feet high?" "I should think not so much," replied the girl. "Very well," said the professor, "you seem to have as near an idea of 15 feet as girls generally get." He stopped one of the older girls, who was explaining something. "You used the word —— ; can you think of any

word that would better express your meaning?"
"No, I cannot," said the girl.   "Can you think of
any word that you might have used in place of it?"
"Yes, I might have said ——."   "Would not that
word express your meaning better?"   "No, the
first word is nearer what I thought." "Very good,"
said the professor.   "I thought that there was a
better word, but, perhaps, the word you first used
is the best."   He took especial pains with the
reading.   "Why do you read in that unhappy
voice?   We want a cheerful tone."   "I can't hear
what you are saying.   I might, perhaps, if I listened
very hard, but it is your business to make me hear
easily."   The negro children read much better than
the whites, probably because they are more
imitative; if asked the meaning of a word, the answer
is promptly given, but with more regard to sound
than sense.   "What is the meaning of the word
narrative?" the professor asked of a small class.
One little ebony thrust out her hand, and was called
upon.   "Narrative means native."   The rest of the
children evidently thought that this sounded well,
and it took some time to explain the word in a
manner which was equally satisfactory to them.

Here, as elsewhere, the white and coloured
children are taught in separate schools.   In almost
every case the teachers who instruct the negroes

maintain that their intellectual capacity is equal to that of white children, and this opinion is generally expressed without any reservation ; but some observant persons contend that during the inceptive period of education the negro is equal or superior to white children of the same age, but when the reflective faculties are called into exercise the whites show greater powers of mind. The most satisfactory point in connection with the negroes is the determination they manifest to educate their children, and the perseverance with which the children are sent to school, even when the family can ill afford to lose their services.

One of the most interesting institutions of Atlanta is the University, for the education of coloured persons, under the superintendence of Professor Ware. The National Government appropriated 270,000 acres of land for school purposes in Georgia. The value of the land is about 300,000 dollars, and the whole revenue accruing from it has been appropriated to the State University at Athens. As whites only are educated at this University, a claim was made on behalf of the coloured people of the State; and after much discussion this claim was recognised by the appropriation of 8,000 dollars annually to the Atlanta University for the education of coloured people. This grant was made by the republicans in 1870, and when the democrats obtained power in 1872 it was discontinued, but only for a year; the march of public opinion in favour of negro education compelled the democratic State Government to renew the grant in 1873, since which it has been continued, and is not likely to be interrupted. This case affords an illustration of the progress of opinion in favour of negro education, which has been general throughout the Southern States, and is now so firmly established that wherever the negroes claim a fair share of the public grants for education their claim is respected.

The Atlanta University has 175 students, half of whom pay the fees and cost of board. Many young negroes have worked and saved up 200 or 300 dollars in order to come to the University. It will thus be seen that the energy which the negroes are manifesting to obtain education is not confined to the ordinary work of the Board Schools, but extends to the higher branches of learning.

About 75 of the students are girls, and their progress is regarded as universally satisfactory.

Professor and Mrs. Ware, who have devoted their lives to this work with true missionary zeal, are now much cheered to find their labours recognised and encouraged in quarters from which persistent opposition was formerly experienced. When they came to Atlanta any manifestation of regard for the blacks was looked upon as an act of hostility to the whites; but a great change has taken place in public opinion, and it is now generally felt that national advancement requires the elevation of the negro race, and those who undertake their education are no longer regarded with disfavour.

There are many societies in the Northern States for promoting numerous enterprises amongst the negroes. Before reaching Atlanta, I noticed a large crowd of negroes at one of the wayside stations, and I found the occasion to be the leaving of a missionary who had been working amongst them for two or three years, and was then changing his station. The marks of respect and regard paid to him and to his wife were pleasant to see; the missionary was a most intelligent travelling companion, evidently devoted to his work in the genuine spirit of Christianity.

WASHINGTON.

When the Americans had to decide upon a location for their government, the large cities which then existed were so jealous of each other that neither of them could be adopted, and so a city had to be created for the purpose. Washington was then laid out on an extensive scale from the expectation that, with the advantage of being the seat of Government, it would speedily become a large city. This expectation has not been realised. The place which has been so much pampered does not prosper, trade and commerce cannot be tempted to the locality, and, with all the advantages afforded by the presence of several thousand employés of the Government, it is in such an unsatisfactory condition that two-fifths of the property in the neighbourhood have been forfeited for the non-payment of taxes.

It is nothing short of a National misfortune that this should be the case. If the seat of Government were placed in some thriving and populous city many persons might see something of its working without the necessity of taking a journey for the purpose. Washington and its institutions are well worth a visit, but it is not every American who can arrange to travel several hundred miles to see them. If these institutions were surrounded by a large population engaged in the ordinary pursuits of life, millions of people, in the course of a year, would be brought in contact with them. During the session Washington is a lively place, but when Congress is not sitting I am told that it is like a city of the dead. For some reason not very apparent the public buildings have been kept a long distance apart, thus, the Capitol in which Congress assembles is nearly two miles from the White House where the President resides, and about the same distance from the Treasury and the War Office. This is not so great an inconvenience as it would be in England, because the members of the Cabinet are not members of the legislative assemblies, but still it seems difficult to understand why such a great quantity of space should have been deliberately placed between the various Government Offices.

I had not been many minutes in Washington before I set off for the Capitol to see the House of Representatives and the Senate, which were both sitting. No greater contrast can be discovered in the manners and habits of the two nations than that which is to be found in a com-

parison of the British House of Commons and
the House of Representatives of the United States.
No one ventures to enter the House of Commons
during the sittings of that assembly except
members, and the few officers whose presence
is absolutely required to carry on the business.
On a recent occasion when, by some unprecedented oversight on the part of the jealous
janitors, two strangers strayed into the house, it
was felt that the British constitution had received a
shock. The consternation created by this trivial
incident indicates the solemnity which attaches
to the position of an M.P., and to the general
conduct of parliamentary business. The severe
rules laid down for the guidance of members
themselves are rarely relaxed. I have seen Mr.
Gladstone called to order from all parts of the house
merely because, when talking to another member,
he was standing a few inches in front of the bar,
beyond which no member is allowed to stand. If
any member passes between the Speaker and the
member who is addressing the house, loud cries of
order resound from all sides. When the Speaker
himself rises to address the house silence at once
prevails.

The admission of strangers to the gallery is
limited to a very small number under most

stringent regulations ; if any stranger assumed an ungainly attitude, or took a note book out of his pocket, he would at once be called to order by the jailors who are responsible for their safe custody and good behaviour. Ladies, as is well known, are admitted only behind a screen, and but few can gain admission to the miserable recesses allotted to them. Under the most exciting circumstance the house may be crammed, but not the slightest disorder or irregularity would be permitted, and, even when nothing of interest is transpiring, no laxity is allowed. If this brief description of the British House of Commons has duly impressed the reader with a sense of the solemn order and general dullness of that respectable assembly, he will be prepared to appreciate the contrast afforded by the House of Representatives at Washington.

With a note of introduction to Mr. Randell, the speaker, I timidly approached the door of the House of Representatives, feeling that if I ventured a step too far I might suddenly find myself in the custody of a Sergeant-at-Arms. With bated breath I enquired, if my note could be sent to Mr. Randell, who was then in the chair. The reply was as usual in America " Oh yes," and almost before I could look round one of the speaker's secretaries came out, and, saying that Mr. Randell

wished to see me, took me at once right through
the floor of the house to the platform, on which the
speaker was standing.   Here, in front of the whole
assembly, I stood talking to Mr. Randell, who was
hammering for order with his left hand, while he
used his right to shake hands with his visitor.   He
at once gave me a card of admission to the floor of
the house for the remainder of the session, and sent
a messenger to introduce me to the Press Gallery.

Instead of the contracted and dingy chamber
at Westminster, I found at Washington a light,
lofty, and spacious assembly room, where each
member had a seat and a desk, leaving room on
the floor of the house for hundreds of visitors.   For
spectators there are extensive galleries which will
accommodate fifteen hundred persons.   A large
portion of this space is open to the public without
any restrictions, one end is devoted to ladies and
the gentlemen who acccompany them, other parts of
the galleries are set apart for the friends of members
and the diplomatic corps, while the space behind
the speaker is given up to the press.

There are also spacious and well lighted rooms
behind this gallery for the use of writers and
reporters connected with newspapers.   Gentlemen who attend here are not burdened like
English reporters with the work of taking several

elaborate reports, as a verbatim report is published at the expense of Government, and newspapers throughout the Union are chiefly supplied by the New York Associated Press. Short-hand writers who take the official report, and reporters for the Associated Press are accommodated with seats on the floor in front of the speaker's platform where they have a better chance of hearing, but if, as often happens, the speaker's voice is feeble, or the tumult in the house is vigorous, reporters will leave their seats and stand by the member who is speaking in order to take their notes.

As a rule no member who speaks in the house is listened to, or expects to be heard. Generally the speeches are read from manuscripts of alarming proportions ; sometimes a member has the good sense to ask that his speech may be taken as read, in which case it is at once handed over to the reporters to appear in the official report, and the next morning the member addresses a sack full of these reports to his constituents. The permission to take the speech as read is always cheerfully accorded. When reading, the members usually make unsuccessful attempts to compete with the general uproar in the house by using a stentorian voice, and as much action as is possible ; action which is seldom graceful, as one hand is occupied

in holding a cumbersome manuscript. The house
is apparently used as a kind of Exchange where
members transact private business. For this
purpose the desk in front of each member affords
every convenience, and amidst the universal din
in which no separate voice is distinctly heard—
private conversation may be successfully carried on.

Anyone wishing to see a member may be taken
to his seat. I believe that the privilege of visiting
members at their seats is not generally extended to
ladies, but on two occasions I saw a girl of about
twelve years of age walk across the floor of the
house apparently for the purpose of informing her
father that it was tea time. After performing this
duty, and, while preceding her parent out of the
house, she was chucked under the chin by a friendly
member who thought this a suitable mode of
shewing respect to her father and herself.

Thirty or forty messengers are employed in the
house who rush hither and thither as they are
called by members clapping hands. These
messengers are lively boys who employ every spare
moment in playing on the floor of the house, when
called they run with great alacrity in the direction
of the loud claps which are constantly heard
demanding their assistance. I saw two boys
starting for the same point from opposite parts

of the house, they cannoned heavily at the angle of convergence, and both fell prostrate on the floor in front of the speaker.

The speaker stands on a platform, upon which he constantly receives visitors, and as constantly he adds to the general din by loud knockings with an auctioneer's hammer, the purport of which I could not quite discover, as no notice appears to be taken of this proceeding. Large numbers of persons make a lounge of the strangers' galleries, and the precincts of the chamber are crowded with multitudes of people who look upon the Capitol as their own property, which in fact it is, although in other countries it would not be used in common by all persons. A large and valuable library is provided for the use of the members, which is open to the public. As if to prevent the possibility of any dignity being attached to the House of Representatives, a table is placed close by the chief entrance, upon which are displayed various packages, and you read on a large placard—

"Mark your Clothes with Rubber Stamp."

What connection this had with legislation I was unable to discover.

I wonder if Colonel Forester and the "Father" of the English Press Gallery are aware that in the

United States women are admitted as reporters to
the galleries set apart for members of the press.
In America you can no longer say gentlemen of
the press ; you must say ladies and gentlemen of
the press. But the ladies did not take the position
without the exercise of much perseverance. The
judicious officer, who corresponds to our active
Sergeant-at-Arms, when he was first applied to for
their admission, appropriated a portion of the
general ladies' gallery for ladies of the press, but
this did not satisfy them. With the gentlemen of
the press the ladies resolved to be. This was conceded, as everything is conceded which ladies in
America demand.

It would take a whole volume to describe the
Capitol in a manner worthy of itself. I can certify
to the correctness of the Guide Book, which states
that it "has a noble and commanding situation
upon the brow of what is called the Capitol Hill."

In this respect, as well as in others, it presents a
contrast to the British House of Commons. I am
sorry to say that the Capitol was destroyed by
the British Army in 1814. Just at the time when
we should have supposed that our Army had something more important to do. It took the Americans
ten years to re-build it. Wings were added in
1851. The building, which has cost $2\frac{1}{2}$ millions

sterling, is 751 feet long and 290 feet wide. The dome, 396 feet from the ground, is four feet lower than St. Paul's. As you enter the Rotunda, an Englishman finds himself confronted with monster paintings which are not flattering to his national vanity. "The Signing of the Declaration of Independence," "The Surrender of General Burgoyne," "The Surrender of Cornwallis," "The Embarkation of the Pilgrims," all recall incidents in our history which we do not care to remember, and which Americans are never allowed to forget.

The Senate Chamber is in the same building, also the Supreme Court of the United States, and a President's Room, "where the President sits during the last hurried days of the session to be nearer the Senate, in order to sign the bills as soon as they are passed"—from which I gather that St. Stephen's is not the only place where legislation is done in a hurry during the last days of the session.

The absence of Cabinet Ministers from the Congress and the Senate deprives these Assemblies of much of the interest which would otherwise attach to them. No one seemed to expect that any good would come of the debates in the House. Indeed, they cannot be called debates, as the time is mainly occupied with the reading of the long essays prepared with more or less care, with the view of

G

satisfying the reader's constituents, for which purpose they are printed at full length in the official
report. Of course there are rare occasions when the
speeches of leading men receive some attention; but
I had not the good fortune to be present on any such
occasion, and I am assured that they are exceedingly rare.

I should be very sorry, however, to convey the
impression that the assembly of Congress has no
influence on the destinies of the nation. It appeared
to me that members who do not listen to speeches
were much influenced by the exchange of ideas
amongst each other in conversation; and, as conversation is continued both in and around the
Chamber, they have, in this way, abundant opportunity of exchanging ideas and getting information. The extent to which private conversation
is carried on will be understood from the fact
that when the Speaker left the chair, on the House
going into Committee, I noticed that he went about
to all parts of the Chamber chatting with members,
while the business of the House was continued
under the guidance of the Chairman of the Committee. Can anyone imagine the Speaker of the
English House of Commons wandering about the
House as a universal chatter-pie, while Mr. Raikes
is in the chair and public business is proceeding?

The Senate is a much more quiet and dignified assembly. Ample provision is made in the Senate Chamber for the presence of spectators; but a large proportion of the work is done in " secret session." All appointments are discussed in secret, and other matters which cannot conveniently be laid before the public.

Public men are easily accessible in the United States. The custom is to give immediate admission, although the official may be engaged at the moment with relays of other visitors. You stand, or sit, and take your turn, hearing in the meantime the conversation which is taking place with your predecessors. This was the case in the provinces with treasurers, secretaries, mayors, and governors of States. I scarcely expected a similar reception at Washington, but I found that even there the custom prevailed.

Provided with a note of introduction to General Sherman, the General commanding the United States army, I called at the War Office. " Is General Sherman here? " " Yes, last door on left." I went, as directed, and repeated the enquiry. " There he is," said a clerk, pointing with a pen to a tall and elderly gentleman who was already engaged with three or four visitors. When my turn came, he entered into conversation in as friendly a manner as if he had known me for twenty years.

I was especially desirous of seeing Mrs. Hayes, and I was informed that anyone could attend her evening receptions without an introduction ; but as I did not wish our interview to be limited to a formal recognition, I obtained such an introduction as would ensure some conversation. On arriving at the White House at eight o'clock, I found some visitors were already in the waiting-room, but none, as yet, had been admitted. At intervals of two or three minutes we were summoned in separate parties to the reception-room. To my surprise, Mrs. Hayes introduced me to each of her previous visitors, and the whole proceeding was quite devoid of stiffness or formality.

She made especial inquiry as to the Southern States ; and with reference to the temperance question she said that she felt it right to maintain the same simple habits which she had always practised in Ohio, meaning that she continued a total abstainer from alcoholic liquors. Mrs. Hayes is a lady of commanding presence, with manners dignified and agreeable. She has set her face against extravagance in dress, and has discouraged some of the popular gaieties. The present visitors to the White House are quite a different class of persons from those who frequented it during the reign of the last President.

As I was passing the White House the next morning, I was preceded by a large party of Americans, rather shabbily-dressed, who rang the bell; and on asking if they could see the President, the porter replied, "Oh yes, walk right up." I, therefore, decided to walk right up, and found myself in a waiting-room where seventy or eighty persons had assembled. An official came in and said, "The President has to attend a Cabinet Council in half-an-hour, and the receptions this morning must be merely formal; no conversation can be permitted, and no petition or business of any kind must be introduced." Of course this did not suit me, so I followed the officer as he left the room, and explained that I was an Englishman connected with the press, leaving Washington to-morrow, and my only opportunity of having a few minutes' conversation was the present, and I asked him if he could now arrange for it. He replied, "I will try; look out for me, and I will look out for you." In two or three minutes the doors were thrown open, and the President appeared in the adjoining room. The crowd streamed in, shook hands, and filed out. In less than five minutes all had passed through, the doors were shut, the crowd had gone, and I was standing alone with the officer. "Now," said he, "you can go in." I, therefore, entered, and in another minute I was talking to the President about the Southern States. He concluded a brief interview by expressing a hope that English capitalists and labourers would feel renewed confidence, and come in still greater numbers to the United States. If my knowledge of Mr. Hayes had been limited to this interview, I should have supposed him to be a gentleman well able to form sound conclusions and give good reasons for them; and I may have something more to say on this point in another chapter.

In going down the stairs I met another crowd of visitors coming up, and among them a young negro girl about thirteen years of age, with a countenance that looked like a note of interrogation. In her left hand she held aloft a jam pot, and her anxiety appeared to be divided between securing this property and seeing all there was to be seen. I turned back to see what would happen. A crowd equal in numbers to the first again occupied the waiting-room, and were also informed that their visit to the President was merely " complimentary." The doors were thrown open, and the former proceeding repeated. The black girl with the jam pot entered the room, stood aside for a moment to see what other people did, and then went up to the President, holding out her right hand, whilst her left kept the jam pot aloft. He gave her a specially cordial reception, and as she came out her face was beaming with satisfaction.

I left Washington with great regret. It is the centre of, perhaps, the most vigorous political system in the world. Energy is stamped upon the features of every officer with whom I became acquainted. Something may be due to the fact that I was a stranger and connected with the press, but it appeared to me that all persons who called on any officials were received with the same energetic courtesy and patient attention. In every case the gentleman whom I saw seemed so thoroughly to understand his work, and so proud of his office and of his country, that I came away with the happiest impressions, and felt that I had spent some days in a bracing atmosphere.

EMIGRATION.

During 1877, emigration to the United States almost ceased, or rather it was nearly balanced by the immigrants from that country. Throughout that year the number of persons of British origin who emigrated to the States was 45,481, but during the same time we received from them 44,878 immigrants, leaving a balance of 603 only as the excess of emigrants over immigrants. It is obvious that the natural movement is from the overflowing population of the East to the unoccupied lands of the West, and, therefore, that some great disturbing cause has been in operation to prevent this natural flow of population. This cause is not difficult to find. Protection has made the United States the dearest country in the world for the ordinary articles of consumption, and, at the same time, has checked the development of industry in natural and profitable channels; thus making employment scarce and living dear, so that the country has ceased to afford the natural advantages which it formerly offered to immigrants.

Since 1815, 5,531,102 emigrants have left British shores for the United States; of whom about one-fifth were foreigners. But after making allowance for these, and deducting the number of immigrants, which may be taken as equal to one-third of the emigrants, the balance of emigrants of British origin who have settled in the United States since 1815 is, as nearly as possible, three millions. This is about twice the number of persons that have emigrated from the United Kingdom to all other places, including British North America and Australia.

We cannot fail to take an interest in a country to which so many of our fellow-countrymen have gone to seek their fortunes, and who do not cease to take an interest in the land of their birth. The friends they have left behind them are not forgotten, for since 1848 more than twenty million pounds sterling have been remitted by settlers in North America to their relatives in the United Kingdom.

It may appear like a paradox, but it is perfectly certain that the more persons emigrate from, the more can live in, the United Kingdom. Our limited land and imperfect knowledge of agriculture do not enable us to provide sufficient food for our people, many of whom have been half starved within the present century. The distressing condition which prevailed forty years ago would have continued and intensified if it had not been

for the advantages derived from those who have
left our shores.   The United States and our
Colonies have sent us abundant supplies of
food, and received payment in manufactures,
which have given profitable employment to our
people.   Every cargo of corn which we receive
and pay for by the produce of our looms enables
so many more persons to live on our soil than
could otherwise have been maintained.   Without
this trade we could not support our existing
population, and the rapid increase which takes place
in our numbers can be provided for only by a
portion of that increase leaving our shores for other
lands, where they employ themselves in producing
food or raw material for our markets, and receiving
manufactures in exchange.   New colonists are
naturally our best clients, as more advanced and
populous communities require for their own use a
larger proportion of the food they produce, and
supply, to some extent, their own manufacturing
requirements ; and thus a constant stream of emigration is necessary in order to maintain our prosperity.

Great Britain has become so pleasant to
live in that emigration is looked upon as a hardship, and there is some danger that this sentimental
and self-indulgent feeling will supersede the spirit
of enterprise which, of late years, has induced our

energetic people to become colonists.   If such
should be the case, we shall soon have a return of
those days of privation and distress which drove so
many people from our shores.   As our own advancement depends upon emigration, so does the prosperity of those of our race in other parts of the world
depend upon their receiving from this country a
constant accession of immigrants, for while our
difficulties arise from too dense a population, their
difficulties are occasioned by a paucity of people.
The present interruption or diminution of the stream
of emigration is, therefore, to be regarded with serious
apprehension ; and if it should continue the consequences will be disastrous to the United States
on the one hand, and to the United Kingdom on the
other.   In this country we look upon the
matter with some indifference, as we are beginning
to regard our own colonies as affording the most
advantageous field for development.   Our colonial
trade is increasing, and our trade with the United
States is decreasing ; at the present moment the
trade with our colonies is, as nearly as possible,
equal to our trade with the United States, which
means that a colonial population of 14 millions
does as much business with us as a population of
47 millions in the United States.

It is, therefore, much more to our advantage to
encourage emigration to the colonies ; but it is not

the less to be deplored that the financial policy of
the States should so contribute to their own im-
poverishment as to limit our trade with them, and
thus shut us out from a country the nearest and
most accessible in which we find a people of our
own race and language.   Their shores are only
eight or nine days from our own, and with free
intercourse between the two countries there would
be little difference to a working man whether he
obtained employment at Newcastle, Cardiff, or
Pittsburgh; and a London capitalist would invest
as freely in New York or Chicago as in Liverpool
or Hull.

The English capitalist has a difficulty in obtaining four per cent. for his money.   The American
agriculturist has a difficulty in borrowing at fifteen
per cent.   Capital invested in American agriculture
means cheaper food for our own people, with
increased comfort and prosperity, and a reduced
manufacturing cost. Thus, in helping the Americans
we help ourselves; capital and labour on the other
side of the Atlantic assist capital and labour on
this side, and the more they get of each the better
for ourselves.   If restriction of trade interrupts the
intercourse between the nations we shall suffer, as
we have before suffered, from congestion, which
causes acute suffering, and ultimately compels our

people to leave their country from destitution and distress. With free trade and free intercourse, the prosperity of the States will attract our labourers and encourage our capitalists, relieving, at the same time, our superabundant labour and our plethora of capital. The question of the moment is whether the stream of emigration to the West is to be attracted by prosperity or driven by adversity, and the answer may be looked for with equal interest in both countries.

Imagine for a moment that a new island had been discovered between Southampton and Jersey containing, say, 100 square miles of good land; how promptly it would be occupied, and what a god-send it would be considered. If the first thousand persons who occupied this island, unable to cultivate more than a third of the land, thought it desirable to limit their intercourse with this country by imposing heavy duties on imported articles, we should wonder what object they could have in view. Yet they might say, "We prefer making our own cloth, calico, and earthenware; and to do these things we will leave a large portion of the land uncultivated, because we know that an agricultural people are a stupid people, and without manufactures there is no development of intelligence or enterprise." Under such a system our emigrants would cease to go to that island where things were made artificially dear; if they did leave our shores they would go further on—to Canada or New Zealand, where a more liberal spirit was manifested, and where enterprise was allowed to develop in a natural manner. The same reasons have operated in reference to the United States. The land which is nearest to this country—the land which, until recently, received the largest portion of our emigrants, has now ceased to attract our working men, because the comforts, conveniences, and necessaries of life have been made artificially scarce and dear.

Not only has the working man been drawn from the States, but capitalists have been scared away, as they know that security is unattainable where the industrial enterprise of a nation is thwarted and disturbed by protective laws instituted for the benefit of class interests. Between the capitalists and the labourers are numerous classes, many of whom are seeking a suitable locality on which to expend the moderate fortune they have acquired; such persons will not go to a place where artificial scarcity and dearness prevail, and thus, no one would think of going to the States to spend money.

We cannot, however, suppose that a policy so retrograde and barbarous as that which now shuts out the States from a fair share of the world's advantages will continue to prevail; ere long a removal of restrictions will cause the tide of emigration again to flow in full force across the Atlantic.

In the meantime let us learn to look upon emigration not as a misfortune, but what in truth it is, the very foundation of our development. Thousands of young men desirous of seeking their fortunes in the world are over-persuaded by weak mothers and sisters to remain at home, often doing nothing, and at best mere quill-driving. How often do we hear that the fortunes of the widow and the orphan are squandered by such young fellows, in whom, through idleness, Satan has found an easy prey. Instead of wasting money at home, let them go and earn it where it is to be found, and where it is obvious that the earth wants subduing and replenishing. Providence has not provided every man or woman with work precisely where they are born ; but no man is justified in complaining that work cannot be found, while well ordered States and Colonies contain uncultivated land, and dense populations are wanting food which that land could produce.

WHO SHOULD EMIGRATE?

To whatever part of the world we turn our
attention we discover the truth of the proverb that
" Providence helps those who help themselves."
There seems to be little room in this part of the
universe for people who do not exercise some degree
of forethought and self-denial.   At the present
moment penniless men or women are not wanted
in the United States.   They certainly would not
have a better chance of employment there than in
England ; and for them emigration would be a
dangerous course, by which they might be exposed
to much suffering.   A time may come when
employment will be so abundant in the States, that
men without means may venture across the Atlantic
with the certainty of finding work on arrival at
their destination ; but such a time is not yet.   The
wages usually paid in the States offer no inducement as compared with those paid in the United
Kingdom, when the difference in the cost of living
is taken into account ; and the difficulty of getting
employment in the States appears to be greater than
in this country.   It is a singular fact that labour is
both more difficult to buy and more difficult to sell

than on this side of the water; if you want employment you cannot get it so easily, and if you want help it is more difficult to obtain. Almost every kind of business is hampered with a licence tax, which prevents competition; and nearly all the necessaries and luxuries of life are raised in price by the prevalence of protective duties. Thus employment is restricted and living is made dearer.

In a Democratic Society the law naturally represents public sentiments, and a traveller in the States discovers an unmistakeable feeling against cheapness; for the existence of this feeling it is difficult to account, but it accords with the idea of protective duties. The small matters purchased at various shops are two or three times as dear as they are in England. Tea and coffee, although untaxed, are certainly not cheaper, and sundry operations such as shaving, boot cleaning, etc., are about three times as costly as in England; but anyone who attempted to reduce these prices would be unpopular rather than otherwise. A grocer said to me, "If a man in this town reduced the price of photographs we would not deal with him, because we know that if one thing was reduced in price other things would come down, and we should lose all our profits." American tradesmen rely upon the slow shilling rather than the nimble ninepence; they prefer

H

large profits and small returns to small profits and
large returns; under these circumstances the expense
of doing business is greatly increased, as everyone
pays dearly for what he requires, and there is much
less business to be done. The prevalent feeling
against cheapness makes it difficult for a stranger
to begin work in the States. If he felt disposed to
shave people for twopence, or clean boots for a penny,
he would not be allowed to do so ; his competitors
would make it too hot for him, and he would get no
assistance or sympathy from the public. This state
of feeling may be broken down by the present
depression of trade ; and, indeed, until it is broken
down, it is difficult to see how trade can become
prosperous. What is the use of cheap production
and cheap manufacture if the cost of distribution
forms a barrier to the free use of the articles produced ? American productions are constantly sold
at a lower price in Liverpool and London than in
New York or Philadelphia, and a return of prosperity in the States must mainly depend upon their
own people being supplied at a moderate cost with
all the requirements of civilised life.

No one who has merely labour to sell should at
present go to the States, and no one who merely
wishes to be waited upon should go there. But
the present state of things affords many good

openings for men with small means and much
energy. A little capital will go a great way in the
States just now in the purchase of land or other
property, and the man who can avail himself
of the natural advantages of the country could
not have a better time than the present for
beginning. It is just the people with small means
who find it so difficult to get suitable investments or
independent employment in the United Kingdom
who would find good openings in the States. Such
persons may do well there at farming, grazing, or
gardening, for all of which purposes land can be
had on such moderate terms, that a sum which
would be trifling for similar purposes here would
there be ample. Suppose a young couple have
betweeen them four or five hundred pounds in this
country, what can they do with it? If invested, it
may bring them in four per cent. If employed, it
is brought into competition with much larger
amounts and will, probably, be lost; but in the States
matters are quite different. It they wish to lend
they can get ten to twelve per cent. on ample
security ; but if they wish to employ it they can
purchase and work a farm of 160 acres, or a good
market garden of 10 or 12 acres, or they can invest
in cattle, look after their own and other people's
herds, and while they are getting a fair living they

may see their property gradually becoming more valuable. The social position which such persons occupy in the States is far above that which is awarded to them here ; and if they like to take an interest in the public work of the locality in which they are placed, they will find any good sense or intelligence they may possess fully appreciated, without prejudice from that feeling of caste by which, in this country, they would be over-shadowed.

In addition to engagements connected with the land, there are other openings for small and industrious capitalists. As shopkeepers they would have better opportunities than are to be found in this country, for the development of new districts is more frequent and rapid than with us. As contractors, there are a variety of undertakings upon which as masons or carpenters they might enter. In wood-work, intelligent mechanics going to the States for the purpose of producing articles of general use, would enjoy an excellent field for their labours. The United States is probably the richest country in the world for timber ; there are 240 kinds of trees in North America suitable for timber, against 40 only which can be found in Europe, and, thus, the carpenter and furniture maker have advantages to which we can lay no claim. The most valuable kinds of wood can be obtained at a fourth part of their cost in England. In the Southern States, where cheap timber and cheap labour can be had, small but thriving manufactories could be established at very little cost, in which could be made any wooden articles which are wanted in this country.

But whatever undertaking might be entered upon in America, the same caution and common sense must be exercised there as would be necessary here or elsewhere. It is seldom that new concerns of any kind prove an immediate success, and if the proportion of capital to the work undertaken be not properly adjusted, failure and disappointment will result. A large proportion of failures arise from want of perseverance, and if a man has insufficient capital he cannot hold on. Whatever a man enters upon, his engagement should be well within his means, and he is not safe unless he allows a large margin for unexpected delays and disappointments. But with the exercise of the same amount of caution and industry the small capitalist has a far better chance in the United States than in this country.

It may be said, that if it be necessary to have four or five hundred pounds before anyone can safely emigrate to the States, there are but few persons who can command that amount of capital who would wish to go. To this I reply that I do not regard

emigration as a refuge for the destitute. I hope it
will be long before any persons will again be
driven from our shores by poverty and distress.
During the last three or four years, while there have
been great want of employment and much increase
of pauperism in the United States, most persons
have had a fair chance of making a living on
this side of the Atlantic ; and working men, without
means, would not better their condition by
going to the States. If employment there
should become abundant, then men, without
means, might safely emigrate ; but it would be
unwise for them to do so until a change has taken
place. For persons with a small amount of
capital, the case is quite different, as for them the time
is specially favourable ; and they may be tempted
to cross the water by the advantageous investments and superior position offered to them on
the other side.

Not only may industrial capitalists, commanding a few hundred pounds, find profitable
occupation and investments, but capitalists seeking
large investments, without employment, might benefit
their position by placing their capital where it will
realise a large interest and stimulate profitable
industry. Farmers and traders in the Western States
pay to bankers 18 per cent. per annum for accom-

modation. Such a rate of interest would be ruin ous in this country, but there it is not so. A farmer with 160 acres of land, surrounded with unoccupied pastures, finds that every spring droves of young cattle are driven past his place from the Southern States which he may purchase at a most moderate price. If he can give them two summers on his land their value will be doubled, and if he has to pay 18 per cent. for the money he can still make a good profit. But it would, of course, be better for him to borrow the money on mortgage at 10 or 12 per cent.; and as mortgages cost the borrower but a few shillings, and give an absolute title to the lender, the business is easily arranged. If the lender has sufficient judgment to form a sound opinion as to the value of property, and sufficient firmness to insist upon the punctual payment of interest, his advances will be perfectly secure, his interest very large, and he would be lending to clients whose profits enable them to pay high interest with advantage to themselves. Thus, persons with small means, whom we may term Industrial Capitalists, and those with large means, who may be styled Investing Capitalists, may emigrate to the States with advantage, and the present time is especially favourable for doing so.

But no one should go to the States who cannot

take their capital and labour with them. Persons who are merely spenders find America an undesirable field for their operations. In Britain an idle man is generally regarded as a gentleman ; in the States his position would be more doubtful, for idleness is not much respected there; and an income which would bring every comfort and many luxuries here would be quite inadequate there. It may be a very sensible thing for a man who has a fixed income in the States to spend it in London or Paris, but the reverse operation would be entire folly. If noble or ignoble ease is wanted let it be taken in the older countries, where the comforts and conveniences of life are more easily and economically obtained.

If, again, anyone has a good position or good prospects in this country let him not risk a change ; but for those, of whom there are always many, just starting in life and seeking a career, they may find it advantageously in the newer States. The wide field opened in America for the investment of capital and energy deprives of all excuse for idleness every man or woman whom Providence has endowed with a moderate capacity.

RAILWAY TRAVELLING.

It is a serious disappointment to an American if you do no admit that their railway carriages are a great improvement upon the " stuffy little boxes used on English railways." After a considerable experience of both, I am bound to say that I greatly prefer the English carriages. This may appear like an obstinate insular prejudice, but some substantial reasons can be given for the preference. On measuring the seats in several of the American railways, I found that the space allowed for two passengers varied from two feet nine inches square to three feet square. In this space two passengers are expected to sit during the days and nights which are consumed on an American railway journey. If both passengers are of moderate size they will find it a very tight fit to squeeze themselves into the space. If their legs are of the usual length it will be very difficult to know how to dispose of them. At every movement their limbs come in contact with sharp angles of iron or wood ; even the arm-rests are made of polished iron with sharp corners. The tops of the seats do not reach above the middle of the back, and thus it is impossible to rest the head or the shoulders.

If anyone wishes to realise the discomfort of
an American traveller, let him mark out a space
three feet on the floor, place two small chairs upon
it, and get two grown-up people to sit within
those limits for twenty-four hours; the victims
will never wish for a nearer approach to purgatory. It is quite a painful sight to witness
the futile efforts of passengers to obtain comfort in a crowded carriage during the night
journeys; they twist themselves into all kinds
of shapes in their frantic efforts to get a little rest
for the head and back. If a passenger obtains the
command of two seats, as he often does, he can build
up a support for the head and make himself tolerably
comfortable; but if a fellow-traveller insists upon
sharing the double seat, then purgatory begins.

In the event of an accident the sharp angles
and ornaments, with the movable seats, are exactly
adapted to cut the passengers into mincemeat.
If a collision occurs a fellow's head must go some-
where, and unless he is so fortunate as to fall against
another passenger, he is bound to hit his head
against the hard wood or iron which occupies the
whole space of the carriage; thus his chances of
escaping without serious injuries are reduced to a
minimum. The Pullman cars are no improvement;
the seats do not afford more room than ordinary

carriages, and are, in fact, lower at the back and still more uncomfortable. The drawing-room cars, with easy chairs for seats, are very good, but these are not provided for the long journeys to the South and West. As all the passengers have to enter and leave the carriages at the ends, it takes a long time to get in or get out, and you frequently have to fight your way against opposing streams of passengers.

The Pullman car system appears to have been introduced throughout America for the purpose of enabling the railway companies to charge more than the maximum rates to which fares are limited under their concessions. These rates vary from three to ten cents. ($1\frac{1}{2}$d. to 5d.) per mile per passenger, and the full rates allowed are usually charged for the ordinary accommodation. No distinction of class is recognised in American railway legislation, but by providing special carriages at a separate cost the railway companies get over the limits of the maximum charge. The more effectually to do this, the tickets for the Pullman cars are sold separately, and each passenger has to get and take care of two sets of tickets, one from the railway company and one from the Pullman Company. Each Pullman car is provided with a conductor and a porter; the position of conductor could be most ably filled by an English gentleman-help, who had failed in every other capacity. The only business which the conductor has to do is to exchange the tickets issued at the office for other tickets ; the object of this exchange is not apparent, but the arrangement gives the passengers some trouble and affords the appearance of occupation to the gentleman-conductor ; moreover, if there were no conductor to wait upon, the porter would have but little employment.

When I left New Orleans there were in the train three Pullman cars, with three gentleman-conductors, three grand porters to look after them, and four passengers. Under such arrangements dividends to shareholders are not likely to be forthcoming, and if obtained they must be got out of the twenty-five passengers who travelled in the ordinary carriages. Only one passenger train in twenty-four hours runs over the line in question, so that the shareholders' prospect is of the most dismal character. In the Eastern States the Pullman cars are well occupied, but in the West and South they are constantly running with only three or four passengers. The system is a heavy burden on the American travelling public, it involves a double set of carriages, and a double staff of ticket clerks, conductors, and porters, and the public get nothing more than the railway companies ought to supply for the maximum fares fixed by their concessions. It may be contended that sleeping cars are essential when the journeys are long; for my own part, I would rather spend seven days and nights in a European first-class carriage than in a Pullman car. The sleeping places are about 6ft. long, 3ft. wide, and 2ft. 6in. high, and as far as possible every breath of air is excluded; the company let this space, and appear to impose no restriction upon the number of persons who occupy it. On one occasion, when I had an upper berth, I found that the lower one was occupied by two women and a child; in another slept a mother with two boys of 13 and 11, and the mother said that her elder boy was sick every morning after sleeping in the car. Not only is the berth shut as closely as possible, but if the night is at all cold no air is permitted to enter any part of the carriage, which is heated to about 80 degrees. On one occasion I felt the heat very oppressive, and some other English passengers were quite overcome by it. I, therefore, appealed to the negro porter to open the ventilators. He replied, pointing to the American passengers, "They don't want no ventilation I guess."

The constant application for tickets is a source of great annoyance to travellers in America; after every stoppage the conductor comes through the carriage to collect the tickets or fares from new comers, and he may or may not choose to remember that you have shown yours. The conductor is frequently changed, and it is the duty of the new comer to investigate every case ; if you happen to be asleep he will screw his thumb into your ribs and thunder the word "tuckets" into your ears without the slightest commiseration.

Everybody in the States has railway tickets for sale. A banker will ask you if you are going to such-and-such a place, as he can supply tickets at less than the regular rates, the hotel-keeper does the same, and there are in most towns special offices for the purchase and sale of tickets. This arises from the circumstance that tickets for long distances are charged less in proportion than short distances ; so that a calculating American buys a ticket for a longer distance than he wants to travel, and sells the balance, or he will take a return ticket and sell the return. The whole system appears to open the door for fraud on every hand ; the conductors constantly take money from passengers without giving any receipt, and they seem to have absolute authority to decide all disputed points. A man's fortune is supposed to be made when he is appointed a railway conductor, and if he does not get rich it is supposed to be his own fault.

FOOD SUPPLIES.

Those who were acquainted with the condition of the agricultural labourer in England, during the thirty years which intervened between the close of the great war and the adoption of free trade, will remember that hard working, industrious men and their families were often without bread to eat, and such a luxury as meat was rarely seen on their tables, The wages of agricultural labourers in Wiltshire and other farming districts were sometimes reduced to six shillings per week; and even at this low price their labour was not cheap, as semi-starvation left them so weak and listless that they had neither strength of body to do their work, nor strength of mind to think of improving their condition. It was pitiful to see the herds of men who wandered from one farm-house to another seeking employment, and caring nothing whether it was obtained or not; for the parish allowance, without work, was just as good as wages with labour. I have known cases in which men came to their work in the morning in so weak a state that the farmers were obliged to give them a little food to enable them to commence.

During this miserable period heavy protective duties were maintained for the benefit of the agricultural classes; and it not unfrequently happened, that, while the labourers were starving, corn was brought to our shores and sent back again without been discharged from the ship, because the duties, under the sliding scale, had risen so high as to prevent the landing of the corn. Notwithstanding the inconceivable folly and wickedness of a protective tariff it was almost unanimously supported by politicians and the press. Whigs and tories advocated heavy duties on corn; and even the radicals declared that what the people required was not cheap corn but political power, and votes were to be given when bread was wanted. The " unadorned eloquence " of Richard Cobden enlightened the people on the value of free trade, and the blessings of plenty and peace have followed the opening of our ports to all the world. Either the people must have eaten a great deal too much since the adoption of free trade, or they were kept very short of food before; for, in addition to the great increase of our home production, we now import more wheat than we grow.

It is to the development of railways in the States that we owe the enormous increase of corn supplies. The quantity of land thus opened up is practically unlimited. Railways can be laid at a small cost over the level prairies, and the whole area of the country will be intersected with railways when the next cycle of prosperity gives increased circulation to capital and industry. Thus, America may be relied upon as an inexhaustible granary upon which we may draw to an unlimited extent.

But the importation of corn is now an old story, and at present our chief interest is excited by the importations of beef which come pouring in from the vast prairies of the West. Although these importations deprive the farmers and landowners in this country of those golden expectations which they were realizing upon beef at a shilling a pound, and, although it is admitted that

> " He who drives fat oxen
> Should himself be fat,"

we do not hear from any quarter that the people ought to be deprived of cheap meat for the benefit of the agricultural class. The subject is therefore reduced to the practical question—Can America supply us with beef as freely as she is sending corn?

There is no question that the beef is there. The enormous herds which the traveller passes on the boundless prairies as the train rushes by grow and fatten with little cost for labour, and none for rent.

I

The low price at which beef can be produced will be best illustrated by a story told by General Sherman, who said that when he was staying in Texas he received a note from his butcher, apologising for charging him 2d. per lb. for beef, but as he supplied the best joints only he could not sell them at a lower price. It is true that the best beef in Texas would be considered inferior to the best beef in London, for the American grazier, like the American farmer, has a rough and ready mode of doing his business; but there is a flavour in prairie-fed beef which is wanting in our stall-fattened oxen, and, with a little improvement in the treatment of bullocks in the States, the beef from them will perhaps be equal to any which we can obtain.

As I have previously explained, the cattle, as a rule, shift for themselves all the year round, and during the winter lose much of the flesh which they put on during the summer. Good beef cannot be made in this way, and some of the graziers, especially in the Northern States, are beginning to see that nature requires a little assistance. Cattle must be protected during the winter. Shedding is cheaply erected in a country where the cost of timber is merely the cost of labour in cutting and sawing; and the corn, which is now sometimes burnt for fuel, can always be supplied in the West at, say 25 cents, or one shilling, per bushel.   It is usually given to the beasts just as it is brought in from the fields—in the husk.   This plan involves some waste, but the hogs, which are kept on the farm, pick up what the bullocks leave, and every grain is thus turned into beef or pork.

The conditions under which first-class stall-fed beef may be produced in the Western States are therefore these :—The farmer obtains 80 or 160 acres of land free, on condition that he lives upon the land for five years, or if he covets a special spot, which has already been appropriated, he can purchase as much land as he requires at a cost of, say 6 dollars, or 24s., per acre.   His farm will be surrounded by unoccupied land, upon which his herds can be supported during six or seven months of the year, at the mere cost of looking after. Any quantity of hay can be obtained for winter use at 3 dollars, or 12s., per ton; and he can either grow Indian corn or buy it at 1s. per bushel.

A similar state of things to the present must continue for many years to come, as the quantity of unoccupied land is enormous, and as cultivation is extended there will be an immense increase in production; the quantities of corn and cattle now produced are but small compared to the supplies which we may in future receive.

Mr. Macdonald, in his letters to the *Scotsman*, estimates the cost of producing corn-fed beef in the Western States, after providing a fair profit to the breeder and feeder, at from 2¼d. to 3½d. per lb. of live weight; and the cost of the same beef dressed and shipped at New York, 4d. to 5½d. per lb. Transit across the Atlantic he estimates at 1½d. per lb., making the cost in Liverpool or Glasgow 5½d. to 7d. per lb. This estimate has evidently been most carefully made, and with a Scottish farmer's view of what the profits on grazing ought to be. We do not quite understand why Mr. Macdonald, in making this estimate, has taken the cost of Indian corn so high as 30 cents., or 1s. 3d., per bushel; he has shown that in Illinois a landlord pays his tenants only 15 cents, or 7½d., per bushel for corn when he provides land, the tenants finding everything else, including seed and labour, and on land costing only a few dollars per acre, it is obvious that the rent and taxes cannot be equal to all other charges. We may, therefore, feel sure that at the prices named in this high estimate good American beef can be supplied. Possibly the supply of the best corn-fed beef will be for a time inadequate to the demand, but the quantity will soon be increased now that the trade has been shown to be practicable and profitable. Improvements will probably be made in the mode of refrigeration, so as to make the preservation of the meat more certain and the transport less costly. We may, therefore, look upon the meat supply as the satisfactory development of a new business, which, on the one hand, will give employment to many energetic young men who want occupation, and on the other will enable a larger number of persons to live in the United Kingdom, where the reduced cost of food will lessen the cost of producing, and increase the demand for manufactures.

With a very small amount of capital a young Englishman might begin as a grazier in the Far West. If he is strong and enterprising he would enjoy life in the saddle, with the boundless prairies for his range. He could attach himself to a Contractor, who has the charge of herds, and any capital he has might be successfully invested in the purchase of cattle, either many or few, which would be allowed to run with the herds of which he assisted in taking charge.

The description which Mr. Macdonald gives of Mr. Gillet's estate in Illinois is sufficient to fire the ambition of any young man who wishes to become possessed of flocks and herds of patriarchal dimensions. Mr. Gillet began cattle rearing at Elkhart, Macon County, in 1846, with 18 native cows, and by attention to improvements in the breed he now has a herd of 2300 head, which so good a judge as Mr. Macdonald describes as the "grandest bestial display he had ever seen in one man's possession." Mr. Gillet now prepares for the market over eight hundred thousand pounds weight of beef per annum, and nearly half as much pork. His estate comprises 12,000 acres of land, much of which is cultivated by tenants, who provide seed and labour, and supply him with Indian corn for his cattle at 15 cents (7¼d.) per bushel.

As a specimen of what may be done by a capitalist, we may refer to the successful operation of the late Mr. Grant, formerly of the well-known firm of Grant & Gask, of London. Mr. Grant, who is a native of the North of Scotland, purchased about 100,000 acres of land from the Kansas Pacific Railway Company at Victoria, in Ellis County, Kansas, and arrived at Victoria in May, 1873. Mr. Macdonald, who visited this colony, writes—" Mr. Grant and his little band of agriculturists found Victoria as nature and the buffalo had left it. They had no precedent to guide their operations, no home comforts such as they had been accustomed to in their native land ; drought and grasshoppers devoured their first two crops, and wolves and

stormy weather played havoc with their stock.
Those who had little lost all, or nearly so, and a few
left in despair ; those having larger purses or
wealthy friends, and extra courage, retained their
hold, and scattered seed for one more chance.
Fickle Dame Fortune could not always frown on
such a beautiful country. Victoria has been bright
with her smiles for two years, and it is only
just to say that those who remained have done
better than those who left. There are now close
upon two thousand souls, where four years ago
there were barely as many dozens; and everywhere
in Victoria I was delighted to find happiness, peace,
and plenty. Mr. Grant finds that his colony is rising
in favour among intending emigrants. He prefers
to sell his land in sections of 640 acres ; and to
farm this thoroughly, and tide over probable
emergencies at the outset, it would be well to have
at least £2,000. The majority of those who have
settled here within the past two years are Russians,
and, being working people without capital, they
have reduced the cost of labour greatly. They break
prairie and plough land at 5s. or 6s. per acre, which
used to cost 12s. or 14s., and for a day's work
Russian women charge only 25 cents, or 1s., and
excellent workers they are. Mr. Grant has about 800
acres under cultivation, and, besides wheat, oats, and

rye, he grows large quantities of Indian corn and millett for food for his stock. Exclusive of calves, he owns over 800 cattle, and has about 11,000 sheep. His wool crop ranges from 3lbs. to 5lbs. per head."

The change from a shop in Oxford Street to the ownership of 100,000 acres of land in Kansas must, indeed, be great, but capital, common sense, and perseverance will carry a man through anything which he pursues with diligence. Mr. Grant developed into a patriarch with unusual rapidity, but free trade between the two nations would make his example more easy to follow. If the 2,000 settlers in Kansas could purchase clothing from England without the interposition of enormous duties, their position would be much better than it is. By her protective duties the States are doing what they can to prevent the occupation of their country by British capital and labour, the advance of which they profess so much to desire. Free intercourse between the United States and the United Kingdom would make the two countries almost as one; with only nine days, and no custom-house between them, we should scarcely regard our friends going to the States as emigrants. Our young men and maidens might go forth to subdue and replenish the earth without those hardships by which this work has hitherto been accompanied.

PROTECTION.

More than a hundred years ago we impressed protectionist principles so thoroughly on the minds of our then fellow-subjects in America that they have not since forgotten the lessons they received.

We prohibited the establishment of cotton mills, iron foundries, and other manufactories, as we contended that these would be inimical to *our interests* which, then, as at present, we thought it our duty to uphold, without an undue regard to the *rights* of other people. Ever since that time it has been the day and night dream of the Americans to make themselves a manufacturing community. Nature has given them abundantly the means for agricultural development, but the nation, like many individuals, despises natural gifts, and determines to gain other accomplishments; therefore, they cheerfully make any amount of sacrifice for the purpose of developing manufactures.

In the United Kingdom, the teachings of Cobden convinced the public of the soundness of free trade principles, and the prosperity which resulted from the adoption of free trade so completely confirmed these views that possibly few persons in

this country will be found disposed even to consider
the grounds upon which Americans advocate the
policy of protection. It would be a mistake to
suppose that in the States protection means merely
a patriotic sentiment. Many of the Americans are so
thoroughly opposed to freedom of trade, and convinced of the value of protection, that they look with
great disgust upon any importations into their native
town, even when these importations come from other
parts of the Union. It is contrary to the constitution
for any State to impose duties upon importations from
other States, but the spirit, if not the letter, of this
provision is evaded by charging a heavy license duty
upon traders importing articles from other States ;
therefore, it is not surprising that they look unfavour-
ably upon importations from Europe.

The argument by which they justify their
feeling against imports often finds expression in a
statement that they have in their town, or state,
unemployed persons; and, under these circumstances, the import of articles which *can* be made at
home is a dead loss. Why, for instance, should
brushes or biscuits be brought from the Eastern
States when, by the exercise of a little energy,
a brush manufactory or a biscuit bakery could be
established in the locality. They argue that home-
made brushes may, for a time, be dearer and more

clumsy than those which can be purchased elsewhere, but for the sake of giving employment to
their own people they are quite willing to pay more
for brushes in order that the industry may be
established in their midst.

They overlook the fact that a community, like
an individual, may prosper, and usually does prosper
most by devoting its energies to one industry
rather than to several—by producing that for which
special advantages are possessed, and exchanging
the results of well directed industry for the products
of other places. In the United States, as in the United
Kingdom, the most thriving places are those which
are noted for a special industry, such as Waltham
for watches, or Johnsbury for scales, Manchester for
cottons, Staffordshire for pottery, or Sheffield for
cutlery. In short, the principle of division of labour
holds good for localities as well as for individuals,
and the best results will be obtained on the
principle of free exchange, leaving each place and
each person to produce that for which they have
special advantages or qualifications.

So thoroughly are Americans imbued with protectionist principles that, in those cases where they
have succeeded in establishing an export trade, in
spite of protection, the persons engaged therein are
still in principle ardent protectionists. I have pre-

viously referred to the Waltham watch factory, near
Boston, where improved machinery enables the proprietors to make watches for England. The manager
there said that he considered the English Government was very unwise in allowing English labour
to be displaced by receiving American watches
which, if we had common sense like the Americans,
we should rigidly exclude. To this observation I
replied that to assume that imports lessened the
amount of local labour is to take appearances for
realities. It is true that American watches coming
to England lessens the work of our own watchmakers, but some other industry is stimulated in
proportion. The Americans do not make us a
present of their watches; if they did it would be
ungracious as well as unwise not to receive them;
but they expect something in return, and we shall
send something which we make better than the
Americans, just as they send us watches which they
make better than we do. The result is that we get
cheaper and better watches; our own watchmakers,
who are not making watches so well as they
ought to do, will lose some employment, but an equal
amount of employment will be given to some
other trade or trades which are carried on more
advantageously.

The Americans believe that protection developes
manufactures, whereas it is about the surest

method of retarding their development. Few men will take more trouble than is necessary in perfecting their own business, and if a manufacturer can secure a good profit by appealing to his Government for protection he will not exert himself to adopt improvements in his production. Just as the British farmers fifty years ago, relying upon protection, cared not to develop agriculture, and often found themselves in difficulties, so the traders in America who have been most protected are now in the most unsatisfactory condition. Instances illustrative of this principle might be given to any extent, but two or three will suffice. The manufacture of woollen cloth is prohibited by a duty of 35 per cent., and 2s. per lb. Wool is cheaper in the United States than in England, but cloth is much dearer, and the best cloth has to be imported in spite of the duty. The long period of protection which cloth makers have enjoyed at the expense of the rest of the community has not stimulated them to manufacture either so well or so cheaply as the cloth makers of other countries. Every man who buys a coat in the States pays from 20 to 50 per cent. more than he would give for the same article in London. A London starch manufacturer, who visited a starch factory in the States, informed me that he was surprised at the wasteful

and extravagant manner in which the work was
being carried on, and he said to the proprietor." If
you were not protected you could not afford to be so
wasteful ; in England a factory carried on like yours
would ruin the proprietors in twelve months." The
American manufacturer replied, " Without protection
we should be shut up." In this he was probably
mistaken ; instead of shutting up his factory he
would improve it — just as English farmers
improved their cultivation when protection was
withdrawn.

The natural advantages of the United States
are so great that nothing but the most egregious,
social, or legislative blundering would have brought
them to the condition of depression through which
they are now passing. With abundant land, a
country which requires development in every
respect, and an energetic people, employment
should be easy to get, and yet workmen find
it there more difficult to obtain than in the older
States of Europe. Natural advantages have been
thrown away by inducing men to direct their
energies into unsuitable channels through the disturbing influence of protection. Had trade been
free, each man would have undertaken work for
which he or his circumstances were naturally
adapted, but protection has diverted labour to less

suitable and, therefore, to less profitable channels, and the increase which it has occasioned in the cost of living has given other nations an advantage in the general trade competition.

At New York I attended, by invitation, a discussion on protection, during which the arguments in its favour were ably and concisely stated. They are with us so old that they are now novel, and I will reproduce them here, in a condensed form, as the best means of showing the state of feeling on the subject. It is of course necessary to eulogise whatever has to be protected, and in our own country, when self-interested patriotism was defending protection to agriculture, we heard much about a "bold peasantry" possessing all the virtues, and manufacturing populations practising all the vices. The able gentleman who introduced the subject at New York gave us the reverse of the medal. He contended that an agricultural nation must be poor. "Mechanical arts, adding a hundred-fold to the power of man, make wealth. Spain, Italy, and Ireland are instances of the miserable condition of nations which depend on agriculture. Not only poverty of wealth but poverty of intellect arises from devotion to agriculture; slavery and priestcraft fasten upon those unhappy countries which limit their industry to the cultivation of the land.   A fertile soil merely increases all these evils, as it leads to an undue increase of population.   The best results are obtained where the greatest variety of work is afforded for the development of man.   In England three centuries ago the competition amongst agriculturists broke prices down until people could not live upon the soil.   Henry VIII. adopted the good wholesome doctrine of protection, and stimulated mechanical arts.   He obliged every farmer to grow flax, and prohibited the importation of linen.   Afterwards England made the mistake of protecting agriculture instead of manufactures, but the manufactures which had been stimulated by the original protection increased in strength, and England withdrew the agricultural protection at a time when starvation was staring her population in the face.   The abolition of protection on food enabled England to compete with all the world, and from that time she dates her advance.   Her insular position and wealth of iron and coal have enabled her to maintain free trade against all the world.   She is the only country which has adopted, or can adopt, free trade.   Her conditions are diametrically opposed to our own.   The problem we have to consider is that of the best development. We have no trouble about land, which is free to all, and agriculture amongst us is sure to

flourish ; our great difficulty is to promote manufactures.

" No country can resist or compete with the
manufacturing power of England without protection.
The iron industry of France could not exist if unprotected. America is in the same position, and without protection we should have to go back to agriculture only, which is a condition not to be thought of
by any sane man. No undue proportion of our
population is employed on manufactures. It is the
duty of Government to make laws to restrain the
selfishness of mankind for the protection of the weak
in order that all may prosper."

Such are the arguments advanced in favour of
protection by an educated and thoughtful American.
They will bear careful study, and it would be
useless to discuss the matter in the States unless we
are prepared to look at it from the American point
of view. We may readily admit the advantages
derivable from variety of employment, and certainly
we shall not be disposed to underrate the value of
manufactures to a community. We may concede
that it is by no means desirable that any people
should be exclusively devoted to agricultural pursuits ; but after making these concessions we are
free traders still. Granted the importance to the
United States of having manufactures, yet even gold

K

may be bought at too high a price, or may be wasted in the endeavour to obtain it, and if the American people realised the effect of protection they would hesitate to make the sacrifices it imposes upon them. Protective duties raise prices, and the dearness of many of the necessaries or conveniences of life in protected countries not only limits the consumption of the special articles, the price of which is thus enhanced, but it places all producers and manufacturers at a disadvantage as compared with their competitors in less protected communities. The true source of manufacturing development is found in the energy, enterprise, and ingenuity of the people, but the pampering influence of protective duties is fatal to the manifestation of these virtues. If before erecting a manufactory a man goes hat in hand to a Government, imploring it to place burdens on the rest of the community for his own special benefit, there is but little hope that such a man will display energy or ingenuity, as he founds his hopes of success not on the perfection or natural value of his work, but on the amount of duty which he can persuade the Government to impose on his competitors.

In conversation with an intelligent and successful manufacturer, he expressed the opinion, which is so common in America, that protection was necessary to start a trade, but when it was well established it should be removed. I asked him what would be the effect on his own business if he gave a large subsidy to the heads of each department so long as the work they did was unprofitable, with the understanding that as soon as it became profitable the subsidy would be discontinued. If the policy of paying for failure instead of for success would not answer in private life, why should we expect it to succeed when publicly applied. The proper reward for a manufacturer is the profit which naturally results from his labours; work that cannot be done with profit had better not be undertaken, for it will merely occupy labour which might be advantageously employed in other channels.

My friend then observed, "Surely it is but common sense to impose import duties on commodities which may be produced and manufactured at home, and to allow the free importation of what we cannot produce or manufacture ourselves." I replied to his question by asking, "What is the object of import duties—to raise prices or to obtain a revenue? If the object is to raise revenue, why do you adopt a course which will raise prices to a greater extent than it produces revenue? If you put a duty on any article which is not produced in the

States you increase the price and get a corresponding revenue. Supposing that some other article is taxed, of which half is produced in the States and one half imported, the duty would raise the price on double the quantity that was imported, and thus the Government would receive only half of what the people paid."

He replied, "If we are willing to make this sacrifice in order to stimulate manufactures, why should we not do so?" It was obvious that our argument was getting into the "vicious circle," but I answered, "It is merely a question of profit and loss, and if, when you have calculated the *cost and results* of protection, you find the balance is on the right side, by all means continue it. Your most experienced financiers estimate that the protectionist policy is costing the nation about 100,000,000 dollars annually. Your unprotected trades have thus placed upon them a burden which often retards their developement, and yet we find that the prosperity you have is in connection with unprotected industries, while your protected trades are languishing. Both theory and experience show that you might as well attempt to establish a forest by growing trees in a hot-house as to develop national trade by the stimulus of protection."

"Heyl's Import Duties" for the United States is a semi-official publication, containing a digest of statutes relating to the subject, which occupies 250 pages, and the list of duties, printed in small type, with double columns, covers 79 pages.

Almost every article which can be recalled by the memory seems to be included in this list; a very few, such as tea, jalap, and skeletons, are "Free." In order to give a sense of equity, articles which are constantly the subject of export instead of import are duly taxed; thus, bacon is charged with a duty of 1d. per pound, and animals, even down to rabbits, are subject to a duty of 20 per cent.; alum is charged 2s. 6d. per 100 pounds; anthracite coal is free, but bituminous is taxed 3s. per ton; cheap cottons are charged $2\frac{1}{2}$d. per yard and 10 per cent.; dearer cottons range from 15 to 35 per cent. on the value; cutlery, 35 per cent.; books, 25 per cent.; glass, 30 to 40 per cent.; gunpowder, 20 per cent.; gutta-percha, 40 per cent.; iron bars for railroads, 2s. 11d. per 100 pounds; steel bars for railways, $\frac{1}{2}$d. per pound; other iron bars, from $\frac{1}{2}$d. to 1d. per pound; linens, 30 per cent.; ale, 1s. 5d. per gallon, or without bottles 10d. per gallon; brandy, 8s. per gallon; wine, 1s. 8d. per gallon; all wines containing over 24 per cent. of alcohol to be forfeited; machinery,

65 per cent. ; mouse-traps, 35 per cent. ; oil-cloth, 45 per cent. ; oils, from 20 to 50 per cent. ; silk, 60 per cent. ; slates, 40 per cent. ; steel railway bars, $\frac{1}{2}$d. per pound ; sugar, $\frac{3}{4}$d. to $2\frac{1}{2}$d. per pound ; tin bars, blocks, or pigs, free ; tin boxes or roofing plates, 35 per cent. ; tobacco, 2s. per pound, and 30 per cent; warming-pans, 35 per cent.; watches, 25 per cent.; woollens, 35 per cent.

Drawbacks are allowed on manufactured articles exported equivalent to the amount of duty paid on the raw material used in their manufacture. Mr. Fernando Wood, of New York, introduced a bill in Congress early in 1877, which contained a serious proposition for modifying the protective tariff of the United States. It was proposed to reduce the number of articles paying duty from about 2000 to 500, and, generally speaking, the duties were to be reduced to 20 per cent. No sooner was this moderate proposition heard of than it excited violent opposition from interested parties. I have previously written of the unrivalled advantages which the neighbourhood of Pittsburgh affords for the production of iron and coal. The inhabitants are not content with these natural advantages, but are anxious that their fellow-countrymen should continue to be taxed for the benefit of Pittsburgh, and they promptly organised a demonstration against the proposed reduction of duties.

The following description of the proceedings appeared in the *Times* of February 28th, 1878 :—

"This Pittsburg demonstration was a procession and mass meeting. For several days preparations were made for it, and all the factories and mills were closed so as to give the workmen opportunity to participate. The day was damp and the clouds lowering, while a heavy rain the previous day falling upon the remains of the last snowstorm made the not over-clean streets a sea of mud. But, nothing daunted, at least 15,000 workmen marched in procession, while half a million people gazed upon the pageant, the surrounding country for miles being almost stripped of inhabitants. Excepting a few coaches containing the city officials, the procession was entirely composed of workmen, marching four and six abreast, and carrying banners displaying mottoes which illustrated the object of the demonstration. The popular belief that England is at the bottom of the proposed reduction of the tariff found expression in a variety of ways. Here are some of the mottoes :—'America first, England afterward;' 'The importation of British iron means starvation to American freemen;' 'Congress must not reduce Americans to the level of European serfs;' 'We want high tariff and prosperity;' 'High tariff guarantees prosperity throughout the country;'

'We want Protection to the last, and nail that to the mast;' 'No British gold for us.' Two companion banners were borne, one inscribed 'Free Trade with America,' and having a picture of John Bull and the British Lion, well-fed and contented; the other inscribed 'Free Trade in America,' representing a hungry and tattered iron-worker tramping along a road and passing a milestone which said 'One mile to the Poor-house.' A banner had on one side an iron mill in ruins, labelled 'Free Trade,' while on the other side a mill in prosperous operation was marked 'High Tariff.' Another bore the inscriptions, 'This is no time to experiment with Free Trade,' and 'Put tea and coffee on the free list, but protect home industries.' Another large display said, 'Free Trade—foreign countries prosper at our expense.' The procession showed that the best feeling existed between the employers and workmen, though times have been very bad at Pittsburg, and such expressions as 'Protection to the manufacturer means prosperity to the working man,' were frequent."

The Exposition building in which the mass meeting was held is an enclosure covering several acres, and a vast crowd filled it, listening to Protectionist orations delivered from three platforms at the same time. The speakers were men of local fame only, and came mostly from the ranks of the procession ; but the leading people of Pittsburg gave the use of their names as officers of the meeting, the sentiment of the city and its neighbourhood being almost unanimous on the subject. The addresses generally advised that the present tariff be let alone, denouncing any change in Protectionist duties, particularly on iron and steel, the chief Pittsburg industries. Free trade was unanimously opposed, and one of the orators declared that "the manufacturing interests of England lie prostrate to-day, the result of Free Trade and open ports." The meeting adopted resolutions expressive of its sentiments, and determined to send Congress a memorial on the subject. These resolutions represent the Protectionist views in reference to the proposed reduction of the tariff, and I therefore quote them :—

"The agriculturists, merchants, manufacturers, and working men of Western Pennsylvania, Eastern Ohio, West Virginia, and Maryland, in mass convention assembled, representing all shades of opinion, having considered the proposed changes in the present tariff laws, and their effect upon our industrial interests and the prosperity of the whole country, do hereby declare :—

"That whereas it is especially important at this time, when *the country is just emerging from the greatest depression known to our history*, that no obstacle be thrown in the way of returning prosperity ; and whereas we believe, and experience has shown, that one of the principal causes of business depression in this country has been the frequent and radical changes in the laws bearing upon our material interests. the constant agitation whereof produces a state of *uncertainty, which is destructive of business enterprise;* and whereas an examination of the provisions of the proposed Tariff Bill shows that its effect will be injurious to many of the industries which we represent, and absolutely fatal to some; and whereas the blighting effect of the agitation of these changes is already apparent in reduced revenues, in the disorganisation of business enterprise, and in the check of that returning confidence so necessary to prosperity; therefore,

" Resolved, That, reiterating our abiding faith in Protection and its beneficial effects on the whole country, we protest against any departure from its principles in the framing of our tariff laws.

" Resolved, That we deem it unwise, inexpedient, and hostile to the best interests of the country to make radical changes in a law which an experience of 16 years has shown to be highly advantageous to the welfare of the nation, and to have been the largest factor in the development of our resources.

" Resolved, That a due sense of patriotism and proper regard for the development of the resources of our country, and a becoming attention on the part of the Government to the welfare of all its citizens, require that the paramount object to be kept in view in all tariff legislation is the protection of the people and their concerns, rather than any concessions to foreign solicitations or interests.

" Resolved, That upon this question the interests of employer and *employé*, of labour and capital, are identical.

" Resolved, That the proposed revision of the tariff must result in the curtailment of the quantity and variety of our products, imposing burdens thereon which cannot but bear heavily upon the class of men who, by their skill and labour, contribute to the production of these varied articles, and that it is neither wise nor humane to take such a step as shall result either in the enforced idleness of thousands of labouring men or in the necessity of such wages as shall afford only the most meagre subsistence to their families.

" Resolved, That the chairman of this Convention shall appoint a committee of fifteen, representing the various interests involved, who shall prepare a memorial, setting forth the especial hardships that will be entailed by the proposed tariff changes, which shall be forwarded to our members of Congress, with the request that they use all fair and honourable means to prevent any radical change in the existing rates and duty."

The first paragraph states that " the country is just emerging from the greatest depression known to our history," and the third deprecates changes in " a law (protective) which an experience of sixteen years has shown to be highly advantageous to the welfare of the nation." It seems a little paradoxical that a "highly advantageous" law should be followed by " the greatest depression known in history." One of the obvious consequences of the duty on iron was that railways in the States paid 30 or 40 per cent. more for their rails than they would otherwise have cost; and, thus, for all time locomotion is made more costly.

More than half of the iron furnaces in the United States were out of blast at the time at which this demonstration took place, in spite of the "highly advantageous" law which has given iron a protective duty of about 40 per cent., and since that time more furnaces have been blown out. Many millions of capital have been invested in industries under the stimulus of protection, which are now valueless, and which, if invested in unprotected industries, would be giving employment to labour, and supplying the varied wants of the people.

That protective duties in the States have been injurious to British trade we do not deny, but they have been doubly injurious to the Americans themselves. That their exports have largely increased is quite true, but this circumstance is attributable to protection only so far as protection has checked prosperity, and compelled the Americans to send abroad what they have lost the power to consume at home. It cannot be contended that import duties have enabled the American farmer to produce corn more cheaply or in greater quantities, and it is obvious that the production of calicoes, watches, sewing machines, and other articles for exportation could not have been increased by protection, which must have the effect of making their production more costly, as it increases the cost of the necessaries or conveniences of life to the producers. One of the most serious consequences of protection is that it presents obstacles to customers. Exports must be paid for, and if difficulties are interposed in payment, the sales will be less or the prices will be lower. Freight from the States to Liverpool is unnaturally high, because the Americans will not allow the free importation of articles which would be brought as return cargoes.

The system of selling at a reduced price for exportation, which is not unknown in this country, is carried to an almost inconceivable extent in America. It is the common custom for manufacturers to form a ring which fixes the price of their productions in their own country, and leaves them free to export at any prices they choose to take. If you want American calico you can buy it 30 per cent. cheaper in Liverpool than in New York at the present moment. The same is the case with sewing machines, watches, and other articles. I found that American ladies were surprised at the discovery that sewing machines made by their favourite makers can be bought at two-thirds of the price in England at which they are obtainable in the United States.

We are quite willing to receive anything from the States which they will send us cheaper or better than we can make for ourselves. No one here will purchase American articles unless it is to his advantage to do so, and we shall not try to hinder anyone from buying them, as a trade which is beneficial to the individual is advantageous to the State. We hear sometimes of one-sided free trade ; there is no such thing. It would be as reasonable to talk of the marriage of one person as of one-sided trade. You must have two people for a wedding, and you must have a buyer and a seller to make a trade. We sometimes hear of persons being compelled to sell at a loss, but whoever heard of persons being compelled to buy at too low a price. Whoever may be hurt by the trade obstacles between the two countries, it is certain that we, as the chief purchasers, are not the chief sufferers.

That the intercourse between the two countries might be greater and more advantageous to both there can be no manner of doubt. The time may come when the shackles will be removed and free exchange allowed, but vested interests die hard, and many years may elapse before the battle of free trade will be won in the States ; or it may be that the present depression of trade on both sides of the Atlantic will be so intensified, and the necessity of relieving industry become so imperative, that the bands of protection will be suddenly torn asunder, and the people of both countries permitted to be happy and prosperous.

A CRISIS.

Wherever I travelled in the States I found that the last Presidential election was spoken of with bated breath, as a man would speak of a chasm over which he had leapt, but down which he might have been plunged; or, to take another simile, it was like a storm which, having strained every timber and rope in the ship, causes some passengers to fear that the craft will never outride such a storm again, and others to be proud of her performances under stress of weather, and to feel confident in the future. From no one in the States did I obtain so clear and connected a description of the terrible contest as I wished for; but on returning to England I met an experienced and intelligent American gentleman to whom I explained my desire for information, and, in responding thereto, he gave such a clear and complete account of the crisis that I have asked, and obtained, his permission to transfer his history of that eventful time to these pages.

He wrote as follows, under the title of

THE PRESIDENTIAL CONTEST.

Rarely have the vicissitudes of fortune presented themselves in more gloomy array than they did in the United States in the winter of 1876-77, when the question of the Presidential succession was, throughout the length and breadth of the land, agitating the minds of the American people. The mischances of the times were full of ill-omen to the peace and stability of the Republic, and even the most sanguine of its friends apprehended events of the deadliest kind.

The canvass preceding the general election held on Tuesday, November 7th, 1876, had been exceptionally keen. Local, state, and national officials, and *presidential electors*, were then chosen. The two great opposing national political parties, the Republicans and the Democrats, had exerted their utmost efforts to win, and thus invested the contest with an intensity of interest unusual even in a fight for the Presidency. The long stagnation in trade, which affected the whole country, had thrown more than a million of men and women into idleness, made the taxes more oppressive, cut down the profits of tradesmen, and depreciated the value of real estate (houses and land) from 30 to 50 per cent., until in New York, Brooklyn, and other cities, prices descended to a depth that they had never touched before, " and the bottom seemed to have fallen out of things." Under such circumstances, it is not to be wondered at that the people, anxious

for relief, enquired closer than ever as to the conduct of their public men, and the principles
enunciated by the rival political parties.   The
Republicans, who had enjoyed a sixteen years'
lease of power, blamed the demon of speculation,
and the inherent stubbornness of the Southern
people to accept the result of the war, as the chief
causes of the evil times.   The Democrats alleged
that the people's misfortunes were due to the
partisan mismanagement and shameless plundering
of their opponents.   In short, with that freedom and
directness of language conspicuous in American
political discussion, each side accused the other of
an endless catalogue of errors and wrong doing.

Paradoxical as it may seem, the machinery by
which political movements are worked in the States,
is of the simplest, and yet of the most complex
character.   Ordinarily, the real manipulators of
political campaigns and the makers of nominations,
are the professional politicians.   Occasionally, and
especially in times of popular excitement, instead of
directing, these men are led by events.   The centre
of the American political party system is the ward
clubs, which give expression to their behests
at what are called " primary elections," whereat
delegates and ward officers are chosen by ballot.
The delegates attend city, county, state, or national

L

conventions, as the case may be. At these conventions the party programme is formulated, and the candidates for office are named. Those eligible to vote at the unlegalised party elections, or "primaries," are, as a rule, known adherents who are registered voters in the ward. Unfortunately, the primary elections are corrupt—the machinery being put in operation by a few ward politicians—and ballot-box stuffing, fraudulent counting, squabbling, and fighting, are by no means uncommon.

The year of grace 1876 was not propitious for politicians in the United States, and their calculations were in many instances woefully disappointing to them. The Grant Administration, which was then in power, as a matter of course and fact, sought to perpetuate the Republican party rule. For that purpose, Mr. Zachariah Chandler, Secretary of the Interior, and Chairman of the Republican National Committee, obtained *pro rata* assessments from the salaries of nearly 200,000 Federal office-holders, including the employés of the Post Office, War, Navy, Treasury, and other departments of the National Government. The money thus procured was applied to defray the expenses of the Republican campaign. In addition to the large sums raised in that way, the ward clubs and the candidates contributed their share towards the costs of the contest. The Republicans were the first to hold their National Convention, make nominations, and announce their political platform, as it is called in the States. Their Convention was held at Cincinnati, Ohio, on the 14th June, 1876. Nearly 1,000 delegates assembled, each State being represented in proportion to its Congressional strength. The prominent candidates for the Presidency, and those who secured the greatest number of votes during the stormy preliminary portion of the sitting, were, in the order named, Senators Blaine, Conkling, and Morton. None of these three gentlemen attained in the balloting the necessary majority for a choice, and Governor R. B. Hayes, of Ohio, ultimately succeeded in obtaining the Republican nominations as the result of a compromise between two of the opposing factions. Appended is a copy of the Republican platform or declaration of principles adopted at the Convention :—

REPUBLICAN PLATFORM.

When, in the economy of Providence, this land was to be purged of human slavery, and when the strength of government of the people, by the people, and for the people, was to be demonstrated, the Republican party came into power. Its deeds have passed into history, and we look back to them with pride. Incited by their memories to high aims for the good of our country and mankind, and looking to the future with unfaltering courage, hope, and purpose, we, the representatives of the party, in National Convention assembled, make the following declarations of principles :

1.—The United States of America is a nation, not a league. By the combined workings of the National and State Governments, under their respective constitutions, the rights of every citizen are secured at home and abroad, and the common welfare promoted.

2.—The Republican party has preserved these Governments to the hundredth anniversary of the nation's birth, and they are now embodiments of the great truths spoken at its cradle—"that all men are created equal ; that they are endowed by their Creator with certain inalienable rights, among which are life, liberty, and the pursuit of happiness ; that for the attainment of these ends governments have been instituted among men, deriving their just powers from the consent of the governed." Until these truths are cheerfully obeyed, or, if need be, vigorously enforced, the work of the Republican party is unfinished.

3.—The permanent pacification of the Southern section of the Union, and the complete protection of all its citizens in the free enjoyment of all their rights, are duties to which the Republican party stands sacredly pledged. The power to provide for the enforcement of the principles embodied in the recent constitutional amendments is vested by those amendments in the Congress of the United States, and we declare it to be the solemn obligation of the legislative and executive departments of the Government to put into immediate and vigorous exercise all their constitutional powers for removing any just causes of discontent on the part of any class, and for securing to every American citizen complete liberty and exact equality in the exercise of all civil, political, and public rights. To this end we imperatively demand a Congress and a Chief Executive whose courage and fidelity to these duties shall not falter until these results are placed beyond dispute or recall.

4.—In the first act of Congress, signed by President Grant, the National Government assumed to remove any doubts of its purpose to discharge all just obligations to the public creditors, and "solemnly pledged its faith to make provision at the earliest practicable period for the redemption of the United States notes in coin." Commercial prosperity, public morals, and national credit demand that this promise be fulfilled by a continuous and steady progress to specie payment.

5.—Under the Constitution, the President and heads of departments are to make nominations for office ; the Senate is to advise and consent to appointments, and the House of Representatives is to accuse and prosecute faithless officers. The best interest of the public service demands that these distinctions be respected ; that Senators and Representatives who may be judges and accusers should not dictate appointments to office. The invariable rule in appointments should have reference to the honesty, fidelity, and capacity of the appointees, giving to the party in power those places where harmony and vigour of administration require its policy to be represented, but permitting all others to be filled by persons selected with sole reference to the efficiency of the public service, and the right of all citizens to share in the honour of rendering faithful service to the country.

6.—We rejoice in the quickened conscience of the people concerning political affairs, and will hold all public officers to a rigid responsibility, and engage that the prosecution and punishment of all who betray official trusts shall be swift, thorough, and unsparing.

7.—The public school system of the several States is the bulwark of the American Republic, and with a view to its security and permanence we recommend an amendment to the Constitution of the United States forbidding the application of any public funds or property for the benefit of any schools or institutions under sectarian control.

8.—The revenue necessary for current expenditures and the public debt must be largely derived from duties upon importations, which, so far as possible, should be adjusted to promote the interests of American labour and advance the prosperity of the whole country.

9.—We re-affirm our opposition to further grants of the public lands to corporations and monopolies, and demand that the National domain be devoted to free homes for the people.

10.—It is the imperative duty of the Government so to modify existing treaties with European Governments that the same protection shall be afforded to the adopted American citizen that is given to the native born ; and that all necessary laws should be passed to protect emigrants in the absence of power in the States for that purpose.

11.—It is the immediate duty of Congress to fully investigate the effect of the immigration and importation of Mongolians upon the moral and material interests of the country.

12.—The Republican party recognises with approval the substantial advances recently made towards the establishment of equal rights for women by the many important amendments effected by Republican Legislatures in the laws which concern the personal and property relations of wives, mothers, and widows, and by the appointment and election of women to the superintendence of education, charities, and other public trusts. The honest demands of this class of citizens for additional rights, privileges, and immunities should be treated with respectful consideration.

13.—The Constitution confers upon Congress sovereign power over the territories of the United States for their government, and in the exercise of this power it is the right and duty of Congress to prohibit and extirpate in the territories that relic of barbarism— polygamy ; and we demand such legislation as shall secure this end and the supremacy of American institutions in all the territories.

14.—The pledges which the nation has given to her soldiers and sailors must be fulfiled, and a grateful people will always hold those who imperilled their lives for the country's preservation in the kindest remembrance.

15.—We sincerely deprecate all sectional feeling and tendencies. We therefore note with deep solicitude that the Democratic party counts, as its chief hope of success, upon the electoral vote of a united South, secured through the efforts of those who were recently arrayed against the nation ; and we invoke the earnest attention of the country to the grave truth that a success thus achieved would re-open sectional strife and imperil National honour and human rights.

16.—We charge the Democratic party with being the same in character and spirit as when it sympathised with treason ; with making its control of the House of Representatives the triumph and opportunity of the nation's recent foes ; with re-asserting and applauding in the National Capitol the sentiments of unrepentant rebellion ; with sending Union soldiers to the rear, and promoting Confederate soldiers to the front ; with deliberately proposing to repudiate the plighted faith of the Government ; with being equally false and imbecile upon the overshadowing financial questions ; with thwarting the ends of justice by its partisan mismanagements and obstruction of investigation ; with proving itself, through the period of its ascendency in the Lower House of Congress, utterly incompetent to administer the Government ; and we warn the country against trusting a party thus alike unworthy, recreant, and incapable.

17.—The National Administration merits commendation for its honourable work in the management of domestic and foreign affairs, and President Grant deserves the continued hearty gratitude of the American people for his patriotism and his eminent services, in war and in peace.

The candidates were : RUTHERFORD B. HAYES, of Ohio, for President ; WILLIAM A. WHEELER, of New York, for Vice-President.

Here it may be seen that the key-note of the Republican campaign is struck in an appeal to the North to excite the people's fears that the result gained by the war would be lost, unless the South was ruled by the strong arm of a Republican Administration. Confessedly, the Republicans attempted "to fire the Northern heart," and re-kindle sectional animosity. They accused the Southerners of ignoring the issues settled by the war, and of ill-treating and murdering their former slaves. Thus the canvass came to be popularly called " The Bloody Shirt Campaign."

The Democrats held their National Convention at St. Louis, on the 27th of June, 1876. Among the prominent candidates were Governors Samuel J. Tilden, of New York ; Thomas A. Hendricks, of Indiana ; and Senator Bayard, of Delaware. Although there existed a bitter personal animosity to Mr. Tilden in a portion of the delegation from his own State, this feeling being attributed to his assaults on Tweed and Tammany, he received a majority of ninety-five votes on the first ballot. Under the rule governing Democratic Conventions, a vote of two-thirds is necessary for a choice. On the second ballot Mr. Tilden received the requisite number, and was declared the Democratic nominee for the Presidency, whilst Mr. Hendricks was named for the Vice-Presidency. In their turn the Democrats issued their platform, which was as follows :—

DEMOCRATIC PLATFORM.

We, the delegates of the Democratic party of the United States, in National Convention assembled, do hereby declare the administration of the Federal Government to be in urgent need of immediate reform ; do hereby enjoin upon the nominees of this Convention, and of the Democratic party in each State, a zealous effort and co-operation to this end ; and do hereby appeal to our fellow citizens of every former political connection to undertake with us this first and most pressing patriotic duty.

For the Democracy of the whole country, we do here re-affirm our faith in the permanence of the Federal Union, our devotion to the Constitution of the United States, with its amendments universally accepted as a final settlement of the controversies that engendered civil war, and do here record our steadfast confidence in the perpetuity of Republican self-government.

In absolute acquiescence in the will of the majority—the vital principle of Republics ; in the supremacy of the civil over the military authority ; in the total separation of Church and State for the sake alike of civil and religious freedom ; in the equality of all citizens before just laws of their own enactment ; in the liberty of individual conduct, unvexed by sumptuary laws ; in the faithful education of the rising generation, that they may preserve, enjoy, and transmit these best conditions of human happiness and hope, we behold the noblest products of a hundred years of changeful history ; but while upholding the bond of our Union and great charter of these our rights, it behoves a free people to practise also that eternal vigilance which is the price of liberty.

Reform is necessary to rebuild and establish in the hearts of the whole people the Union—eleven years ago, happily rescued from the danger of a secession of States, but now to be saved from a corrupt centralism, which, after inflicting upon ten States the rapacity of carpet-bag tyrannies, has honeycombed the offices of the Federal Government itself with incapacity, waste, and fraud, infected States and municipalities with the contagion of misrule, and locked fast the prosperity of an industrious people in the paralysis of " hard times."

Reform is necessary to establish a sound currency, restore the public credit, and maintain the national honour.

We denounce the failure, notwithstanding all these eleven years of peace, to make good the promise of the legal tender notes, which are a changing standard of value in the hands of the people, and the non-payment of which is a disregard of the plighted faith of the nation.

We denounce the improvidence which, in eleven years of peace, has taken from the people in Federal taxes thirteen times the whole amount of the legal tender notes, and squandered four times their sum in useless expense, without accumulating any reserve for their redemption.

We denounce the financial imbecility and immorality of that party which, during eleven years of peace, has made no advance toward resumption, no preparation for resumption, but instead has obstructed resumption, by wasting our resources and exhausting all our surplus income ; and, while annually professing to intend a speedy return to specie payments, has annually enacted fresh hindrances thereto.   As such a hindrance, we denounce the resumption clause of the Act of 1875, and we here demand its repeal.

We demand a judicious system of preparation by public economies, by official retrenchments, and by wise finance, which shall enable the nation soon to assure the whole world of its perfect ability, and its perfect readiness to meet any of its promises at the call of the creditor entitled to payment.

We believe such a system, well devised, and, above all, entrusted to competent hands for execution—creating at no time an artificial scarcity of currency, and at no time alarming the public mind into a withdrawal of that vaster machinery of credit by which ninety-five per cent. of all business transactions are performed—a system open, public, and inspiring general confidence, would from the day of its adoption bring healing on its wings to all our harassed industries, set in motion the wheels of commerce, manufactures, and the mechanic arts, restore employment to labour, and renew in all its natural sources the prosperity of the people.

Reform is necessary in the sum and mode of Federal taxation, to the end that capital may be set free from distrust and labour lightly burdened.

We denounce the present Tariff, levied upon nearly 4,000 articles, as a masterpiece of injustice, inequality, and false pretence. It yields a dwindling, not a yearly rising, revenue.   It has impoverished many industries to subsidise a few.   It prohibits imports that might purchase the products of American labour. It has degraded American commerce from the first to an inferior rank on the high seas. It has cut down the sales of American manufactures at home and abroad, and depleted the returns of American agriculture—an industry followed by half our people. It costs the people five times more than it produces to the Treasury, obstructs the processes of production, and wastes the fruits of labour. It promotes fraud, fosters smuggling, enriches dishonest officials, and bankrupts honest merchants. We demand that all Custom House taxation shall be only for revenue.

Reform is necessary in the scale of public expenses—Federal State, and Municipal. Our Federal taxation has swollen from sixty millions, gold, in 1860, to four hundred and fifty millions, currency, in 1870 ; our aggregate taxation from one hundred and fifty-four millions, gold, in 1860, to seven hundred and thirty millions, currency, in 1870 ; or, in one decade, from less than five dollars per head to more than eighteen dollars per head. Since the peace, the people have paid to their taxgatherers more than thrice the sum of the National Debt, and more than twice that sum for the Federal Government alone. We demand a rigorous frugality in every department, and from every officer of the Government.

Reform is necessary to put a stop to the profligate waste of public lands, and their diversion from actual settlers, by the party in power, which has squandered two hundred millions of acres upon railroads alone, and out of more than thrice that aggregate has disposed of less than a sixth directly to tillers of the soil.

Reform is necessary to correct the omissions of a Republican Congress, and the errors of our treaties and our diplomacy, which have stripped our fellow citizens of foreign birth and kindred race recrossing the Atlantic of the shield of American citizenship, and have exposed our brethren of the Pacific coast to the incursions of a race not sprung from the same great parent stock, and in fact now by law denied citizenship through naturalization, as being neither accustomed to the traditions of a progressive civilization nor exercised in liberty under equal laws. We denounce the policy which thus discards the liberty-loving German and tolerates a revival of the coolie trade in Mongolian women imported for immoral purposes, and Mongolian men held to perform servile labour contracts, and demand such modification of the treaty with the Chinese Empire, or such legislation within constitutional limitations, as shall prevent further importation or immigration of the Mongolian race.

Reform is necessary, and can never be effected but by making it the controlling issue of the elections, and lifting it above the two false issues with which the office-holding class and the party in power seek to smother it :—

1.—The false issue with which they would enkindle sectarian strife in respect to the public schools, of which the establishment and support belong exclusively to the several States, and which the Democratic party has cherished from their foundation, and is resolved to maintain without prejudice or preference for any class, sect, or creed, and without largesses from the Treasury to any.

2.—The false issue by which they seek to light anew the dying embers of sectional hate between kindred peoples once estranged, but now re-united in one indivisible Republic and a common destiny.

Reform is necessary in the Civil Service. Experience proves that efficient, economical conduct of the governmental business is not possible if its Civil Service be subject to change at every election, be a prize fought for at the ballot-box, be a brief reward of party zeal, instead of posts of honour assigned for proved competency, and held for fidelity in the public employ ; that the dispensing of patronage should neither be a tax upon the time of all our public men, nor the instrument of their ambition. Here, again, promises, falsified in the performance, attest that the party in power can work out no practical or salutary reform.

Reform is necessary even more in the higher grades of the public service. President, Vice-President, Judges, Senators, Representatives, Cabinet Officers, these and all others in authority are the people's servants. Their offices are not private perquisites, they are public trusts.

When the annals of this Republic show the disgrace and censure of a Vice-President ; a late Speaker of the House of

Representatives, marketing his rulings as a presiding officer; three Senators profiting secretly by their votes as law-makers; five chairmen of the leading committees of the late House of Representatives exposed in jobbery; a late Secretary of the Treasury forcing balances in the public accounts; a late Attorney-General misappropriating public funds; a Secretary of the Navy enriched or enriching friends by percentages levied off the profits of contractors with his department; an Ambassador to England censured for dishonourable speculations; the President's private secretary barely escaping conviction upon trial for guilty complicity in frauds upon the revenue; a Secretary of War impeached for high crimes and mis-demeanours—the demonstration is complete, that the first step in reform must be the people's choice of honest men from another party, lest the disease of one political organisation infect the body politic, and lest by making no change of men or parties we get no change of measures and no real reform.

All these abuses, wrongs, and crimes, the product of sixteen years' ascendency of the Republican party, create a necessity for reform confessed by Republicans themselves; but their reformers are voted down in conventions and displaced from the Cabinet. The party's mass of honest voters is powerless to resist the 80,000 officeholders—its leaders and guides.

Reform can only be had by a peaceful civic revolution. We demand a change of system, a change of administration, and a change of parties, that we may have a change of measures and of men.

Resolved, That this Convention, representing the Democratic party of the United States, do cordially endorse the action of the present House of Representatives in reducing and curtailing the expenses of the Federal Government, in cutting down salaries and extravagant appropriations, and in abolishing useless offices and places not required by the public necessities, and we shall trust to the firmness of the Democratic members of the House that no committee of conference, and no misinterpretation of the rules, will be allowed to defeat these wholesome measures of economy demanded by the country.

Resolved, That the soldiers and sailors of the Republic, and the widows and orphans of those who have fallen in battle, have a just claim upon the care, protection, and gratitude of their fellow-citizens.

The candidates were: SAMUEL J. TILDEN, of New York, for President; THOMAS A. HENDRICKS, of Indiana, for Vice-President.

There were so-called " Greenback " (United States Notes), " Prohibition," and " American " parties, but their following was unimportant. With the issuing of the " platforms," the fight for political supremacy began in earnest. Partisan pamphlets, squibs, and bills were strewn broadcast, and the press, especially the rural newspapers, indulged in those reckless personalities which, on such occasions, too frequently disgrace young nations. Mr. Hayes was accused of double dealing, and evading the burden of his share of the Ohio State Tax. He was also said to be a member of the " American Brotherhood," a secret society to exclude *foreign-born citizens* from office. Mr. Tilden was charged with being a sham reformer, and cheating the Government out of the Income Tax. Each party did its utmost to attract adherents. Out and in-door meetings were held every night in the different villages and wards in the cities. Speeches—argumentative, inflammatory, and otherwise—were made by the million, *con amore* and for pay. As

election day drew near the hubbub increased. More
drink was consumed, more speeches were made,
more music was clanged, more flags displayed,
more illuminations exhibited, more fireworks
burned, and more and longer processions appeared.

The American political procession is of
indigenous growth. Take for illustration that which
filed before Mr. Tilden, in Brooklyn, New York, on
Saturday, November 4th, 1876, three days before
the general election. The weather was cold, and
the wind circulated about the wooden platform
placed in the rear of the City Hall. On this
platform Mr. Tilden and his friends stood for hours,
and far into the Sunday morning, saluting the processionists as they passed. It was nearly midnight
before the head of the column made its appearance.
Since night-fall the whole city had been disturbed
by the turmoil of its preparation, and miles of
streets were occupied by men on foot, on horse-
back, and in vehicles. On they came at last,
masses of men and youths marching in files
eight and twelve abreast, each processionist bearing
aloft a lighted kerosine torch-lamp fastened on
something like a broom-handle. Between the
masses of pedestrians were troops of horsemen, men
bearing flags, banners, emblematic devices, and
transparencies inscribed, "Tilden and Reform,"

"Vote for Sammy," &c., in numbers bewildering. There were triumphal chariots, and prison cells on wheels, wherein were seen men in convict garb, labelled "Republican Statesmen." Uniformed policemen, firemen with their steam-engines ready for work, and political volunteers, "Boys in Blue," dressed in cheap imitation soldier attire (an American cloth cap and cape), stepped past with military precision. Limelights mounted on waggons brilliantly illuminated the scene, and fireworks let off in continuous succession marked in the frosty air the line of the procession. Though over three score years, and of spare figure, Mr. Tilden continued for hours on his feet saluting the processionists and exchanging remarks with his more enthusiastic followers. Like many public men in the States, he is by profession a lawyer. Without being cold, he is, even in his best efforts, a self-conscious orator, and the twinkle of his grey eyes betrays that he holds the subject matter of discussion well under control.

The executive power in the United States is vested in the President, who holds office during the term of four years. The Vice-President is chosen for the same term. The Constitution prescribes :—

Each State shall appoint, in such manner as the Legislature thereof may direct, a number of electors equal to the whole number of senators and representatives to which the State may be entitled in the Congress ; but no senator or representative, or person holding an office of trust or profit under the United States, shall be appointed an elector.

The law under which the Presidential election in 1876 proceeded was :—

The electors shall meet in their respective States, and vote by ballot for President and Vice-President, one of whom, at least, shall not be an inhabitant of the same State with themselves. They shall name in their ballots the person voted for as President, and, in distinct ballots, the person voted for as Vice-President ; and they shall make distinct lists of all persons voted for as President, and of all persons voted for as Vice-President, and of the number of votes for each, which lists they shall sign and certify, and transmit sealed to the seat of government of the United States, directed to the President of the Senate. The President of the Senate shall, in the presence of the Senate and House of Representatives, open all the certificates, and the votes shall then be counted. The person having the greatest number of votes for President shall be the President, if such a number be a majority of the whole number of electors appointed ; and if no person have such majority, then from the persons having the highest numbers, not exceeding three, on the list of those voted for as President, the House of Representatives shall choose immediately, by ballot, the President. But in choosing the President the votes shall be taken by States, the representation from each State having one vote ; a quorum for this purpose shall consist of a member or members from two-thirds of the States, and a majority of all the States shal be necessary to a choice ; and if the House of Representatives shall not choose a President, whenever the right of choice shall devolve upon them, before the 4th day of March next following then the Vice-President shall act as President, as in the case of the death or other constitutional disability of the President.

The person having the greatest number of votes as Vice-President shall be the Vice-President, if such number be a majority

M

of the whole number of electors appointed, and if no person have a majority, then from the two highest numbers on the list the Senate shall choose the Vice-President. A quorum for the purpose shall consist of two-thirds of the whole number of senators, and a majority of the whole number shall be necessary to a choice.

By legal enactment the election is held on the first Tuesday in November. The polling places are open from sunrise to sunset. Of the eight and a half millions who voted in the elections held on Tuesday, November 7th, 1876, nearly every individual felt satisfied that his party would receive the popular endorsement. Long before dawn on that day the rival political partisans were astir in the streets, establishing themselves in little wooden booths stationed near the different polling places. From these places were given out the party ballots to the voters. The public-houses were closed, and business was suspended. Crowds loitered around the polling places all day, but the voting proceeded peaceably, and there was a general observance of law. After night-fall dense throngs of people assembled in front of the newspaper offices, the different political headquarters, and in the public halls. At these places were displayed huge illuminated bulletin boards, on which were written the election returns as telegraphed from all parts of the country. The tide of partisan hopes ebbed and flowed several times during the evening, as the returns put one candidate and then the other at the head of the poll. By midnight it was announced that many Northern States had given Democratic majorities, and that all the Southern States had chosen Tilden electors. The supporters of Mr. Tilden, assured of his election, became wild with delight. To celebrate the Democratic victory, they cheered by the hour, made speeches to one another, and kindled bonfires in the streets.

On the morning of November 8th the newspapers proclaimed the election of Tilden and Hendricks. The thirty-eight States returned three hundred and sixty-nine Presidental electors, and of this number it was asserted that the Democratic candidates had a majority of from ten to twenty votes. Journals of all shades of political opinion published leaders addressed to "President-Elect Tilden." There was one ominous exception to this acknowledgment of the Democratic success. The *New York Times*, the leading Republican organ, maintained that Mr. Hayes had been elected by a majority of one. The assertion was at first received with incredulity. When it became apparent, however, that the Presidential succession hinged on the electoral votes of Florida, South Carolina, and Louisiana, general alarm prevailed. The extent of the excitement was such, that, on the

9th and 10th of November, business was everywhere suspended. The agitation of the public mind was increased by the knowledge that the government of the three States in question was in the hands of notoriously unscrupulous partisans. Two years previously Congressional investigating committees had revealed a state of matters existing in Louisiana and the adjoining States so dangerous to Republican institutions that it drew down the condemnation of the whole country upon the adventurers who were ruling and ruining the South. It was owing to the disfranchisement and apathy of many Southerners, following the close of the war, that their State Governments passed into the control of political hucksters, who kept the ascendency by managing the negro votes. Even when out-voted, these "carpet baggers," receiving the aid of the Federal Government, managed to maintain themselves in power. In December, 1872, the Conservatives, or Democrats, succeeded in carrying the election of Louisiana. The "carpet bag" rulers of that State, aided by Judge Durrell (a district court United States judge), and the Federal troops, nullified, by their arbitrary acts, the result of the election, which would otherwise have forced the political adventurers to leave the State. A Republican Congressional Committee, in a report on

Durrell's conduct in the matter, said : " It was
" impossible to conceive a more irregular, illegal,
" and inexcusable act—a more flagrant offence and
" abuse of authority, destructive of every principle
" of right ; in the highest degree dangerous to
" Republican government, and a high crime and
" misdemeanour under the Constitution of the
" United States." (*43 Congress, H.R. 732.*) Durrell
escaped impeachment by immediately resigning.
To the State Government thus imposed, and to its
appointees, was, in 1876-77, entrusted the counting
of the votes which were to determine whether eight
Republican, or eight Democratic Presidential
electors should be returned.   The political condition of things prevailing at the time in South
Carolina was much the same as in Louisiana, and in
Florida it was only a degree better.   The character
of the " carpet baggers " is best inferred from the
language of some of themselves.   " There are still
" a few years' good stealings to be got out of
" South California," said one who did not con-
template emigration, although the State was bank-
rupt.   Another said that by means of " the greatest
" political contrivance ever invented," viz., State can-
vassing, or " returning boards," over which their
appointees presided, the ballots of entire counties
could be thrown out, or counted as best suited their
interests.

A troublous week for the country passed, and whilst the returns still showed majorities for Tilden, the more ardent Republicans began to insist that their candidate (Hayes) had been elected. They demanded that the Southern " returning boards " should throw out enough Democratic votes to elect a Republican President, on the pretext that their political opponents had " bull-dozed " the negro voters.   " Bull-dozed " is a comprehensive Americanism, and means anything, from bluster to murder, that may be resorted to in order to intimidate. An order of President Grant's did much to calm the people.   He wrote :   " Should there be " any ground of suspicion of fraudulent counting on " either side, it should be reported and denounced " at once.   No man worthy the office of President " should be willing to hold it, if counted in or placed " there by any fraud.   Either party can afford to be " disappointed in the result, but the country cannot " afford to have the result tainted by the suspicion " of illegal or false returns."   By the middle of November there was less threatening talk of commotion.   An incident, however, occurred to mar the spreading and deepening of the trust that the demand for a fair count would be respected.   It was the discovery that Zachariah Chandler, United States Secretary of the Interior, had, early on the

8th November, telegraphed to the Republican leaders in Oregon, North and South Carolina, Florida, Louisiana, and other States : " We are now " absolutely certain of 184 votes for Hayes if " Florida (or Louisiana, as the case might be) is " safe, and Tilden is sure of the rest. Can you " certainly defeat all Democratic attempts by fraud, " false counting, or bribery to capture ? Answer " when sure. Chandler." Yet at that date it was notorious that Hayes could not count on more than 166 electoral votes, and it required 185 to elect the President. In response to a demand from all quarters, which President Grant himself recognised, prominent and trusted citizens connected with both political parties were sent into the States of Florida, Louisiana, and South Carolina to witness the counting of the votes. Party feeling was running at such a height, however, that the visiting Republicans in one of those States refused to act jointly with the visiting Democrats, to ensure a just declaration of the result of the polling. The returning boards in the three disputed States met in November, and by the close of that month, despite all protests, they had thrown out thousands of Democratic ballots, and given the election to Hayes and the different local Republican leaders. In Florida and South Carolina, the State Supreme

Court Republican Judges issued processes which compelled a re-count of the legislative and gubernatorial votes, and ensured a quasi-recognition of the actual Democratic majorities.   Two judges, Bond and Wood, of the United States district courts, intervened and prevented a re-count of the votes cast for State electors.   In each of the three States, Republican and Democratic governors and legislators contended for the mastery, the Democrats refusing to recognise the decisions of the returning boards.

Congress met on the 4th of December, and the Presidential electors met in their respective States on the 6th of December, and voted for the next President and Vice-President of the United States. Democratic as well as Republican electors met in Oregon and the three disputed States, and the first-named electors cast their respective States' electoral votes for Tilden and Hendricks, whilst the Republican electors cast their votes for Hayes and Wheeler.   Issues were raised that the votes of many of the electors were void, by reason of political disqualifications, the persons alluded to being Federal office-holders.   The two Houses, the Senate, and the House of Representatives, sent investigating committees to the contested States, but their reports only commanded the approbation of the partisans whose side their clashing narratives favoured. As the Democrats had a majority of seventy-four in the House of Representatives, they did not despair, notwithstanding all that had occurred, of seating their candidate. The United States Constitution gives the power to the Representatives, in certain contingencies, to elect the President, and to the Senate authority to elect the Vice-President.

The new year dawned ominously for the peace of the Union. In the South, thousands of armed citizens—the White League Soldiers as they were called—were marshalled in the streets of New Orleans, Louisiana, Columbia, and South Carolina, to assist in the installation of Democratic governors in these States. The opposing Republicans, aided by negro militia and United States troops, barricaded and loop-holed the public buildings in their possession. It needed but a spark to have re-kindled the embers of another and deadlier civil war. Fortunately it was wanting.

The closing scenes in this memorable struggle for party ascendency were near. The voice of the monetary interests, always in favour of public tranquility, and the better judgment of all classes, were overwhelmingly for compromise, and a speedy settlement of the question of the Presidential succession. Congress responded to this public demand by appointing, on the 7th January, 1877, a committee, consisting of five members from each House, to arrange some joint plan for counting the electoral votes. This committee, on the 18th January, urged a speedy termination of the dispute, " as it was impossible to estimate the material loss " the country was suffering from the existing state " of uncertainty." With their report they submitted for enactment the draft of a bill creating an electoral commission or tribunal to determine the disputed issues. The bill in detail directed the manner in which the two Houses, the Senate and Representatives, should meet in joint session and count the electoral votes of the States. The returns were all to be opened, and acted upon in the alphabetical order of the different States. In the event of a disagreement as to which set of returns from any State (the votes of the Hayes and the Tilden electors) should be counted, the bill provided : that a Commission, consisting of five of the Associate Justices of the United States Supreme Court, five Senators, and five Representatives, should decide which set of returns were valid, and were to be counted. To the Commission the same power was given, for the purpose of executing its task, as was vested in both Houses ; the United States Senate and Representatives acting together or separately. Power was not given to either House, once the Commission was constituted, to dissolve it, until the Presidential electoral count was completed.

The extreme Republican and Democratic partisans viewed the bill with suspicion. The former preferred to trust to President Grant and the army rather than to an Electoral Commission. The discussion that followed the introduction of the measure was not confined to the capital, but was participated in by all citizens. The unexpected election by the Legislature of Ohio, on the 25th January, of Associate Justice Davis, of the United States Supreme Court, as United States Senator, affected an instant, and more favourable change of opinion regarding the bill among Republicans, for by the aid of votes of members of that party, who were in a majority in the Senate, the measure was carried. It was known that Justice Davis was a Democrat, and that by right of seniority he would be one of the five justices in the Commission, and that this would give the Democrats a preponderating vote in its deliberations. The Electorate Bill passed the Senate on the same day by a majority of 47 to 17, and on the 26th January it passed the House of Representatives by a vote of 191 to 86. Of the Senators who voted for the bill, 21 were Republicans and 26 Democrats. Of the Representatives who supported the bill, 158 were Democrats and 33 Republicans. Its opponents in the Senate were 16 Republicans and 1 Democrat; in the House of Representatives, 68 Republicans and 18 Democrats. President Grant signed the bill on the 29th January, and it became the law of the land. In his Message approving the measure he wrote as his reasons for signing the bill: " Because of my apprehensions of the immediate " peril to the institutions of the country from which, " in my judgment, the Act affords a wise and con- " stitutional means of escape. . . . Industries " are arrested, labour unemployed, capital idle, and " enterprise paralysed by reason of the doubt and " anxiety attending the uncertainty of the double " claim to the chief magistracy of the nation." At the same time the Administration took extraordinary precautions against any outbreak, by hurrying troops and munitions of war into Washington and other points they considered it advisable to thoroughly guard. The passage of the bill destroyed a partisan pretence, reputed to be favourably regarded in the highest quarters, that the Republican Vice-President of the Senate, T. W. Ferry, had the sole right to open and count the Presidential electoral votes. The Electoral Commission was composed of eight Republicans and seven Democrats, namely :—three Justices, three Senators, two Representatives—Republicans ; Two Justices, two Senators, and three Representatives—Democrats.

The final count began in Congress on the 1st of February, 1877, which was one of the great days in Washington. Policemen guarded the approaches to the Capitol, and kept back the surging crowd of spectators which sought to enter the building. The two bodies met in the hall of the House of Representatives, and while they continued in joint session Vice-President Ferry presided. The admission of the public to the galleries was restricted by the issue of tickets. The proceedings were begun with more than usual solemnity. The counting proceeded smoothly until Florida was reached. From this State there were three sets of returns, one of which gave the four votes of the State to Hayes, the other two giving them to Tilden. Objection being made to their being counted, the two Houses separated, and the electoral votes of Florida were sent to the Electoral Commission for disposal. The Commission met the same afternoon in the Supreme Court-room, and adopted a body of rules for their guidance, which allowed of counsel being heard on behalf of the respective Presidential claimants. The Democratic case was, that fraud vitiated everything, an offer to prove that the Tilden electors had been chosen, and that Florida, by its highest executive, legislative, and judicial authority, had pronounced the Tilden electors' votes as the only genuine ones. The Republicans took the ground that the Hayes' electors' returns were *prima facie* the only legal ones, and that Congress had judicial power only in respect to the personal disqualification of the electors, but could not interfere with the discharge of their functions by the different States. After hearing extended arguments, the Commission decided, by a vote of eight Republicans to seven Democrats, that "They would not go behind the returns."

The excitement produced by this decision is difficult of appreciation by anyone unacquainted with the American character. Only the most ultra Republicans were pleased. There was a far more general and profound regret that the United States Supreme Court Justices should have been found dividing by political lines. The Democrats charged that the decision was in violation of the spirit, if not the letter, of the compromise, which was to unearth and defeat fraud. Justice Bradley, who had been chosen in place of Justice Davis, was their especial *bête noir.* He was accused of being subservient to two great railroad corporations, the managers of which were opposed to Tilden's election. It was shown that his written opinion and decision conflicted, and from this it was said he had altered his mind at the last moment. Angry Democrats called for the assembling of 100,000 men in Washington, on the 4th of March, to install Mr. Tilden as President, regardless of Congressional decisions. Mr. Tilden was counselled to assert his rights by force, but he advised patience to the end, and he declined the many proffers of armed assistance. On the 11th of February, the Senators, by a party vote, decided to count Florida for Hayes, and the Representatives, by an equally strict party vote, agreed that it should not be so counted. The two Houses not agreeing under the law creating the Electoral Commission, the Florida electoral votes were counted for Hayes. The next contest was over the vote of Louisiana, from which State there were two sets of returns, Hayes and Tilden. On the 16th of February the Commission, by its party vote of eight Republicans to seven Democrats, decided that the eight votes of Louisiana should be given to Hayes. On receiving this intimation, the House of Representatives adjourned until the 20th February. On that day, the two Houses having again disagreed as to how the votes should be counted, Louisiana's eight votes went to Hayes. Objection being taken on the 21st February to the counting of Oregon's three electoral votes, the question was referred to the Commission. In this instance the Democrats had a *prima facie* case, but on the 23rd February the Commission, by eight Republicans to seven Democrats, decided to give the State's votes to Hayes. The ground of the decision was that the disqualification of Watts (a postmaster) did not operate to elect Coghlen (the Democratic elector), and the latter was not entitled to a certificate as an elector. A report which was circulated at this period, that Mr. Hayes intended, when elected, to pursue the Southern policy of Grant's Administration, came near, by uniting the Democrats, to defeating the further progress of the count. The friends of Mr. Hayes, and that gentleman himself, published denials of the story. In addition thereto, they also reiterated their previously expressed sympathy with Hampton and Nicholls, the contesting Democratic governors in South Carolina and Louisiana respectively. This affair made the Democratic Congressmen more cautious, and strengthened a wing of that party in the House of Representatives known as " Filibusters." The " Filibusters " comprised the Democrats who were

resolved to strain Parliamentary usages "to prevent the Republicans cheating them out of the
election," as their spokesman bluntly put it. The
next and the last serious objections were made to
the double returns from South Carolina. The
Electoral Commission, on the 27th of February,
decided, by eight Republicans to seven Democrats,
to give the seven electoral votes of that State to
Hayes. The " Filibusters " fought to delay the proceedings with increased audacity. Objection was
taken to counting the vote of a Hayes elector when
Vermont was reached. Prominent Southerners, fear-
ing that the count would not be completed in time,
made personal appeals to their friends to hasten
matters. They claimed that Hayes had given
written guarantees that Hampton and Nicholls
would be recognised as the legal governors of South
Carolina and Louisiana, and that it was worth the
Presidency to free those two States from " carpet
baggers' " rule. Vermont's votes were counted for
Hayes, and on March 2nd the votes of Wisconsin,
the last of the 38 States, came up for consideration.
Objection having been taken, the case was referred
to the Commission, which, on the same day, by its
former vote of eight to seven, decided that all the
State's votes should be counted for Hayes. The
Senate at once concurred, but in the House of

N

Representatives the "Filibusters" made a last desperate effort to defeat the count. Personal appeals diminished their number from over 120 to 70 votes in the all-night struggle that ensued. Representative Mills, of Texas, sought recognition for a resolution providing for an immediate election of a United States President, but it was ruled out of order by Speaker Randell. Mr. Blackburn, of Kentucky, denounced the Electoral Commission as a fraud. "The people," he said, "might yet rise " and demand what their representatives had " surrendered, even at the expense of blood." About 4 a.m. on the 3rd March the Representatives, by a vote of 136 to 79, declined to count Wisconsin for Hayes. The Senators immediately entered, and for the last time the two Houses met in joint session. The ten electoral votes of Wisconsin were counted for Hayes. By common consent, the Democrats withdrew from the floor of their hall, and, standing near the doorways, watched what followed. Amid impressive silence, Vice-President Ferry declared the result : 185 electoral votes for R. B. Hayes ; for S. J. Tilden, 184 votes ; and then he made the formal announcement that Mr. Hayes had been elected President of the United States for the four years beginning March 4th, 1877. No demonstration followed the declaration.

The people received the news calmly, and there were none of the customary celebrations. The House of Representatives met on the afternoon of Saturday, March 3rd. Proctor Knott, as Chairman of the Select Committee on the Privileges of the House, offered for adoption a resolution declaring that S. J. Tilden, of New York, having received 196 electoral votes, had been elected President of the United States, and T. A. Hendricks Vice-President. The resolution was adopted on a party vote of 137 to 88. Another session was held on the following day, at which an effort was made by the Republicans to have the army supplies voted. The Democrats had steadfastly refused to do so, in order to prevent the troops being again used to coerce the Southern people in the exercise of their right of local government. At the last minute, and just before the clock struck twelve, Mr. Foster (Republican) asked for three months' supplies for the army. The Democrats answered by shouting "No, not for three days," "Not for a day," "Not for a minute," and a scene of disorder ensued. Mr. Foster rejoined, "Then the responsibility must rest with you." To which Mr. Morrison replied, "We accept the responsibility." And so ended the forty-fourth United States Congress on Sunday at noon. The army had to be maintained for six months by issuing certificates of indebtedness, which were disputed, but ultimately paid.

Rumour had it that both Mr. Hayes and Mr. Tilden took the oath imposed on the President on Sunday, in order to be prepared for any contingency that might arise. If Mr. Tilden did so, it must have been taken at New York, for he went about his affairs as usual, and took no further steps to vindicate his title. The public inaugural ceremonies attending Mr. Hayes' installation took place at the Capitol on the 5th of March. They were of the usual character—a military and civic procession, the delivery of the inaugural address, and taking the oath of office. The reception of the new President by the populace was not unqualifiedly enthusiastic, for hisses as well as cheers greeted him as he passed with General Grant to and from the Capitol. Mr. Hayes did not prove ungrateful to his supporters, and even his enemies admit that he has kept his engagements. His promises to recognise Hampton as governor of South Carolina, and Nicholls as governor of Louisiana, were also observed, and by that means " carpet-bag " rule in these two States came to an immediate and inglorious end, for many of the " carpet-baggers " became fugitives from justice.

The fever of four months' intense excitement must have exhausted the subjects of it, or the

disappointment to which more than one-half of
the nation was subjected would not have been
borne without manifestations more violent than
those which occurred.   It is true that many strong
protests were made ; that the *New York Sun* published a portrait of President Hayes for several
weeks, with the word

F R A U D

in large letters across his forehead ; and that Mr.
Tilden received numerous offers of physical support
from those who thought themselves able at least
to begin a civil war, but, like a true patriot, he
turned a deaf ear to all such suggestions.   Still it is
doubtful whether a physical contest would have been
avoided but for the judicious conduct of Mr. Hayes.

It will have become apparent from the history
of the election that Mr. Hayes was not a party man
in the ordinary sense of the word.   At the first
ballot of the Republican party he received only an
insignificant number of votes, and he was accepted
as a candidate simply as a compomise between
the adherents of two men whose supporters
were each numerous but not sufficiently strong
to win, and they were ultimately satisfied to
defeat each other, by concentrating their votes
upon an outsider, whose small chances had not
excited their jealousy or mistrust.   Thus it was that

Hayes became the candidate of the Republicans, although, in a party sense, he was by no means up to the usual standard of that hatred, malice, and all uncharitableness which are supposed to be essential in a sound party man.

Mr. Hayes was no sooner installed President than he declared that he represented not a party, but the nation ; and that in all his appointments and proceedings he would be governed by the interests of the public, and not by the interests of a party. That the spoils of war belonged to the victors had been a maxim in American politics, and it was thought that the winning side was bound to make all appointments from its own supporters. Mr. Hayes took a different view, and this manifestation of an equitable spirit contributed greatly to allay the popular irritation caused by his election. It is probable that as a Republican he has been able to do for the Southern States what a Democrat would have failed to accomplish. Had Mr. Tilden been elected it would perhaps have been impossible for him to have satisfied the great expectations which his election would have raised in the South, and all the energy of the Republicans would have been aroused to oppose him. With Mr. Hayes as President, the Southern States accepted his concessions as more than they hoped for or expected, and the Republicans were unable to oppose the man whom they had placed in the Presidential chair. There remains, however, the fact that in the last election for President fraud was triumphant, and to this day it remains unpunished. If this fraud had been committed personally by Mr. Hayes the situation would be intolerable, but few, even in the violence of party conflicts, charge Mr. Hayes with any departure from the path of rectitude. His calmness, moderation, and firmness are on all sides acknowledged, and should he finally succeed in establishing freedom and justice in the Southern States, and permanence in the civil service, he will earn the everlasting gratitude of his fellow-countrymen.

CONSTITUTION AND GOVERNMENT OF THE UNITED STATES.

In the article on " Kin Beyond the Sea," which appeared in the *North American Review*, of September, Mr. Gladstone writes : " The struggle with the South for the first time has definitely ·decided that to the Union, through its Federal organisation, and not to the State Governments, were reserved all the questions not decided or disposed of by the express provisions of the Constitution itself." I have read this paragraph with some surprise, as it appears to me to be distinctly in opposition to the Constitution of the United States, and to the principles and sentiments which one hears on every side when travelling in America. In a judgment given in the Supreme Court of the United States, in October, 1875, Chief Justice Waite, in delivering the opinion of the Court, said : " The Government of the United States is one of delegated powers alone. Its authority is defined and limited by the Constitution. All powers not granted to it by that instrument are reserved to the States or the people. No rights can be acquired under the Constitution or laws of the United States, except such as the Government of the United States has the authority to grant or secure. All that cannot be so granted or secured are left under the protection of the States."

The principle thus laid down is universally regarded in the United States as the cardinal principle on which the Union is based, and each State strictly reserves all the rights of government which it has not surrendered to the Union. What the States have surrendered is defined by the Constitution with so much clearness that the leading principles on which the Federal Government is based are quite unmistakeable.

The Constitution of the United States provides that the Congress shall have power

1.—To lay and collect taxes, duties, imposts, and excises; to pay the debts and provide for the common defence and general welfare of the United States; but all duties, imposts, and excises shall be uniform throughout the United States.

2.—To borrow money on the credit of the United States.

3.—To regulate commerce with foreign nations, and among the several States, and with the Indian tribes.

4.—To establish a uniform rule of naturalization, and uniform laws on the subject of bankruptcies throughout the United States.

5.—To coin money, regulate the value thereof, and of foreign coin, and fix the standard of weights and measures.

6.—To provide for the punishment of counterfeiting the securities and current coin of the United States.

7.—To establish post offices and post roads.

8.—To promote the progress of science and useful arts, by securing for limited times to authors and inventors the exclusive right to their respective writings and discoveries.

9.—To constitute tribunals inferior to the Supreme Court.

10.—To define and punish piracies and felonies committed on the high seas, and offences against the laws of nations.

11.—To declare war, grant letters of marque and reprisal, and make rules concerning captures on land and water.

12.—To raise and support armies, but no appropriation of money to that use shall be for a longer term than two years.

13.—To provide and maintain a navy.

14.—To make rules for the government and regulation of the land and naval forces.

15.—To provide for calling forth the militia to execute the laws of the Union, suppress insurrections, and repel invasions.

16.—To provide for organizing, arming, and disciplining the militia, and for governing such part of them as may be employed in the service of the United States, reserving to the States, respectively, the appointment of the officers, and the authority of training the militia according to the discipline prescribed by Congress.

17.—To exercise exclusive legislation in all cases whatsoever over such district, not exceeding ten miles square, as may, by cession of particular States, and the acceptance of Congress, become the seat of Government of the United States, and to exercise like authority over all places purchased by the consent of the Legislature of the State in which the same shall be, for the erection of forts, magazines, arsenals, dock-yards, and other needful buildings ; and,

18.—To make all laws which shall be necessary and proper for carrying into execution the foregoing powers, and all other powers vested by this Constitution in the Government of the United States, or in any department or officer thereof.

It will be seen that the Federal Government of the United States exercises exclusive jurisdiction over a district which is limited to ten miles square ; outside of that all powers of Government belong to

the respective States, except such as are expressly
defined as belonging to the Federal Government.

In direct limitation of the powers of the
Federal Government, the Constitution declares that
Congress shall not suspend the privilege of the
writ of *habeas corpus* unless when, in cases of
rebellion or invasion, the public safety may require
it ; and that no bill of attainder or *ex post facto* law
may be passed, and no title of nobility may be
granted.

The powers of the separate States are limited,
as follow :—

SECTION X.

1.—No State shall enter into any treaty, alliance, or confede
ration ; grant letters of marque and reprisal ; coin money ; emit
bills of credit ; make anything but gold and silver coin a tender
in payment of debts ; pass any bill of attainder, *ex post facto* law
or law impairing the obligation of contracts ; or grant any title
of nobility.

2.—No State shall, without the consent of the Congress, lay
any imposts or duties on imports or exports, except what may be
absolutely necessary for executing its inspection laws ; and the net
produce of all duties and imposts, laid by any State on imports o
exports, shall be for the use of the Treasury of the United State s
and all such laws shall be subject to the revision and control of
the Congress. No State shall, without the consent of the Congress,
lay any duty of tunnage, keep troops or ships of war in time o
peace, enter into any agreement or compact with another State, or
with a foreign Power, or engage in war, unless actually invaded,
or in such imminent danger as will not admit of delay.

3.—No person held to service or labour in one State under
the laws thereof escaping into another shall, in consequence of

any law or regulation therein, be discharged from such service or labour, but shall be delivered up on claim of the party to whom such service or labour may be due.

This recognition of slavery was insisted upon by the slave-holding States, and the difficulties to which it gave rise are matters of history.

Articles of Amendment have been added to the original Constitution from time to time, but none of these infringe the cardinal principle of limiting the powers of the Federal Government to such matters as have been expressly delegated to it.

At the first session of Congress ten amendments were adopted, the first of which declared that Congress shall make no laws respecting an establishment of religion, or prohibiting the free exercise thereof; or abridging the freedom of speech, or of the press ; or the right of the people peaceably to assemble, and to petition the Government for a redress of grievances.

The second article is as follows :—

"A well regulated militia being necessary to the security of a free State, the right of the people to keep and bear arms shall not be infringed."

This article restores to each State the authority to make itself a military Power. Wonderful it is that a central authority which allows its constituents to bear arms independently of itself should have held together for over a century.

The thirteenth article of amendments, adopted on the 18th December, 1865, just after the war, declares that

Neither slavery or involuntary servitude, except as a punishment for crime, whereof the party shall have been duly convicted, shall exist within the United States or any place subject to their jurisdiction.

On July 20th, 1868, an important amendment was adopted, which declares that

All persons born or naturalized in the United States, and subject to the jurisdiction thereof, are citizens of the United States, and of the State wherein they reside. No State shall make or enforce any law which shall abridge the privileges or immunities of citizens of the United States ; nor shall any State deprive any person of life, liberty, or property without due process of law, or deny to any person within its jurisdiction the equal protection of the law.

It seems that this article did not sufficiently secure the voting power of citizens, for on March 30th, 1870, another amendment was passed, which declared

That the right of citizens of the United States to vote shall not be denied or abridged by the United States, or by any State, on account of race, colour, or previous condition of servitude.

The large powers given to the President of the United States are defined as follow :—

The executive power shall be vested in a President of the United States of America.

The President shall be commander-in-chief of the army and navy of the United States, and of the militia of the several States, when called into the actual service of the United States. He may require the opinion, in writing, of the principal officer in each of the executive departments upon any subject relating to the duties of their respective offices ; and he shall have power to grant reprieves and pardons for all offences against the United States, except in cases of impeachment.

He shall have power, by and with the advice and consent of the Senate, to make treaties, provided two-thirds of the Senators present concur ; and he shall nominate, and, by and with the advice and consent of the Senate, shall appoint, ambassadors, other public ministers, and consuls, judges of the Supreme Court, and all other officers of the United States whose appointments are not herein otherwise provided for, and which shall be established by law. But the Congress may, by law, vest the appointment of such inferior officers, as they think proper, in the President alone, in the courts of law, or in the heads of departments.

The President shall have power to fill up all vacancies that may happen during the recess of the Senate, by granting commissions which shall expire at the end of their next session.

He shall, from time to time, give to the Congress information of the state of the Union, and recommend to their consideration such measures as he shall judge necessary and expedient ; he may, on extraordinary occasions, convene both Houses, or either of them, and, in case of disagreement between them with respect to the time of adjournment, he may adjourn them to such time as he shall think proper ; he shall receive ambassadors and other public ministers ; he shall take care that the laws be faithfully executed; and shall commission all the officers of the United States.

The President, Vice-President, and all civil officers of the United States shall be removed from office on impeachment for, and conviction of, treason, bribery, or other high crimes and misdemeanours.

The legislative powers granted by the Constitution are vested in a Congress of the United States, which consists of a Senate and House of Representatives.

The House of Representatives is composed of members chosen every second year by the people of the several States, each State sending one Representative for each 30,000 males over twenty-one years of age.

The Senate is composed of two senators from each State, chosen by the Legislature thereof for six years. One-third of the Senate is chosen every two years.

All bills for raising revenue must originate in the House of Representatives.

The President may veto any bill, which may then be re-considered by the House in which it originated, and, if approved by two-thirds of that House, it becomes law.

The Constitution provides that the judicial power of the United States shall be vested in one Supreme Court, and in such inferior courts as the Congress may from time to time ordain and establish, the judges holding their offices during good behaviour.

In Washington's Farewell Address to the people of the United States he thus speaks of the Federal Government :—

The unity of government which constitutes you one people is now dear to you. It is justly so ; for it is a main pillar in the edifice of your real independence ; the support of your tranquility at home, your peace abroad – of your safety, of your prosperity, of that very liberty which you so highly prize. But, as it is easy to foresee that from different causes and from different quarters much pains will be taken, many artifices employed, to weaken in your minds this truth ; as this is the point in your political fortress against which the batteries of internal and external enemies will be most constantly and actively—though often covertly and insidiously—directed, it is of infinite moment that you should properly estimate the immense value of your national union to your collective and individual happiness ; that you should cherish a cordial, habitual, and immovable attachment to it ; accustoming yourselves to think and speak of it as a palladium of your political safety and prosperity ; watching for its preservation with jealous anxiety ; discountenancing whatever may suggest even a suspicion that it can, in any event, be abandoned ; and indignantly frowning upon the first dawning of every attempt to alienate any portion of our country from the rest, or to enfeeble the sacred ties which now link together the various parts.   *   *   *

To the efficacy and permanency of your union a government for the whole is indispensable. No alliances, however strict, between the parts can be an adequate substitute ; they must inevitably experience the infractions and interruptions which alliances in all times have experienced.   *   *   *

The base of our political system is the right of the people to make and to alter their constitutions of government ; but the constitution which at any time exists, until changed by an explicit and authentic act of the whole people, is sacredly obligatory upon all. The very idea of the power and the right of the people to establish government presupposes the duty of every individual to obey the established government.

The comprehensive character of the Union which Washington contemplated is indicated in the following sentences :—

I have already intimated to you the danger of parties in the State, with particular reference to the founding of them on geographical discriminations. Let me now take a more comprehensive view, and warn you, in the most solemn manner, against the baneful effects of the spirit of party generally.

This spirit, unfortunately, is inseparable from our nature, having its roots in the strongest passions of the human mind. It exists, under different shapes, in all governments, more or less stifled, controlled, or repressed ; but in those of the popular form it is seen in its greatest rankness, and is truly their worst enemy.

The alternate domination of one faction over another, sharpened by the spirit of revenge natural to party dissension, which, in different ages and countries, has perpetrated the most horrid enormities, is itself a frightful despotism. But this leads at length to a more formal and permanent despotism. The disorders and miseries which result gradually incline the minds of men to seek security and repose in the absolute power of an individual, and, sooner or later, the chief of some prevailing faction, more able or more fortunate than his competitors, turns this disposition to the purposes of his own elevation on the ruins of the public liberty.

Without looking forward to an extremity of this kind (which, nevertheless, ought not to be entirely out of sight), the common and continual mischiefs of the spirit of party are sufficient to make it the interest and duty of a wise people to discourage and restrain it.

The prophetic mind of the writer seems to have foreseen the convulsion by which the Union was so nearly severed. The great contest between the North and the South was the result of a combination of "geographical distinctions," and "the baneful effects of the spirit of party generally."

The country was not spared the great calamity of civil war, but it has been delivered from the still greater calamity of disruption.

Washington's advice is, however, not the less applicable because one great danger has been

o

surmounted. If the "spirit of revenge," as carried out under the presidency of General Grant, had been prolonged, there would have been no satisfactory or permanent re-union. Under the more rational and judicious administration of President Hayes, and his able Ministry, the wounds occasioned by civil strife are healing, and the great nation is making steady advances towards a real union and substantial prosperity.

As to the government of the Government, the power is theoretically vested in the Supreme Court of the United States of interpreting the Constitution when any moot point arises ; but it may be questioned whether Congress does not really exercise that function.

The Constitution vests in the United States Supreme Court power in all controversies to which the United States is a party, and in controversies between two or more States, or between citizens of different States ; and to Congress is given the power of altering or amending the Constitution, under compliance with certain rules. The Article which refers to this subject directs that whenever two-thirds of both Houses shall deem it necessary to propose amendments to the Constitution, or, on the application of the Legislatures of two-thirds of the several States, Congress shall call a Convention for presenting the proposed amendments, which amendments shall be valid to all intents and purposes as part of the Constitution when ratified by the Legislatures of two-thirds of the several States, or by Conventions in three-fourths of the States.

As each State retains and exercises all the powers of government which are not delegated to the Federal authority, it is scarcely necessary to define the powers of the State Government. In practice these powers include whatever the people desire that the Government should undertake. But each State has a " Constitution," the main object of which is to prevent the Executive Government from exercising or acquiring powers which may be used for the repression of individual freedom.

The Constitutions of the several States very generally agree in their main features; in nearly all of them there is the same form observed as in that of the United States, and the same principles lie at the foundation. First, there is generally a brief preamble, beginning " We, the people of ——, acknowledging, with gratitude, the grace of God, in permitting us to make a choice of our form of government, do hereby ordain and establish this Constitution." Then follow the Articles of the Constitution of the State, commencing usually with the " Bill of Rights;" next, " Division of the

Powers of Government," "Legislative Department," "Executive Department," "Judicial Department," "Right of Suffrage," "Militia," "Impeachment," "Public Schools," "Land Office," "General Provisions," or, if a Southern or Western State, "Immigration." Under the heading "Bill of Rights," the Constitution of many of the re-constructed States, or Southern States engaged in the rebellion, begins by first abjuring the doctrine of secession, and holding the laws and treaties of the United States supreme. The citizens' personal rights are next defined, and these ordinarily consist of:—the right of conscience or freedom of religious worship, liberty of speech and publication, the right of trial by jury, and of speedy trial. The right of the accused to be heard in his own defence as a witness, and the right to bear arms. The citizens are secured from search or seizure of person or property, except under due process of law, and from imprisonment for debt. (In some States the jury determine not only as to the facts, but, under advisement of the judge, as to the law. In others the judge is the sole exponent of the law; and judges, by consent of parties, in certain actions, may dispense with a jury, and themselves decide on the law or facts, or may act as a court of arbitration). Class legislation is excluded under a declaration that no person or persons shall be entitled to exclusive privileges. No bills of attainder or *ex post facto* law can be made. The military are subordinate to the civil authorities, and perpetuities, monopolies, primogeniture, and entailment are declared contrary to the genius of free government. The right of assembly and petition is given ; and other matters necessary to protect the person or property from the arbitrary exercise of power by whomsoever sought to be exercised. To guard against transgressions of the delegation of Powers, it is declared that everything contained in the " Bill of Rights " is excepted out of the general powers of government, and shall for ever remain inviolate.

The powers of the State Governments are, as a rule, divided into three departments—legislative, executive, and judicial, just as in the case of the United States. The powers delegated to these several departments are fully expressed, and cannot legally be exceeded, although in practice they frequently are ; and they must be exercised solely within the respective departments, the person or persons connected with one having no authority except in his or their own department, unless where otherwise expressly defined.

Under the Legislative Department is defined the qualifications of electors, their privileges from arrest at elections, or while proceeding to vote; but in the latter respect the several State laws differ very much. It may be here noted that manhood suffrage does not prevail in all the States; in Rhode Island and elsewhere a property qualification is necessary, and under the laws of New York State negroes were required, in some towns, to possess 300 dollars worth of property before having the right to vote. Legislative functions are exercised by two bodies called Representatives or Assemblymen, and Senators, both of whom are chosen by the people at elections, held generally every second year for Assemblymen, and every four or six years for Senators. The Senate is usually a permanent body, the members retiring in rotation—one-third every two years as a rule—as their respective terms expire. The mode of voting is by ballot, the time of polling and all kindred matters relating thereto being minutely laid down in the State Constitutions. The payment of State Legislators, the outline of rules for their procedure, and their necessary qualifications, liberties, and functions, are fully defined under the Article that deals with the Legislative Department in the several State Constitutions.

The number of Assemblymen and Senators in each State is fixed by the Constitution of the State.

The State Assemblymen, who are always the most numerous, together with the State Senators, are returned on a population basis. For this purpose, an apportionment is made so that districts, townships, or counties, are grouped into Senatorial and Assembly districts, containing, as nearly as possible, in each a like number of people, or at any rate as many as will entitle the district to return a Senator or Assemblyman. Increase of population is provided for by a re-apportionment of the State every decade, on the basis of the United States census, or as often as may be directed by the State Constitution. The question of the apportionment of a State into Senatorial, Assembly, Judicial—for the judges in most States are elected—or other election districts, is one that perpetually agitates the mind of the American politician, for apportionment gives free scope to what is called political " gerry-mandering." The word " gerrymander," as applied in this sense, may not be so well-known in Britain as the practice it defines. It means dividing a State into election districts, irrespective of all geographical or natural and orderly features, so that the party directing the apportionment shall possess political advantage ; for instance, an over-whelming Democratic district would be made, if possible, more so by the Republicans, who had

nothing to gain there, in order that they might
the more easily defeat their political rivals in the
adjoining districts. Assembly district " A " might
be so shaped as to contain 8,000 Democratic voters
and but 2,000 Republicans ; while Assembly
districts " B " and " C " might have each but a
bare Republican majority of 5,100, as against 4,900
Democrats. " Gerrymandering " runs all the way
down to the division of municipalities into wards,
and counties into townships. As a rule, the State
Constitutions seek to limit this evil by requiring
that all the voting precincts in any district shall be
contiguous ; and, in addition thereto, no political
party dare, for its own sake, push the practice to
extremes. In New York State, for instance, the
Republican Legislature of 1878 adjourned without
re-apportioning the State, as it was constitutionally
required to do. As to the fixing of the capital of a
State, that is done by a majority vote of the people,
and by the same vote the capital may be changed.

The Executive Department in the different
States is entrusted to a Chief Magistrate, styled the
Governor, a Lieutenant-Governor, Secretary of
State, Comptroller, Treasurer, and an Attorney-
General, all of whom are elected by the people ; and
ordinarily a Commissioner of the General Land
Office and a Superintendent of Public Instruction are

also chosen. But the chief executive power is vested in the Governor, whose duties are in general analogous to those of the President of the United States, so far as the several State Governments are similar to the Federal Government. He is elected by the people, and his term, whether for two, four, or more years, is fixed by the Constitution, which also defines how any contest as to the result of the election may be settled. The Governors have the nomination of many important State officers, superintendents, and inspectors of different public works and departments, canals, prisons, &c., but the persons cannot be confirmed in office except by the approval of a majority of the Senate. Like the President, the Governors are commanders-in-chief of the State militia, except when the latter is called into the actual service of the United States. Governors make recommendations to the State Legislatures, publish messages, and take care that the laws are enforced. They have power to pardon criminals, and they may themselves be removed from office for cause by impeachment, initiated by the State Assemblymen or Representatives. In America judgment on impeachment extends only to removal from office and disqualification to hold public office in future. Offences against the common or statute laws are punishable at all times by the legal tribunals, and the fact that an official had been impeached and removed from office would not save him from the penalties otherwise provided by law. The duties of the Secretary of State, Comptroller, and other State officials are sufficiently suggested by the titles of the offices they hold. It frequently happens that political parties are so evenly balanced in the State Governments that the people elect a Republican or Democratic Governor, and a Comptroller or Secretary of State of adverse politics. In practice it cannot be said that when this happens the public interest suffers. The chief power of the State Governors rests in the authority vested in them to exercise the right of veto over any measure or bill passed by the Legislature. If a Governor vetoes any bill, it can only become law by being passed by a two-thirds majority in both branches of the Legislature. It ought to be mentioned that every bill must refer to one subject only, which must be clearly expressed in the title, and the amending of any bill can only be carried out by re-enacting the whole bill in its new form.

The State Judicial Department consists usually of one supreme court and district and other courts. As a rule, three or five judges comprise what is known as the Chief Supreme Court, which has only appellate jurisdiction. The terms and powers of the judges are, within certain limits, defined both by the Constitution and by statute, and in nearly all the States the laws are codified. From time to time the laws are revised and recodified.

Among the miscellaneous subjects provided for in the State Constitutions are the calling out of the militia, impeachment of judges, banking, usury, and public schools, wherein free instruction is provided for all children between, say, the ages of six and eighteen years. The public schools are used, as a rule, by all classes, and private academies are few. Separate schools are provided for coloured children, in Northern as well as in Southern States, in those places where there is a sufficient number of negroes to justify the erection of a school for them. Various other measures affecting the rights of persons and property are also defined in the different State Constitutions, but a good deal has been said and written of late about the necessity of getting Congress to enact laws affecting certain liberties of person, rights of property, and contracts, marriage and divorce, so as to bring about a more general uniformity in these matters than now exists in the States.

The power of establishing counties and county governments, and townships, or municipalities, is

vested in the Legislature, which, in this case also, has
a reasonable amount of discretionary power entrusted
to it, for the creation of counties or the granting of
municipal charters to towns and cities. The action
of the Legislature in such matters is usually
obtained on the petition or application of the
inhabitants, and charters are altered and amended
at the instance of the people, civic officials, and,
occasionally, in the interest of politicians, when
their friends are in a majority in the Legislature.
The county governments are conducted under
different systems, each State having its own mode.
In many of the States, boards of supervisors, who
manage the affairs of their respective counties,
see to the building of bridges, construction of
roads, maintenance of the local poor, erection
and keeping in repair of armouries for militia,
and generally supervising the collection and
expenditure of the local revenues. Their
powers and duties are always defined by statute,
general laws, or specific charter, and, in cases
where the supervisors wish to borrow money for
some projected local improvement, they have to
apply to the Legislature for leave to do so. A
county treasurer attends to the actual financial
department, a county judge, county justices,
constables, and the sheriff to offences against the

laws, and a county registrar keeps the deeds and titles to property ; whilst surrogate judges and county clerks attend to the duties arising in their respective departments, namely, the probate of wills, the filing of all necessary documents connected with the law courts, and the record of companies incorporating under the general State laws for conduct of business, &c.

In some States the county Government is even of a simpler description, and the only officials are the judges, sheriff, treasurer, county clerk, who is also registrar, and justices of the peace, the people arranging for the conduct of their local affairs at public meetings held at stated periods. In fact, in what are called " towns," it is at such recurring public meetings that direction is given to the justices of the peace, or other officials, for the levying of a special district tax for improvements ; under which I include a town hall, police force, street making, and the introduction of gas or water.

In regard to the government of cities, these are all conducted under charters, of special creation by the Legislature of the State. The charters of municipalities much resemble each other, in that the local governing power is vested in a Board of Aldermen or Councillors, who are elected by the different wards into which the city has been divided, and as set forth, together with the municipal boundary, in the charter. A mayor, who also is elected, together with a comptroller, treasurer, and other civic officials, complete the parallel which makes of a municipality a government within a government. The mayor has, in a lesser degree, but subject to aldermanic approval, the power to appoint persons to office, or he may veto any measure passed by the Board of Aldermen, who, to carry it over his veto, must do so by a two-thirds vote. The duties of the municipalities are ordinarily lighting, cleansing and paving streets, the supply of water and gas, sewerage, police, fire, and all other departments comprised in the ordinary conduct of civic affairs.

It was not to be expected that a number of sovereign and independent States would yield all authority to a central power, and place their lives and fortunes ent'rely at the disposal of a Government which individually they could not control. The Federal Government did not, therefore, attempt to usurp more authority than was essential for the purpose of an effective union. It has been said of the British House of Commons that it can do anything short of making a pint cup hold a quart, but the Congress of the United States has neither sought nor obtained such varied powers as are wielded with more or less success at Westminster. A careful perusal of the Constitution will show how extremely limited are the powers given to Congress as compared with those of the British House of Commons. And in practice we do not find Congress occupied with a debate as to whether a provincial town should be allowed to carry out certain proposed sanitary arrangements, or to make a railway tunnel under a river. Neither would it require several years of discussion in Congress before an obnoxious toll bridge in a distant State could be removed. If the Union had been hampered and strained by the exercise of such local duties it would never have held together until the present time. Not only is intolerable inconvenience occasioned in the United Kingdom by the necessity for referring these purely local matters to a tribunal which knows little about the subject, and cares still less, but it is obvious that the British Legislature is hampered and overwhelmed by the necessity for attending to both imperial and local legislation. Enterprise is unduly checked, and social matters neglected, because nothing can be done without the sanction or initiation of an overworked Parliament, which cannot attend to all its multifarious duties.

This is especially the case when any great question arises in home and foreign politics.

Practical legislation is then set aside for a more convenient season, which season, if it comes at all, comes very late. Nor is this the worst evil which attaches to the mixing up of local and imperial affairs. It is notorious that the best and most influential members in imperial politics are the worst in a local sense, and constituencies who elect prominent politicians do so at a sacrifice of local interests ; therefore, such men are often passed over for those who will attend to the pressing local matters, which are so unnecessarily taken to the Imperial Parliament.

The desire which prevails in the United Kingdom to avoid, as far as possible, all legislative interference arises, in a large degree, from the delay and inconvenience usually connected with legislative action. As I have said elsewhere, the sentiment which prevails in the States is very different. There Government is regarded with more friendly feelings, and it is felt that many public advantages can be secured more suitably by legislative action than by any other means.

The Federal Government of the United States is not only free from those local matters which require so much attention in the British House of Commons, but in their foreign affairs their duties are much lighter than those of the English Government.   The complications of European politics are highly interesting to the Americans, and the people have a keen appreciation of whatever takes place in Europe; but their Government is not called upon to take a part in those complicated foreign questions which occupy so much of the time and attention of the English Cabinet.

The members of the administration at Washington are, therefore, free to devote themselves to those questions in which the welfare and prosperity of their own people are immediately concerned; the State Governments are able to carry on their work unembarrassed with either foreign or federal politics.

The result has been a degree of energetic development which is probably without parallel in the world's history.   In the United States we have the spectacle of a Government aggregating to itself surrounding nations, not by the force of conquest, but by the centrifugal power of beneficent administration.   We see law and order prevailing over territories thirty times the extent of the whole surface of the United Kingdom, and it may be said that in almost every part of that vast country life and property are as secure as in the suburbs of London.   We find the unwonted spectacle of a people gathered from all nations

P

welded into a harmonious whole, and not only submitting to, but cordially upholding, the Government under which they are placed.   We find patience with intelligence, and order with energy. The "law-abiding" character of the people is in no degree the result of that inert listlessness which we see in Eastern nations, or the sullen and unavoidable submission to crushing despotism which is not unknown in Europe.

ENGLISH AND AMERICAN AGRICULTURE.

Land in England is far better cultivated than land in America. The farmer in the States can extend the area of his cultivation, and economy is seldom practised, except under necessity; therefore, the Americans do not economise land.

The Government of the United States committed a cardinal error in making land free; under a sound policy, land would have been sold and the proceeds expended in providing good roads and public buildings. This would have induced concentration instead of wasteful expansion.

Virgin land in its native condition, and unappropriated, is useful for grazing purposes, but land which has been allowed to go out of cultivation is an unmitigated nuisance; instead of producing useful grasses it grows noxious weeds, which impede the cultivation of adjoining farms. The profusion and waste of land have been the bane of American agriculture, and so long as it is abundant we shall look in vain for those concentrated efforts which produce such wonders in thickly populated countries.

If the produce per acre in the States is compared with the produce in the United Kingdom, we
might at once award the palm of success to ourselves; but this is not the only question to
determine. While the English agriculturist has
been obliged to economise land, the American has
been compelled to economise labour, and both have
succeeded in overcoming natural difficulties. Land
is more productive here; labour is more productive
there. An Englishman visiting the States is struck
with the waste of land; an American visiting
England is astonished at the waste of labour.

From a social point of view the waste of labour
is by far the most distressing malady, more difficult
of adjustment, and less likely to be cured by the
natural course of events.

That we are not altogether indifferent to the
great dangers we are in by reason of our unhappy
divisions into unsatisfactory class distinctions is
evidenced by the attention which the subject
receives.

The *Daily News* of November 9th, in an article
on the agricultural strike in Sussex, writes:—
"Whatever the coming winter may be as to
weather, it is likely to be a hard one to the
agricultural labourers in Kent and Sussex. Some
of them have already accepted wages of from

twelve to fourteen shillings a week, and others are being locked out for refusing to accept the reduction. Farming for the last two or three years has been as unprofitable as cotton-spinning, and the chance of improvement is more remote in the case of the farmer than in that of the cotton-spinner. The low price of wheat is a direct consequence of the increasing competition of the foreign producer. The farmers, like other people, are anxious in these circumstances to cut down their expenses, and the outlay which it seems most easy to reduce is that which goes in wages. Mr. Dring told the Farmers' Club, at its late meeting, that the only chance for the tenants is for their wives and daughters to give up their servants, do the housework, and, we suppose, the dairy work, themselves, and 'take to the wash-tub instead of the piano.' He might as well have told the farmer that he must give up his horse, dismiss his ploughman, and himself and his sons drive the team afield as in the very olden time. This would be something like the attempt of a manufacturer to compensate for the badness of trade by going to the loom himself, and making his sons and daughters weavers and spinners. The farmers need to be more of capitalists rather than more of labourers."

The *Times*, of the following Monday, thus writes of the agricultural labourer :—" Our

politicians, economists, and philanthropists, educa-
tionists, and improvers generally are now daily
trying their skill on the English agricultural
labourer. What is to be done to make him fit in
not only with modern ideas, but even our new laws,
for neither seem to reach him? He will not respect
himself and rely on himself. He will not put by
for a rainy day. From first to last he is an actual
or potential pauper. He does not care the value of
a pot of beer for liberty, independence, the citizenship of a great empire, intellectual progress, and all
that we and the better part of the world are boasting
of. We run over the world expressing our opinion
freely on the people we come across, all the time
remembering in a corner of our political conscience
that we have left a peasantry at home that will not
stand much criticism."

What a burlesque it is to call upon the agricultural labourer to put by for a rainy day, when we
give him a weekly sum for the maintenance of
himself, his wife, and his children, which would not
pay the washing bill of an average middle-class
family.

But what seriously concerns the people of
England is the fact that we are entering into
competition with the Americans in every department of industry; and we have to consider

whether English agriculturists can compete with American farmers, when they have on the one hand to meet the demands of landlords who expect annually more than the fee simple value of good land in the States, and on the other to get their work done by under-fed, uninterested labourers; and, at the same time, provide costly establishments for themselves and their families, while taking no active part in the actual work of the business in which they are engaged.

The *Daily News* speaks of the English farmer as not having to work, but to organise—at least, we presume that that is what is meant by the statement that they should become more of capitalists rather than more of labourers; but, at the present moment, the American farmer, who does heavy work, beats the English farmer hollow in the matter of organisation.

The cheese and butter factories in the dairy districts of the States have long since relieved the American farmer of the most difficult part of the work in connection with a dairy farm, and produce far more excellent results than can be obtained from several single dairies. I have previously shown how dairy farms, of say 150 acres, are carried on by the landlord and his wife doing most of the work, hiring one man, who lives with the family, and is treated as a member of it.

In corn districts a similar organisation prevails. Steam engines and thrashing machines are taken round to one farm after another, and the working landlord farmers go with the machines to help their neighbours and each other. It is a pleasant sight to see a dozen American landlords gathered round a thrashing machine, not to look at it, but to work it. They keep it going from early morn till dewy eve, as if they intended to get through the work. If you enter the farm-yard whilst these operations are going on you are welcome to see what you can, and your presence will not be regarded as an intrusion, and the work will not be suspended, as no one will be anxious for an opportunity of doing the civil for the purpose of getting a small tip. They are working for themselves, and are not to be tempted by backsheesh.

It may well be asked, what is the effect of severe personal labour on the classes who ought to be leaders in refinement and intelligence? I do not pretend to have had sufficient experience on either side of the Atlantic to enable me to answer this question completely, but, so far as my experience goes, I am bound to say that I think a comparison between the United Kingdom and the United States would be largely in favour of the latter, so far as the agricultural districts are concerned.

Whatever may be the degree of refinement and general excellence to which our landlords have attained, they can have but little influence on our farmers or labourers, for there is little or no association between them. The farmers see their landlords rarely, and never in a social manner. The labourers do not see either the farmers or landlords in the way of social or friendly intercourse. In the States the labourer lives with the landlord-farmer for whom he works, and he is really treated as one of the family, both by the farmer and his visitors. The man expects to be a farmer himself some day, and circumstances place this expectation within his reach. He earns good wages, and can save the small amount of capital necessary to enable him to start on his own account. The labourer on this side of the Atlantic has none of these social advantages, and no prospect of raising himself above his present position. There is, therefore, no sympathy or community of interest between him and the classes above him, and we therefore look in vain for the development of that energy and intelligence which are often found amongst the working men in the States.

As to the effect of their physical activity upon the farmers themselves, I should like to quote the evidence of Mr. Dale, who thus relates his experience amongst the farmers of the Eastern States. At the first farm-house which he entered he found that " the farm belonged to a widow. She met us at the door, and received us with a quiet dignity and grace which would have done no discredit to the lady of an English squire, owning an estate worth four or five thousand a year. Her English was excellent—the English of a refined and educated woman. Her bearing and manners had an ease and quietness which were charming. The house had three good sitting-rooms, well furnished. Books and magazines were lying about ; and there was a small but pretty green-house. I went into one bed-room, and saw that it was extremely neat, and that the linen looked as white as the driven snow. I found that the farm was an unusually large one, being about 200 acres. The farm work was done by the lady's two sons, and either two or three 'hired men' who lived in the house." So much for his first experience.

As to the effect of continuous personal labour upon the farmers themselves, Mr. Dale was assured by " one of the most learned and accomplished men in America, that the New England farmers were generally men of strong shrewd sense and sound judgment, rather slow in their intellectual movements, but with a healthy appreciation for solid thinking. Many of them had a considerable number of excellent books, and read them. On the other hand, I was told by a distinguished lawyer that the intellectual development of the farmers was seriously checked by the severity of their outdoor work. On the whole, however, the testimony which reached me from those who had the largest acquaintance with them supported very strongly the most favourable estimate both of their intelligence and their morals. What I heard about the farmers' wives and daughters was still more decisive. These ladies generally rise early, and spend ther mornings in house work; but after an early dinner, which most of them cook with their own hands, they 'dress,' and are generally free to visit their friends or to occupy themselves with their books, their music, or their needle. They take a pride in cultivating the refinements of life. At dinner and supper the table-cloth is as white, and the silver as brilliant, as in the houses of wealthy merchants in Boston or New York. The farm-houses are planted so thickly over the country that evening entertainments are very numerous, and at many of these—so I was assured—the conversation is very bright and intelligent."

In America, landlords, as we have them, are unknown, and we cannot, therefore, compare

English and American landlords, as there are none on their side to compare with ours. That they suffer nothing from the want of them it would be rash to say. We owe something to the landlords of England in preserving for us the noble parks and splendid domains, the equal of which could be found in no other country under the sun, and these would have been impossible here under a general system of small landlords working their own land. Many Americans lament the absence of an aristocracy, to whom they might turn for assistance in legislation and governmental administration. The subject is one too large to be discussed in these pages, but purely in the matter of agriculture we cannot but see that our threefold system of landlords, farmers, and labourers places us at a great disadvantage in comparison with a more practical system, which develops physical energies, and leaves the land without those heavy burdens which rest upon it here. The question will scarcely be settled by leaving landlordism as it is, and interposing capitalist farmers between landlords and labourers. The whole system is too cumbersome for a simple operation such as the cultivation of the soil. If capitalist farmers are wanted, let the landlord undertake that duty, let him provide machinery and stock for working his land, and then let it in moderate quantities to really working farmers, who would not be above soiling their own hands, or having dinner with their own labourers. In this way it may be possible to restore the impaired energy of the farming population, and inspire the working classes with renewed hope and vitality.

BANKING.

In common with other subjects of Her Majesty, I have sometimes attempted to pass a provincial bank note in London, and I have found that almost any purveyor would rather that I should leave my dinner unpaid for than ask him to change a five pound note from the provinces, although the note was issued in due conformity with the Bank Charter Act, under which Peel guaranteed to give stability to our finances.

I was, therefore, surprised to find, when in the States, that the paper issued by banks thousands of miles distant was received as cash without the slightest hesitation; even the shabbiest, dirtiest, and oldest notes which I could find in my pocket-book were always accepted. During the whole of my travels, no one to whom I had to make a payment looked a second time at a note, whereas the new gold and silver coins were constantly regarded with suspicion, as it was known that they could be, and were, imitated.

It is well worth while to inquire into a system which has given uniformity to a currency throughout three millions of square miles, and which imparts to a ragged bit of paper a value which is not called in question. Why is it that if you bring a bank note from Bristol to London no one will look at it, and if you take it from Minnesota to New York it finds currency as readily in one place as the other? This is one of the questions which I determined to solve, and the answer will be readily understood by any one who takes the trouble to read the following details respecting the laws of banking and currency in the United States.

By the Act of February 25th, 1863, a Bureau was established, charged with the execution of the laws passed by Congress relating to currency, the chief officer of which is called the Comptroller of the Currency. His salary is 5,000 dollars per annum, and he performs his duties under the general direction of the Secretary of the Treasury. The Comptroller is appointed by the President on the recommendation of the Secretary of the Treasury, by and with the advice and consent of the Senate. He holds his office for five years, unless sooner removed by the President upon reasons communicated by him to the Senate. He gives bonds in the penalty of one hundred thousand dollars for the faithful discharge of his duties. A Deputy-Comptroller is appointed, with a salary of two thousand five hundred dollars per annum. I give these particulars as an illustration of the mode in which officers are appointed in the States, and the comparatively small salaries which are paid in cases where, as in this instance, the office is one great importance. The gentleman who is appointed to the office of Comptroller, with a salary of a thousand pounds per annum, is charged with the examination of the National Banks, and the custody of all the plates and "other valuable things" belonging to his department. He has to make annually to Congress a report of the most elaborate character, occupying a closely printed volume about three inches in thickness. It is his business to make arrangements for the examimation of all the National Banks, and upon him devolves the very responsible duty of recommending that banks, under certain circumstances, shall be liquidated or allowed to continue their business.

The law provides that any number of " natural persons," not less than five, may form a National Bank. The capital must not be less than fifty thousand dollars where the population does not exceed six thousand, one hundred thousand dollars where the population is over six thousand, or two hundred thousand dollars where the population exceeds two hundred thousand, and in all cases one-half of the amount must be paid up before a bank can commence business. The shareholders are "held individually responsible, equally and rateably, and not one for another, for all contracts, debts, and engagements of such association to the extent of the amount of their stock therein, at the par value thereof, in addition to the amount invested in such shares."

The private estates of trustees are not responsible, as in this country, as the National Bank Act distinctly provides that "persons holding stock, as executors, administrators, guardians, or trustees, shall not be, personally, subject to any liabilities as stockholders; but the estates and funds in their hands shall be liable."

"All National Banking Associations, designated for that purpose by the Secretary of the Treasury, shall be depositories of public money." The association, thus designated, must give satisfactory security, " and must take and receive at par all national currency bills by whatever association issued."

Every National Bank, before it commences business, must deposit with the Treasurer of the United States any United States registered bonds bearing interest, to an amount not less than one-third of the capital stock paid in. Powers of attorney are given to such National Bank or

Q

association to receive the interest on the bonds so transferred to the Treasurer. Upon a deposit of bonds the association making the same are entitled to receive from the Comptroller of the Currency circulating notes equal to ninety per cent. of the current market value of the bonds, but not exceeding ninety per cent. of the par value thereof, if bearing interest of not less than five per cent. per annum, but the proportion of notes to the capital of the bank must not be more than ninety per cent. on a capital not exceeding five hundred thousand dollars, eighty per cent. where the capital does not exceed one million of dollars, seventy-five per cent. where the capital does not exceed three millions, or sixty per cent. where the capital exceeds three millions.

The expenses of printing notes and other expenses of the Currency Bureau are paid out of the proceeds of the taxes or duties collected on the circulation of National Banking Associations.

"Not more than one-sixth part of the notes furnished to any association shall be of less denomination than five dollars. After specie payments are resumed no association shall be furnished with notes of a less denomination than five dollars."

After the notes supplied by the Treasury have been signed by the President or Vice-President of the association receiving these notes, "the same shall be received at par in all parts of the United States in payment of taxes, excises, public lands, and all other dues of the United States, *except duties on imports.*"

The Comptroller receives worn out or mutilated notes to be cancelled and " destroyed by maceration," and delivers other circulating notes to an equal amount.

Imitation or defacement of any circulating note is prohibited.

In the large cities of the Union the National Banks are compelled "at all times to have on hand in lawful money of the United States an amount equal to at least twenty-five per cent. of the aggregate amount of its deposits, and banks in other places must have fifteen per cent." Whenever the lawful money is below the standard, "such association shal not increase its liabilities by making any new loans or discounts, nor make any dividend until the required proportion has been restored." "And the Comptroller of the Currency may notify any association whose lawful money reserve shall be below the amount above required to be kept in hand to make good such reserve ; and if such association shall fail for thirty days thereafter to make good its reserve of lawful money, the Comptroller may, with the concurrence of the Secretary of the Treasury, appoint a receiver to wind up the business of the association.

Every National Banking Association shall receive at par, for any debt or liability to it, any notes or bills issued by any lawfully organised National Banking Association.

National Banks may charge the rate of interest allowed by the laws of the State in which they carry on business ; where no rate is fixed by the laws of the State, the banks may charge a rate not exceeding seven per cent. Twice the amount of interest fixed may be recovered by any person who has been charged more than the legal rate.

One-tenth of the net profits made must be carried to the reserve fund, until that amounts to twenty per cent. of its capital stock. Loans to one person or company must not exceed one-tenth of the capital. Loans on their own stock are prohibited. All debts on which interest is past, due, and unpaid for six months, shall be considered as bad debts. A list of shareholders is kept for inspection, and a copy sent annually to the Comptroller. Every association must report to the Comptroller five times annually, giving in detail the resources and liabilities of the association, which reports must be published in a local newspaper at the expense of the association.

"In lieu of all existing taxes every association shall pay to the Treasurer of the United States, in the months of January and July, a duty of one-half of one per centum each half year upon the average amount of notes in circulation, and a duty of one-quarter of one per centum each half-year upon the average amount of its deposits, and a duty of one-quarter of one per centum each half-year on the average amount of its capital stock beyond the amount invested in United States bonds." . . . "Nothing herein shall be construed to exempt the shares or real property of associations from either state, county, or municipal taxes."

It will be seen that the National Banks are required by law to retain, in lawful money, and have in their possession, twenty-five per cent. of their deposits in large towns, and fifteen per cent. in smaller places. Whenever their lawful money is below this standard they must cease to make advances; and, if the proportion is not restored within thirty days, the bank may be wound up at the discretion of the Comptroller. It is not easy to see what good can arise from keeping in the coffers of the bank so large a proportion of the deposits, and not allowing this reserve to be used. If the law is adhered to it may often intensify a panic, for with large funds in hand the bank would be compelled to decline assistance to a customer, under whatever circumstances he applies or whatever securities he offers. It is probable that the law is evaded, and that the evils which would otherwise arise from it are thus mitigated, but it is a bad system to have a law which, like our own Bank Charter Act, will only work by being broken whenever a strain comes upon it. If this law were made more elastic, and the taxation adjusted, the National Banks of the United States would probably be the most perfect banking system in the world.

The efficient working of these institutions has been due in a large measure to the impartial and judicious exercise of discretion on the part of the Comptroller. The exigencies of the agricultural population require very large advances during the few weeks immediately preceding the harvest, and I am told that during that period the amount of "lawful money" in some of the National Banks is often reduced to four or five per cent., with the knowledge and consent of the Comptroller. In England we should not think of giving such important discretionary power to any person, much less to an officer with a salary not exceeding a thousand a year.

During the last four years, National Banks, like all other financial institutions in the States, have been subjected to a strain of almost unprecedented severity. The reaction from the previous inflation has been destructive to credit, and has brought about a reduction in values which might account for the overthrow of any financial enterprise. The laxity of morals occasioned by the war, and the carelessness which resulted from exceptional prosperity, produced or permitted a development of fraud which is, perhaps, without parallel in commercial and political circles. Throughout this tremendous test the National Banks have maintained their credit to a remarkable degree.

The complete system of returns, with constant inspection, show to a dollar the amount of losses which have been sustained by depositors and other creditors during the last fifteen years, and the total of these losses has not exceeded 6,400,000 dollars, or rather more than $1\frac{1}{4}$ millions sterling. It must be remembered that this security to depositors has been obtained without resorting to the terrible system of unlimited liability, and without dragging into the vortex of bank failure the estates of trustees, upon whom, in this country, we fix the liability without allowing them to participate in the profits of the venture.

It is not easy to understand the principles upon which the taxation of National Banks has been founded. These banks are supplied by the Government with notes to which the attributes of currency are legally attached. It is true that the banks give security for these notes ; but the revenue from the bonds which are deposited as security is received by the banks, and therefore, they suffer no loss by giving this security, and they benefit by the use of circulating notes to the extent of the interest which they receive for their use. The tax upon them ought, therefore, to be nearly equivalent to the ordinary rate of interest. The notes of the National Banks put out of circulation about an equal amount of the United States legal tender notes, upon the issue of which the Government benefit by the interest on their value ; and unless the National Banks pay an equivalent the Government loses by the transaction.

But while the Government taxes the circulation of the banks one per cent. per annum only, they place a tax on their deposits of one-half per cent., and they also tax their capital stock one-half per cent., except such portion of it as is invested in United States bonds as security for the circulation. The effect of this arrangement of taxation is to give the banks an excessive profit on the issue of notes, which they are, therefore, unduly tempted to force into circulation, while it deprives them of their legitimate profit on deposits. The banks are, therefore, the less disposed to receive deposits, and in consequence they pay to depositors less interest than they would otherwise pay. In short, the circulation of notes is unduly stimulated, and the deposits are checked.

Mr. Knox, the Comptroller of Currency, in a report issued in November last, shows that the claims against all the National Banks which have failed since their establishment have been £4,679,781, of which £2,802,062 have been paid, and he estimates the eventual loss at £1,303,085. He then adds: "The average number of failures during each of the past fifteen years has been less than five, and the average annual loss less than £86,000. The City of Glasgow Bank, which recently failed in Scotland, had a capital and surplus of less than £1,600,000, and liabilities of more than £10,000,000. The deficiency of the assets is nearly £5,250,000, which is four times as great as the losses of all the creditors of National Banks which have failed since the organisation of the system."

"The Bank Superintendent of the State of New York reports the liabilities of twenty-two Savings' Banks which have failed in that State during the last six and a-half years at £2,437,755, and estimates the losses to their creditors at £860,723. He estimates the losses during the last three years at £680,000, which is more that one-half of the estimated losses to the creditors of all the National Banks in the United States from the beginning of the system until now."

" The losses from five State Banks in the city of Chicago during the last two years, which banks were organised under special charters under which neither State supervisions nor reports were required, are estimated to be £763,700, on liabilities of £1,157,112 The losses from the State and Savings' Banks of the country during the present year only, are known to have been greater than the total loss resulting from all the failures which have occurred of National Banking Associations since their establishment. The Government has had large amounts on deposits continually with a great number of National Banks throughout the country, for its convenience in making disbursements, but has suffered no loss during the past twelve years. Upon the circulating notes of the National Banks there has been no loss whatever."

It will be seen from this statement that the National Bank system of the United States compares favourably not only with that of other countries, but shows to great advantage when

compared with other banks in the States.
Twenty years ago banking in America was
gloriously free; all kinds of banks were in
existence, each State did that which was right in
its own eyes, and the States seem to have com-
peted with each other as to which could sanction
the wildest schemes. A traveller at that time was
subjected to constant difficulty and loss in the
matter of currency—no one would change a note
without reference to a book to discover whether
the bank from which it emanated was on the black
list. The rate of exchange between different cities
in the States usually involved a loss of about one
per cent.; thus, if you paid in a hundred pounds at
New York you would receive ninety-nine pounds
only at Chicago. At the present time one shilling
or one shilling and sixpence, instead of twenty
shillings, would represent the cost of remitting a
hundred pounds from New York to a Western City,
and as I have previously stated, the Nationel Bank
notes are taken everywhere without the slightest
hesitation.

In establishing the National Banks, and giving
legal circulation to their notes, the Federal
Government were unable to control or supersede
the operations of other banks which were often
established by Charters granted by the different

State Governments. The Government did, however, put a stop to the issue of bank notes by these banks by imposing a tax of ten per cent. upon the issue of all notes other than the notes of National Banks.

The relative position of the National and other banks in respect of capital and deposits will be seen by the following table, which gives the total average capital and deposits of all the State Banks, Savings' Banks, and private bankers in the country, for the six months ending May 31st, 1878.

	NUMBER.	CAPITAL.	DEPOSITS.
State Banks	853	£24,869,452	£45,896,523
Private Banks	2856	15,559,645	36,766,593
Savings' Banks, with capital...	23	645,468	5,235,993
	3732	41,074,565	87,899,109
National Banks..................	2056	94,178,000	135,432,000
	5788	135,252,565	223,331,109
Savings' Banks, without capital	668		160,659,869
	6456		383,990,978

The total amount of the circulating notes of the National Banks outstanding on November the 1st, 1878, was £64,198,559, and of Greenbacks or Federal Currency £67,336,203. On January 1st, 1879, the Greenbacks, or legal tender notes, became redeemable in gold " on presentation at the office of the assistant treasurer of the United States in the City of New York." The Treasury had made ample preparation for any possible demand by accumulating coin to the extent of £46,531,929, which was the amount in hand on October 1st, 1878. When the 1st of January arrived there was but little demand for gold, and thus the great object of equalising the value of Greenbacks and gold coin was successfully accomplished.

The present position of the American Currency is, therefore, this :—The Greenbacks are legal tender for all payments, and may be exchanged for gold at the office of the sub-treasurer at New York. The notes issued by the National Banks must "be received at par in all parts of the United States in payment of taxes, excises, public lands, and all other dues to the United States, and also for all debts and demands owing by the United States, except interest on the Public Debt and in redemption of the National Currency." All National Banks must receive the notes of any other National Bank for any payment due to them. These notes are, therefore, practically a legal tender at all places except the bank of issue, where they must be redeemed on demand by Greenbacks or coin.

In a letter under date October 31st, Secretary Sherman gives, as collected from the best

authorities, the following statement of the paper
currencies of the several countries named :—

	CIRCULATION.	POPULATION.	PER CAPITA.
France	£92,181,500	36,905,788	12·48
United Kingdom..	42,793,000	33,474,000	6·30
Germany	29,615,000	42,727,360	3·46
United States......	137,715,454	47,000,000	14·65

It will thus be seen that the note circulation of the
United States exceeds that of either of the other
countries mentioned. During the last few years there
has been a slight decrease in the note circulation in
the States, probably from the fact that with
improved banking arrangements a smaller number
of notes are sufficient.

Twenty years ago a comparison of the banking
system in this country and in the States would
have been altogether in favour of our own arrangements. At the present time the case is entirely
reversed ; we have nothing to compare either
in convenience or security with the National
Banking system of the United States. Public
attention is now directed to our own banks, and
if we are wise we shall take advantage of this
opportunity to introduce such arrangements as will
give the same degree of security as has been
obtained elsewhere under circumstances much more
disturbing than any which we have had to
encounter.

The Savings' Banks of the United States are
very peculiar and dangerous institutions. Some

of them have a small amount of share capital, and others are mutual deposit institutions.   None of these banks correspond to the British idea of a Savings' Bank, or afford any substantial security to investors.   There seems to be no kind of limit to the investments which the directors may make, and such investments are very generally of a speculative character.   It appears to be the easiest thing in the world to commit a fraud upon a Savings' Bank in America ; and during the last two years these institutions have been failing on all sides.   In many cases the failures have arisen from the enormous depreciation in the value of property, which has been accelerated by the rapid appreciation or increase in the value of Greenbacks.   Many investments were made when Greenback dollars were worth only 2s. each instead of 4s., as at present, and the property on which advances were made with Greenbacks at 2s. is often insufficient to meet a repayment with Greenbacks at 4s.   But the failure of Savings' Banks is frequently the result of sheer and barefaced fraud.

One of the largest of the Savings' Banks at Chicago had a capital of one hundred thousand dollars, and deposits of over six millions of dollars. It occurred to an ingenious speculator that sixty thousand dollars, or twelve thousand pounds,

invested in the capital of the bank would command
the whole concern. He, therefore, bought shares
to that amount, appointed himself and his creatures
directors, lent the money to himself, lost a good
part of it, and when he could keep matters no
longer afloat pocketed what was not lost and went
off to Paris, where he has since been living in good
style, laughing at the poor credulous dupes who
took him for an honest man.

    We see that a direct influence for good is
exerted by the respective Governments of the United
Kingdom and the United States on banking
institutions. In the United Kingdom the Government has undertaken the superintendence of
Savings' Banks, and has succeeded in providing a
perfect security for depositors, whereas other
banks on this side of the water have been left
without control or supervision, and the result is
manifest in recent failures. In the United States
the process is reversed. Savings' Banks are left to
take care of themselves, and National Banks are
placed under Government supervision ; consequently
Savings' Banks go to pieces, and National Banks outride the worst financial storms. Both Governments
have succeeded in providing for the convenience
and security of the public so far as their interference extends, and beyond its range inconvenience and insecurity remain.

THE TEMPERANCE QUESTION.

No notice of the present condition of the United States would be complete without a reference to the subject of temperance, which, during the last half century, has attracted, at least, as much attention there as it has received in the United Kingdom.

Since the union, various licensing laws have been passed in the several States, all, however, so far unsatisfactory that they have been made the subject of frequent change. Legislators seem to have studied the character of the publican rather than the nature of the liquor which he sold ; they appear to have thought that if the seller was a good man alcohol would do no harm. After taking infinite pains to obtain pious publicans, and constantly failing in the attempt, the clever device was adopted in Massachusetts of requiring the County Commissioners, or Selectmen, to take an oath that they would "faithfully and impartially, without fear, favour, or hope of reward, discharge the duties of their office, respecting all licenses, and respecting all recommendations ;" but after all this swearing, alcohol continued to intoxicate, and drunkenness continued to increase.

R

What may be called the modern temperance
movement began in the United States about
the same time as in this country, and in very
much the same manner. It occured to certain
persons that it might be as well to do without the
liquor which caused so much trouble; they gave it
up, and persuaded other people to do the same.
This "moral suasion" was continued for many years
in both countries with more or less vigour. The
idea then arose in the minds of some temperance
reformers that it would be desirable to prohibit the
sale of this dangerous article. In the States ideas
spring into legislation more quickly than in
older countries; and the State of Maine adopted
what is known as the Maine Law, in 1851.

Since that time the contest between the liquor
trade and prohibition has been severe, no other social
question having engaged so much attention. The war
partly put a stop to this conflict, but after the war was
over, the battle between the liquor trade and temperance was renewed with more energy than before, with
varying results. The polling booths are the usual
grounds for pitched battles; but the contest rages in
all places and at all times with more or less activity.
The temperance reformers appear to have been to
a large extent successful, and, as compared with

this country, temperance opinion in the United States is far more advanced.

We constantly hear from travellers in the United States that the use of alcoholic liquors in that country is much less frequent than in our own, but I have not seen that this general impression has been brought to the test of actual comparison by a reference to official statistics.

In order to enable me to make this comparison I applied to Mr. Nimmo, the Chief of the Bureau of Statistics at Washington, and he has kindly supplied me with a detailed statement of the consumption of alcoholic liquors in the United States, compiled from official sources for the year 1877.

The statement is as follows.   The prices quoted are the average retail cost in the States :—

United States Expenditure.	Dollars.
Whisky and other spirits, 56,848,525 gallons, at 6 dollars (24s.) retail	341,091,150
Fermented Liquors, 9,074,306 barrels, at 20 dollars (80s.) retail..............	181,486,120
Imported Brandy and other spirits, 1,386,670 gallons, at 10 dollars (40s.)	13,866,700
Wines, 5,723,469 gallons, at 6 dollars (24s.)	34,340,814
Domestic Wines, Brandies, &c.	25,000,000
Total Dollars	595,784,784
Or in Sterling......	£113,156,957

The excise returns for the United Kingdom
have recently been issued for last year, from
which it appears that the consumption of alcoholic
liquors in the United Kingdom was as follows for
the year 1877, the prices quoted being the average
retail cost :—

UNITED KINGDOM EXPENDITURE.

British Spirits, 29,889,176 gallons, at 20s. £29,889,176
Foreign Spirits, 10,618,564 gallons, at 24s. 12,742,277
Wines, 17,671,273 gallons, at 18s. 15,904,146
Beer, 30,267,641½ barrels, at 54s......................... 81,722,632
British Wines, Cider, &c., estimated at 17,500,000
 gallons, at 2s. 1,750,000

£142,008,231

In order to make a comparison of the total
quantity consumed in each country, it is necessary
to take the consumption in each at the same
standard of value.   I have, therefore, compiled the
following table, showing

AMERICAN QUANTITIES AT ENGLISH PRICES.

Whisky and other spirits, 56,848,525 gallons, at 20s. £56,848,525
Fermented Liquors, 9,074,306 barrels, at 54s.......... 24,500,626
Imported Brandy and other spirits, 1,386,670 gallons,
 at 24s 1,614,004
Wines, 5,723,469 gallons, at 18s. 5,151,123
Domestic Wines, Brandies (American estimate) 5,000,000

£93,114,278

Taking the population of the United States at
47 millions and the consumption at 93 millions

sterling, we see that a pro rata consumption in the United Kingdom, with a population of 33 millions, would amount to 63 millions sterling, whereas the consumption is actually 142 millions sterling, showing an excess of 79 millions, and that the consumption of alcoholic liquors in the United Kingdom is considerably more than double that of the same population in the United States.

The correctness of a pecuniary test in a comparative statement has been called in question. I have, therefore, prepared a statement giving the alcoholic test, taking the alcohol in spirits at 50 per cent., wines at 15 per cent., and beer at 5 per cent.

UNITED KINGDOM.

Spirits, 40,507,740 gallons, containing 20,253,870 gallons alcohol
Beer,   30,267,611 barrels, containing 54,481,752   „
Wine,   17,671,273 gallons, containing   2,635,690   „

                                         77,371,312   „
Add British Wines 1¼ per cent...   967,141   „

                                         78,338,453   „

UNITED STATES.

Spirits, 58,235,901 gallons, containing 29,117,600 gallons alcohol
Beer,   9,074,806 barrels, containing 16,333,740   „
Wine,   5,723,469 gallons, containing   858,520   „

                                         46,309,860   „
Domestic Wines, &c., 4 per cent...   1,852,394   „

                                         48,162,254   „

This shows that in the United Kingdom 33 millions of people consume 78 million gallons of alcohol per annum, or 2·37 gallons per head. In the United States 47 millions of people consume 48 million gallons per annum, or 1·024 gallon per head.

Since 1870 the consumption in the United States has diminished, whereas during the same period that of the United Kingdom has grown from 118 millions to 142 millions.

In American hotels intoxicating liquors are rarely asked for at meal times, and persons who come to visit friends, or lounge in the entrance-hall, are not in the habit of calling for liquors. A native American will enter an hotel and burn his shins in the neighbourhood of a red hot stove for hours without taking a drink for the good of the house ; he appears to be quite welcome to shelter without drinking what he does not require, and companies of men will lounge in conversation or silence for hours without a glass among them. Of course there is drinking and, as a consequence, there is drunkenness, but custom does not require constant drinking as in England.

There is, probably, a much larger number of total abstainers in the States than in this country, and the moral suasion movement is carried on there with great vigour. At Pittsburg I found that crowded meetings were held twice a day, and many of the worst characters were reformed. In the women's crusade something more than moral suasion appears to have been exercised towards the publicans.

The liquor traders do not like temperance movements in any shape, but their hostility is chiefly manifested against the advocates of legal prohibition. They have a great objection to being put down by law. At a meeting of the " United States Brewers' Association," held at Cincinnati, in June, 1875, the following resolutions against prohibition were adopted :— " Resolved, That where restrictive and prohibitory enactments exist every possible measure be taken to oppose, resist, and repeal them ; and it is further resolved, that politicians favouring pro- hibitory enactments who offer themselves as candidates for office be everywhere strenuously opposed, and the more so if it be found that their personal habits do not conform to their public pro- fession." It appears that between 1873 and 1876 nearly one-third of the brewers were annihilated; there were 3,554 in 1873, and only 2,524 in 1876. Mr. Louis Shade, of Washington, agent of the Brewers' Congress, in addressing the Convention, said:—" There is no doubt that the temperance agitation and prohibitory laws are the chief causes of the decrease as compared with the preceding year. Had our friends in Massachusetts been free to carry on their business, and had not the State authorities constantly interfered with the latter, there is no doubt that, instead of showing a decrease of 116,583 barrels in one year, they would have increased at the same rate as they did in the preceding year."

Whatever opinions other people hold on the subject, it is clear that the brewers do not regard prohibition as a " failure."

As against the rights of separate States to prohibit the sale of alcoholic liquors, the publicans have appealed to the Constitution of the United States, and with some show of reason. The Constitution prohibits any State from imposing duties on the produce of another State ; and it has been contended that, under this law, liquor made in one State cannot be excluded from sale in another. It is also contended that, as the internal revenue officers of the Federal Government charge and receive duties on liquors, this charge involves the right of selling the liquor on which the duties have been paid.

These points have been urged and combated in various courts with all the forensic ability which

traders and teetotallers could command. The
result has been a confirmation of the power of
States to control and regulate or prohibit the sale
of alcohol. The substance of the principles laid
down by the judges is contained in the following
brief extracts from the judgments delivered in
various courts where the question has been tried :—

In the Supreme Court of the United States, Chief
Justice Taney said :—" If any State deems the
retail and internal traffic in ardent spirits injurious
to its citizens, and calculated to produce idleness,
vice, or debauchery, I see nothing in the Con_
stitution of the United States to prevent it from
regulating or restraining the traffic, or from prohibiting it altogether, if it thinks proper."

In the Supreme Court, New Jersey, in 1872,
the Judge said :—" It is an established principle,
essential to the rights of self-preservation in every
organised community, that, however absolute may
be the owner's title to his property, he holds it
under the implied condition 'that its use shall not
work injury to the equal enjoyment and safety of
others who have an equal right to the enjoyment of
their property, nor be injurious to the community."

The law was laid down in the Michigan
Supreme Court in the following terms :—" In the
exercise of its police power, a State has full power

to prohibit, under penalties, the exercise of any trade or employment which is found to be hazardous or injurious to its citizens, and destructive to the best interests of society, without providing compensation to those upon whom the prohibition rests." From which it appears that the subject of compensation has been raised in the States as well as in this country.

So much uncertainty prevails respecting the action of prohibitory laws in the United States, that a brief statement of the present condition of the question may be useful.

The first prohibitory law was enacted in Maine in 1851, and, with the exception of the two years 1856 and 1857, has been continued, and it remains the law of the State to the present time. After the two exceptional years, legislators were chosen by large majorities, who, in 1858, re-enacted the prohibitory law, and since that time Governor Dingle states that "The opposition to the law obviously grew weaker from year to year, and although there were frequent attempts to secure a Legislature favourable to its repeal, yet they always failed."

The State of Maine contains 35,000 square miles, with a population in 1870 of 626,915.

Throughout the whole of the State there is not a single distillery in operation. The law is not actively enforced in every town or district in the State, but that it has upon the whole been effective in a degree which must be highly satisfactory to its advocates is evident from the fact that the liquor revenue from Maine in 1873 was 49,237 dollars, whereas from Connecticut, with a population 90,000 less than that of Maine, the revenue was 336,743 dollars, and from Maryland, where the population is one-fourth more than in Maine, the revenue was 1,285,700 dollars. In the year ending June 30th, 1876, the revenue from Maine was 27,773 dollars.

Official testimony as to the effectiveness and advantages of the law might be quoted to any extent, but the following brief extracts will give a fair idea of the nature of this testimony :—

General Chamberlain, who was Governor of Maine from 1867 to 1871, and is now President of Bowdoin College, writes :—" The law is as well executed generally in the State as other criminal laws are. Many persons think that there is not one-tenth so much liquor sold in the State as there was formerly. While we prefer not to certify to any particular degree of repression of the traffic, we say without reserve that if liquors are sold at all it is in very small quantities compared with the old times, and in a secret way, as other unlawful things are done."

General Connor, Governor in 1876, states :—" It is a matter of common knowledge that the laws prohibiting the sale of intoxicating liquors have been very generally enforced, especially in the cities and large towns, where the traffic is most persistently attempted to be carried on in defiance of them. The law, as a whole, fairly represents the sentiment of the people. Maine has a fixed conclusion on this subject. It is that the sale of intoxicating liquors is an evil of such magnitude that the wellbeing of the State demands, and the conditions of the social compact warrant, its suppression."

Walcott Hamlin, the Superintendent of Internal Revenue, writes, in 1872 :—" In the course of my duty, as an Internal Revenue Officer, I have become thoroughly acquainted with the state and extent of the liquor traffic in Maine, and I have no hesitation in saying that the beer trade is not more than one per cent. of what I remember it to have been, and the trade in distilled liquors is not more than ten per cent. of what it was formerly."

The Ex-Mayor of Portland, who was elected by the Democrats at a time when they openly opposed the law, and who stated that he was unable to approve of the principles of Prohibitory Liquor Laws, writes, in 1872 :—" At the present time the law is probably enforced, even in large towns and cities, as thoroughly, at least, as any other penal statutes."

The Mayor of Bangor, writes, in 1872 :—"Last year the law was seldom enforced in our city ; this year it has been. The records of our police-courts show only about one-fifth the number of cases before it as compared with last year."

The number of persons in Maine convicted of crime in 1860 was 1,215 ; in 1870 the number had fallen to 431, and the number of paupers from 8,946 to 4,619.

Almost any county or town in the United States may adopt prohibition by electing officers who will not grant licenses, and thus what is called here the Permissive Bill, or local option, is in practical operation. The permissive principle appears to afford the most suitable and effective form in which social legislation can be applied. It is useless to attempt the enforcement of a law which is opposed to the pecuniary interests of a large class of traders, unless the principle on which it is founded is abundantly sustained by public opinion. This is not likely to be the case in every town throughout a large State; and, therefore, a Permissive Bill, allowing its adoption where public sentiment is sufficiently advanced, may be useful when legal prohibition for the whole State may be a failure.

Local self-government is better understood and more fully adopted in America than with us; there, each town or village does that which is right in its own eyes. Many towns, and even large cities, are governed by two, three, or four officers annually elected, who are thus immediately amenable to public opinion. Vested interests are little thought of. If a traveller asks, How do you compensate the liquor sellers when you stop the traffic? he is stared at, and asked in return, Why should private interests be allowed to stand in the way of public good? and he is told that if a man is carrying on a trade which is discovered to be injurious to the community he ought rather to compensate the public for the harm he has done than the public compensate him for not doing harm any longer. There cannot be a doubt that in districts where the liquor traffic is excluded, in accordance with public opinion, a degree of prosperity and contentment prevails which is unknown in other communities. I did not travel in the States where the Maine Law is in operation; neither did I make any special efforts to discover temperance communities. I wished to see the country in all respects as it is without exaggerating any one feature; but without looking for them I came upon temperance towns where the sale of liquor is entirely excluded, and upon others where such stringent licence laws are in force as greatly to check the evils of drunkenness. In some of these temperance towns other vices such as prostitution and gambling, had disappeared with the vice of drunkenness.

At Greely, in Colorado, I was assured that not one abandoned woman could be found in the town, and if such a person came to the place public opinion would compel her to leave. As there are many towns and cities in the Union where every kind of vice is rampant, so there are others where the cardinal virtues appear to be triumphant.

We are often assured that most alarming consequences would result if the social virtues were rigidly enforced in any community; such uncomfortable anticipations might be greatly alleviated by witnessing the substantial prosperity, practical freedom, and general happiness which are enjoyed in those localities of the United States in which custom, habit, or law have contributed to the adoption of a high social standard.

RAILWAYS.

The promoters of new railroad lines in the States may be fairly divided into two classes—first, those who seek to build a road for purely local reasons, such as owning land, or having property, or other direct interests in the neighbourhood which they conceive will be benefited by improving the means of communication; and second, those who project lines for purely speculative purposes, one of their objects frequently being to acquire land along the line of the contemplated railway.

If a new railway is projected, and there is a general incorporation law in the State in which the road is to be built, the promoters may avail themselves of that. The rule, however, is to apply to the State Legislature for a Charter. The Charter defines the scope, character, and powers of the Company to be formed, and describes within certain limits the line of the proposed railroad, or places it will pass through, within what time it is to be built, and how operated. Should the line be projected through several States, the Legislature of each must be applied to for the necessary powers, or, if the route lies through United States territory, Congress has to be asked to pass a bill giving the requisite authority to enter upon the National land.

After a Bill or Charter to build a railroad has become law, the promoters, before they enter upon land (other than that held by themselves) must file, with the clerk or other authorities of the different counties through which the railway is to be run, an official copy of their Charter, together with maps or tracings of the line of the new road. When property owners dispute the sufficiency of the compensation offered them by railroad projectors, the State laws prescribe the course to be followed before the line can be actually laid. The legal solution of difficulties of the kind in question is usually the appointment of local arbitrators or commissioners to appraise the property, and injury that may be done thereto, the Courts having power to require a speedy decision.

In the case of a railway built by those resident in the neighbourhood of the proposed line, not for speculative purposes, but to improve communications, cheapen the price of what they have to buy, and open up new markets for what they have to sell, a few leading citizens meet together

s

and each agrees to contribute so much in money
or land towards the scheme. The local representatives in the State Legislature see to the
securing of a Charter, and, when once the latter is
obtained, the rest is comparatively easy, provided
the people are in earnest about getting a railroad.
The residents may go on with the building of the
road themselves, or they may call in a contractor
cr contractors, to take the whole matter off their
hands.

Whichever course they decide to adopt
rarely affects what follows, namely, disposal
of the new Company's stock, paying up of
the requisite amount of the same as required by
law before the Charter becomes operative, and
securing aid from the municipalities or counties in
the shape of subscriptions or bonds to assist in
building the railway. If the contemplated railway
is an important through line, or has some special
feature about it of value to the State at large, the
projectors seek for and frequently obtain assistance
towards its construction in the shape of bonds from
the State Authorities. So American railway promoters look for, and often obtain, assistance towards
the building of new lines from the State Governments, counties, municipalities, and private owners of
property, and not infrequently aid is obtained from

the National Government, in addition to all other sources. Private individuals are not niggardly in giving, and owners of land in the West and South have been known to devote one-half of their property, as well as the right of way, to have a railroad run through their neighbourhood. But there are instances to be found the reverse of this, as when some seclusion loving settler would freely give half his wealth to keep the steam horse away from his locality.

The State Government of Texas had up to 1876 contributed twenty millions of acres to railroad companies, under her general railroad law, which grants 16 sections, or 10,240 acres, of land to every mile of road put in running order. Funds at the rate of 6,000 dollars per mile, at six per cent. per annum, secured on mortgage on the road, have also been lent to railways in that State, whilst other States have not been behindhand in grants of various kinds to their local railroads. The people of Galveston and San Antonio, two Texan towns, each voted a donation of 500,000 dollars for the speedy construction of a line which was to be run between these places.

It appears to be almost a work of supererogation to point out the many ways open to speculators in the State to coin money out of railroad schemes.

What the General, State, or other Authorities do there to aid railroad enterprise indicates how widely the door has been opened for individuals, who have little commercial morality, to take advantage of the public in order to line their pockets. Nearly every State Legislature has its attendant clique of railroad promoters, who secure Charters on speculation to sell to contractors or bankers. The means taken to procure the passage of these bills is seldom free from reproach. The Great Pacific Railway scheme was aided in Congress, as all new railway projects are, by a "lobby," or clique of lawyers, and men who act as "go-betweens" between Congressmen and the speculators.

Poor's Railroad Manual of the United States gives the following statement showing mileage, capital, cost, earnings, &c., of the railroads of the United States in 1876, compared with those of Great Britain for 1875 :—

	UNITED STATES.		UNITED KINGDOM.
Miles of Railroad	73,508	....	16,658
Cost of Railroads	£893,718,387	....	£630,223,496
Capital Stock............	£449,671,675	....	£466,794,056
Funded Debt............	£444,046,712	....	£163,429,438
Freight Moved......tons	197,082,000	......tons	200,069,651
Receipts from Freight	£72,227,475	....	£33,268,072
	(℔ ton, 7/4)		(℔ ton, 3/5)
Gross Earnings.........	£99,451,591	....	£58,982,735

	UNITED STATES.		UNITED KINGDOM.
Operating Expenses...	£62,161,041	....	£32,198,196
Net Earnings	£37,290,550	....	£26,784,539
Dividends................	£13,607,933	....	£9,634,276
Gross Earnings ⅌ Mile	£1,353	....	£3,540
Net Earnings ⅌ Mile...	£507	....	£1,607
Cost of Construction ⅌ Mile	£10,711	....	£37,863
⅌ Cent. of Dividend to Capital	3·03	....	4·54

To the cost of American railways, as given in this table, must be added the value of the land allotted to the companies which undertook the construction of the lines.

It must not be imagined that the construction of a railway in America bears any near relation to what we understand by a railway in this country. Most of the railways in the West are laid upon level prairies ; the work consists in opening a small ditch at each side, the earth from which is thrown into the centre, sleepers are laid upon this earth, and the rails are placed upon the sleepers, and tacked on them by small dog nails. The sleepers are generally cut on some part of the line, and cost nothing but the labour of sawing and carriage. If streams have to be crossed light timber staging is erected barely strong enough to carry the train, the timber costing nothing more than labour and carriage.

In dry weather the road can be used for trains not exceeding 25 miles per hour, but during the few wet days speed is reduced in order to meet the danger occasioned by the softness of the road. Not even a tramway from a stone quarry could be thus laid in the moist climate of Britain; but in the States such lines can be worked with comparative safety during a considerable portion of the year. Two thousand pounds, or ten thousand dollars, per mile would be a large price to pay for constructing such a railway; and, bearing in mind this fact, it will be interesting to note the arrangements which have been made with persons and companies by whom railway construction has been undertaken.

As a specimen of these arrangements we will refer to the Union Pacific Railway, which was Chartered by Acts of Congress on July 1st, 1862, and July 2nd, 1864. By the first named Act the company was endowed with a land grant equal to 12,800 acres per mile, the right of way to a width of 200 feet, and a bond subsidy as a loan in aid. The latter amounted to £3,200 per mile for the line from the Missouri River to the base of the Rocky Mountains, £9,600 per mile for the distance of 150 miles through the mountain range, and

£6,400 per mile for the remaining distance to the western terminus of the road. The Government subsidy was to be a first mortgage on the road and other property of the Company. By the Act of July 2nd, 1864, however, it was changed from a first to a second mortgage, the Company being authorised to create a first mortgage for an amount equal to that of the subsidy lien. For the liquidation of the Government loan and the interest thereon the Government was empowered to retain one-half of the charges for transportation services on its own account, and the Company was obliged to pay to the Government, as a sinking fund, five per cent. of the whole net earnings from transportation, which so far it has failed to do.

The cost of the road and the equipment has been £23,042,917, and the Company has invested about 2½ millions in other undertakings. As the length of the road is 1,030 miles, it shows an average cost of £22,371 per mile. The greater part of this line passes over level land, where the legitimate expenditure on construction ought not to have exceeded £2,000 per mile. For a distance of 150 miles it crosses the Rocky Mountains, but even on this part of the road nothing like an expenditure of £22,000 per mile could have been reasonably incurred. There is no doubt that four or five times as much as the line should fairly have cost has been paid for its construction, and it is, therefore, not surprising that Mr. Hussey Vivian should be able to inform us that five of the promoters of this railway are now enjoying an income of £700,000 per annum between them. In the meantime the Government are left without interest on their advances.

The promoters had the assurance to ask in the first instance from the Government, as a subsidy in land and money, twice as much as was necessary for the construction of the line, and this they obtained. Two years afterwards they persuaded the Government to make their advance a second instead of a first charge upon the railway, and this was conceded. Not satisfied with this second triumph, the Company contended that the interest on the subsidy bonds was not due to the Government until the bonds arrived at maturity, and this monstrous claim has been decided in their favour by the United States Supreme Court, which shows how much cleverness was practised in manufacturing the agreement with the Government. By making the subsidy of the Government a second charge, the Company were enabled to obtain money on their bonds, which they did to an extent exceeding twelve millions sterling.

The total receipts of the Company on capital account were :—

Government Subsidy in Land, 12,046,712 acres, In Cash	£5,447,302
Funded Debt Bonds, bearing interest from six to eight per cent.	12,792,400
Capital Stock	7,352,460
	£25,592,162
Of which there has been redeemed up to end of 1876	2,571,600
	£23,020,562

The company have still on hand more than ten million acres of land, which, at $2\frac{1}{2}$ dollars per acre, are worth five millions sterling.

The railway appears to be remarkably well managed, the operating expenses and maintenance of way not exceeding 40·88 per cent. of the receipts. The net earnings of the line in 1870 were £589,482, which had increased in 1876 to £1,523,729.

The Company commenced paying dividends in 1875 at the rate of four per cent. per annum, and as the charge upon the Funded Debt bonds is under £700,000 per annum, or less than half their net receipts, they must have ample funds for dividends. Had the concern been otherwise conducted, and the outlay kept within reasonable limits, the railway would have been a splendid investment for the original stockholders.

In the States, however, railway promoters become rich and stockholders become poor, a circumstance which will surprise no one who has had an opportunity of comparing the outlay on railway with the work which has been accomplished.

A large proportion of the American railways are lightly constructed tramways over perfectly level land, made as I have before explained, without an ounce of ballast. Such lines can be easily laid down at the rate of a mile per day, and sometimes four miles have been laid in less than twenty-four hours. These lines would be dear at two thousand pounds per mile. I repeatedly call attention to this fact, which it is essential to remember with reference to the cost and value of American railways.

The Union Pacific is not the only railway for which four times as much has been paid as the line should reasonably have cost. The Central Pacific, which is a continuation from the Union Pacific to San Francisco, shows a similar style of procedure, as do many other railways ; but it is not necessary to multiply examples.

It must not be supposed that the men who have thus overreached the Government and the stockholders, to their enormous personal advantage, are by no means unpopular. On the contrary they afford striking examples of the proverb that "Men will praise thee when thou doest well for thyself," and as a matter of fact these men have done well not only for themselves, but also for the public, who have benefited immensely by the development of railways, which perhaps contribute more to national prosperity in America than in any other part of the world.   If the work had been carried out with a moderate degree of honesty, the public advantages and profits to shareholders would have been enormous.

Not only does dishonesty prevail in connection with railway construction, but in working the line the interest of the directors and managers is systematically pursued at the expense of the public and of the shareholders. It is usually taken for granted that the directors of a line will manipulate rates and arrangements for their own personal advantage. Whatever may be the law on the subject, there has hitherto been no observance of equality in rates. These are arranged as it may suit the interests of the directors, or rather director, for it often happens that the control of a railway falls entirely into the hands of one man. An amusing and well-known story is told of two railway magnates who controlled separate lines between Chicago and New

York. Mr. A. puts down his rates for freight to a
very low point.   Mr. B. not only followed suit, but,
after the ordinary manner of competition, he went
still lower. A. reduced again and B. went still
lower ; but Mr. A. had other objects in view, and
having got Mr. B. down to a point at which the carriage of goods would involve a serious loss, he engaged, through his agents, with B. for all the freight
which B. could provide for some months.   A. who
had previously purchased enormous quantities of
produce at Chicago, had the pleasure of seeing B.
take it to New York at losing rates, and at the same
time, knowing that B. was fixed with contracts, put
up the prices on his own line, and carried for the
public at a profit.

Localities are often sacrificed to personal
interests in these railway contests, and certain
industries are ruthlessly destroyed at one place by
preferential rates being given to some other locality
in which the directors are interested.   Thus the
charge for goods from Chicago to New York was
only one-third of the rate from Pittsburg to New
York, although the distance from Chicago was
twice as great.

It must not be supposed that all this chicanery
and fraud is allowed to pass unnoticed by the
public, or by politicians.   It is well-known that

the public interest demands an equalisation of
rates, and this principle is now an important plank
in some political platforms ; but it seems to be
very difficult in the States to frame an Act of
Congress through which interested parties cannot
manage to drive a railway train.

"OLD PROBABILITIES."

In a recent speech, Mr. Hayes, the President, said :—" We have with us to-day the gentleman who is at the head of the Signal Service of the United States.   He is known popularly as ' Old Probabilities,'   He is not old, and, I fear, he is not always probable, but, certainly, in the science of meteorology he has gone farther than any other ; and what does he tell us ?   He says that this atmosphere of ours, this circumambient air that surrounds the globe, is one as a unit, and that it has been discovered, by observations all over the globe, that a great commotion and a great disturbance on any sea or any continent, sooner or later, is felt on every other sea and every other continent."

This observation refers to General Meyer, whose proper designation is Chief Signal Officer of the War Department.   I can bear testimony to the fact that he is devoted to the duties which he has undertaken, for when I called upon him at Washington, although he was suffering from serious illness, he received me in his bedroom and explained his views with an earnestness which could not have been exceeded if he had been in robust health.

It was not until February, 1870, that a resolution of Congress authorised the Secretary of War to take meteorological observations at military stations throughout the United States for giving notices of the approach and force of storms.

For this purpose General Meyer modestly demanded for his office an appropriation of 15,000 dollars, and with that small sum he commenced arrangements for obtaining weather reports from all parts of the States. The issue of synopses and probabilities was commenced on February 19th, 1871, and since that time synopses and prognostications have been issued three times daily, without rest for holidays. or saints' days.

Perhaps no part of the world affords so good an opportunity for making and using these observations as the continent of North America. It stretches more than 3,000 miles from west to east, with a population chiefly in the east. Changes usually advance from west to east, and thus the prognostications which can be made from watching these changes are useful mainly in the Eastern States. Cyclones originate in the Gulf of Mexico, and sweep over the whole Eastern portion of the United States, in the vicinity of the sea.

I visited the Signal Office at Washington, and was much interested in seeing the large maps upon which are displayed all the observations made several days previously. The very obliging gentleman in charge of the office pointed out the various indications on the maps by which he was enabled to trace the progress of storms and infer the direction and rate of their progress, so that he could foretell with precision the time at which they would arrive at certain places. These prognostications are now so carefully made that over 95 per cent. of them are realised, and so thoroughly has the system obtained the confidence of the public that nearly all kinds of business and pleasure are more or less regulated by the weather-wise information telegraphed from Washington. For purposes of navigation of course these prognostications are invaluable, and such implicit reliance is placed upon them that if any captain failed to notice or to act upon warnings when issued he would vitiate his insurance.

The farmer sows and reaps in accordance with the bulletins, which tell him what weather to expect. The butchers slay or reprieve their cattle and pigs according to the indications in the matter of temperature. The doctor reads the forecasts before he sees his patients, and modifies his treatment accordingly. The tourist consults the oracle, and acts upon its directions. No pic-nic would be carried on without anxious reference to the statements issued by " Old Probabilities."

Like every other department in the States, the Chief Signal Officer issues annually an elaborate report, which in this case consists of 500 pages of closely printed letter-press, containing tables innumerable and no fewer than eighty maps, each one devoted to some special subject.

These reports will carry down to posterity a varied and interesting mass of information. They will tell them when the ice broke up in certain ports, when swallows appeared or departed, when wild geese put in an appearance, when grasshoppers or winged ants became numerous, the height of rivers on any day of the year, when frosts commenced and terminated, when the days were cloudy, rainy, or dry, when auroras, solar halos, lunar halos, or mirages were recorded, when cucumbers ripened, when strawberries and blackberries were gathered, when jessamine blossomed, and cherries were in bloom, when meteors were noticed, zodiacal light observed, earthquakes happened, and Polar bands were seen.

Of course such large results have not been accomplished on the original estimate of 15,000 dollars per annum; the amount has been gradually increased, until the sum now voted amounts to

T

150,000 dollars per annum, or ten times the original sum. This expenditure is regarded as trifling when compared with the great advantages which directly arise from the operations of the Signal Bureau.

A Meteorological Congress was held at Vienna in 1873, when it was arranged that at least one observation should be taken daily, and simultaneously at various stations throughout the world. Since that time these observations have been continuously made, and the records are exchanged semi-monthly. Such reports are obtained from Algiers, Austria, Belgium, Great Britain, Denmark, France, Germany, Greece, Italy, Japan, the Netherlands, Sweden, Norway, Portugal, Russia, Spain, Switzerland, Turkey, British North America, the United States, Sandwich Islands, West Indies, and South America.

General Meyer supplements his reports by observations taken at sea by the captains of steamships, and thus provides as complete a record as it is possible at present to obtain. His chief desire is to establish ships of observation on the great oceans, at distances of about 500 miles, connected by telegraphic cables, so as to obtain regular observations from the ocean as well as from the land. These vessels might be useful for other purposes, but the great advantages that would accrue from meteorological observations would be worth all the cost.

Great Britain is in a position to benefit more largely than any other nation by such a system, both from the extent of her commerce and from the circumstance that her limited area does not afford on land that scope which is necessary to enable a forecast of changes to be made sufficiently early to be useful. The world is indebted to an Englishman, Captain Fitzroy, for the first systematic attempts to utilise observations by telegraph, but what he commenced has been carried out far more efficiently in the United States than in this country.

With the limited means at his disposal, and the small area under his observation, Mr. Scott, the Superintendent of our Meteorological Department, is doing all in his power, but, as compared with what is being accomplished in the States, we are doing but little, and until observations are made on the ocean we do not see how the work can be effectively carried out in this country. The observations made in the United States would be of great advantage to us if we could continue them across the ocean, and thus be enabled to trace the western gales for six thousand miles before they reach our shores.

General Meyer has recently opened a bureau at Paris, in order to enable him to make observations in Europe in connection with his own system.

LAND AND LAND LAWS.

What must be the feelings of an Irishman when he finds himself on the other side of the Atlantic, and receives from the Government a present of land, which in the old country would be a handsome fortune? He may miss the moist climate, the green fields, and the contiguity of a melancholy ocean; but his land hunger is satisfied, and he finds himself in the presence of a friendly Government instead of a Government which he too often regards with feelings of hostility. He will, however, see but little of the new Government; it will never assist his landlord to extort rent, for he is now his own landlord; and as for taxes, sixpence per acre per annum will often cover all these. Hard times may come, but he sees the silver lining behind the cloud, which, in his own country, he could seldom see. Amidst all his new hardships he feels independent, and he knows that he has a good chance of being prosperous.

When the thirteen original States formed a union, one of the problems which the Government of the United States had to solve was how to utilise the vast extent of land which had come under its dominion. The extensive regions beyond the State confines, and all unowned land passed under the control of the general Government; and the management of the public lands of the United States was entrusted to the Department of the Interior, the head of which is a member of the Cabinet. The actual superintendence of the lands is centred in the General Land Office, Washington, the chief of which is known as the Recorder.

A system of surveying the public lands was inaugurated as early as 1785 by Congress. Since then immense tracts of country have been surveyed, and accurate maps and records filed in the General and District Land Offices. Before being offered for sale, the unoccupied lands are surveyed in ranges of townships, each six miles square. A township is afterwards divided into thirty-six sections, each section containing one square mile, or about six hundred and forty acres. The divisional mark of the six hundred and forty acre sections is made by lines crossing each other from east to west and from north to south. These sections are further sub-divided into quarters of one hundred and sixty acres each, and one-eighths (eighty acres) and sixteenths. The surveyors put up distinguishable marks in the field indicating the corner of townships, the sections, and quarter sections.

The American Almanack informs us that "The public lands are divided into two great classes. The one class have a dollar and a quarter an acre designated as the minimum price, and the other two dollars and a half an acre. Titles to these lands may be acquired by private entry or location under the homestead, preëmption and timber-culture laws; or, as to some classes, by purchase for cash, in the case of lands which may be purchased at private sale, or such as have not been reserved under any law. Such tracts are sold on application to the Register of the Land Office.

The homestead laws give the right to one hundred and sixty acres of a dollar and a quarter lands, or to eighty acres of two dollar and a half lands, to any citizen or applicant for citizenship over twenty-one who will actually settle upon and cultivate the land. This privilege extends only to the surveyed lands, and the title is perfected by the issue of a patent after five years of actual settlement. The only charges in the case of homestead entries are fees and commissions, varying from a minimum of seven dollars to a maximum of twenty-two dollars.

The timber-culture acts of 1873-78 give the right to any settler who has cultivated for two

years as much as five acres in trees, to an eighty-
acre homestead, or if ten acres, to a homestead of
of one hundred and sixty acres. The limitation of
the homestead laws to one hundred and sixty acres
for each settler is extended in the case of timber
culture so as to grant as many quarter sections of
one hundred and sixty acres each as have been
improved by the culture for ten years of forty acres
of timber thereon, but the quarter sections must not
lie immediately contiguous."

By the Homestead Law no land acquired
under its provisions " shall in any event
become liable for any debt contracted prior to
the issue of the patent therefor."

In America the title to land is in fee simple,
and the purchaser has everything free from the sky
to the centre of the earth. There are no United
States taxes levied on land. As long as the fee is
in the United States there are no taxes whatever,
but the moment the title passes to the State it
becomes subject to the local legislative enactments.

In most of the States, the land is taxed in
proportion to its value, and it is at present a ground
of complaint that people who improve their land
have to pay high taxes, while unimproved land
held for speculative purposes escapes with the payment of a comparatively small sum. Legislation

is, however, being directed towards the lessening of this grievance. In nearly all the States, there is a Local Homestead Law, which prevents the seizure and sale of the actual homestead of citizens, except for taxes, the amount subject to exemption being limited from 500 to 5,000 dollars

In 1844-5, when Texas, which had wrested her independence from Mexico, became a member of the Union, she, by treaty, expressly reserved her own public lands, which then amounted to nearly 200,000,000 acres, and also the right of dividing her territory into other States if she saw fit.

Whenever patents have been issued on public lands of the United States, the patents in question are required to be filed or recorded in the County Record Offices of the different States, and this record takes the place of the patent as establishing the title.

In nearly all of the States statutes of limitation have been passed barring suit for recovery of land where peaceable or undisputed possession has been had for a number of years. In New York State the limit in which the State may bring suit is forty, and in the case of individuals twenty, years. In other States it is even less.

The chief difference in respect to the laws governing succession to heritable property between

the United States and this country is that there
the widow is entitled to one-half of the deceased
husband's real and personal estate, acquired after
marriage, and the remainder is divisible in equal
shares among all the children. If the wife dies,
her half belongs to the children.

Most of the States impose assessments on real
estate (land). No taxes are collected, as a rule, on
property under 200 dollars in value, and the assessment rate varies in the different States. Annual
assessments are a lien, and interest accrues on
each year's assessment. In some States the per
centage on value to which property may be
assessed is limited by the State Constitutions. In
Texas the State is not empowered to raise more
than one-half per cent., or 10s. on each £100 of
valuation, and the counties and towns are restricted
to one-half that sum. Such provisions are not
uncommon in the States.

It is not an unusual thing to find some very
poor men in the States who own from 10,000 to a
million acres of land. The people who actually till
the soil naturally resent the withholding of land
from sale or occupancy by speculators, and, having
the government (State and Municipal) in their
own hands they generally take care that
no large tracts of valuable land shall be per-

mitted to remain unproductive. The States do this by exempting from high valuation improved property. The counties carry the same point by passing ordinances laying out roads, requiring fences to be built, weeds to be eradicated, and prairie or wood fires checked. In Texas, so hard did the taxes press upon many of the holders of large tracts four or five years ago, that almost anywhere (and now in some places) an actual settler could get a 100 acre farm of splendid land from these men for nothing, because its disposal to a settler enhanced the value and improved the chances of making profitable use of what remained. In Ohio fifteen years ago land speculators were glad to be rid of their bargains owing to the onerous character of the local taxes.

Texas, which is, and has been, burdened by land speculators as much as any State, had recently to repeal its law allowing the owner of property which had been sold for taxes to reclaim it within forty years on payment of the tax purchase price, plus 10 per cent. interest. Since that date titles obtained at tax sales have been as good there as in the majority of the States. All sales of property for taxes are made by decree of some Court of competent jurisdiction.

The general law of tenancy in the States is that it can be created by implication, agreement,

or by lease. The only process to get rid of a bad
tenant is by writ of ejectment. Distraining for rent
is prohibited by statutes in nearly all the States.
Under other enactments, household and personal
effects, varying in amount in the different States
from 200 dollars to about 3,000 dollars, are protected and cannot be seized and sold for
any debt. In this category of exemption from
seizure is also included the tools of workmen, and the books or apparatus of professional men. The legal principle involved in all
these cases is, that no person should be deprived
of the means of supporting himself by his own labour.

In many of the States there are laws against
usury. In New York, if more than seven per cent.
interest is exacted the debtor can plead the usury
law, and thus cancel whatever obligation he may
have entered into with a creditor. The rate of
interest borrowers on real estate have to pay for
money depends altogether on the locality and the
condition of the times. The usury laws in the
States, as well as in Canada, are always got over
in some way, either by premiums, or by the
borrower getting but a fraction of the sum
ostensibly borrowed. Borrowers on real estate
have to pay from six per cent. in the
older settled Eastern cities and townships,

to ten, twenty, and even thirty per cent. in the Southern and Western States. A married man cannot mortgage his property without his wife's consent, as she is half owner with him. Whenever money is borrowed on mortgage or real estate, the mortgagee may file the bond in the County Record Office, where it is transcribed, and the entry thus made is a legal notice to all the world. Priority in recording a mortgage (which is marked the minute it is received) entitles the mortgagee to a first lien, although mortgages may have been executed ante-dating it, but not recorded.

There is another feature of the laws affecting land in the States that demands notice. What are called mechanics' liens have, by statute, a priority over all others. A carpenter, mason, or other mechanic who has been engaged in building a house, and who has not received payment for his labour, or for the materials furnished, is entitled to a first lien on the premises as against all comers. The same rule in law extends to the man who erects a fence, builds a barn, or assists in the cultivation of the crops. The Courts, by process, protect the workmen in securing the fruit of their labour, and the owner of the land can be restrained from interfering in any way with the property to which there is a claim made by the labourer

until the matter is equitably adjusted. For
this purpose the Courts appoint receivers of the
property, and on the issue of a suit the character
or amount of the claim made is determined by the
Court or a jury, as the case may be.

The Federal Government grants land for school
purposes and for internal improvements. The States
do the same, and even the counties have power to
donate land for purposes held to redound to the
general welfare. The United States has also granted
tracts for the founding of agricultural colleges, and
most of the States have followed suit. In these
institutions scientific farming is taught. As a fair
specimen of what has been done by States, it may
be stated that in Texas there have been surveyed
and set apart for State University, 221,400 acres ;
and for educational purposes 17,712 acres in each
county. Texas has 168 organised counties, thus
giving to the counties for free schools over twenty
millions of acres.

Success must be held to justify the means
adopted by the United States in the management of land. No other part of the world
has attracted so many immigrants as the United
States have received during the last 100 years, the
population having increased from three millions
to over forty-seven millions ; the whole of

the British Colonies in all parts of the world attain to only one-third of this number.   Our American Colonies had the start of all others, and, therefore, it is not surprising that they have kept the lead since their formation into independent States; and they are still attracting from Europe the majority of those who seek new fields for enterprise, thus proving that they continue to afford greater inducements than are to be found elsewhere.

But notwithstanding the great success which has attended the American system, I cannot help thinking that it would be better not to give away land.   Wherever farms are established it is necessary to provide roads, schools, and other public arrangements, and if land is sold at a moderate price, and the proceeds expended upon these essentials, either better roads could be made or a lower rate of taxation would be sufficient.   At present the American Government gives the land and then taxes it for public works.   This makes it easy to enter upon but difficult to hold, and thus we find many cases in all parts of the Union where land has been taken up and afterwards abandoned. Land once cultivated and then allowed to return to waste is a public nuisance, as it produces injurious weeds instead of useful pasture.

For want of good roads the expense of farming is greatly increased; if roads had been made as fast as land was occupied the settlements would have been more concentrated; settlers, appreciating the value of easy communication, would have kept within the limits of the roadways.

The prosperity of New Zealand appears to have arisen in a great degree from the fact that Government lands have always been held for a stiff price, and the amount received for their sale appropriated to public purposes. In America the cheapness of land has made farmers careless in its use, and thus the style of farming is wasteful, the crops are very small, and no means are taken to prevent the land from being exhausted.

The freedom allowed to selectors in the choice of a location has produced another serious difficulty which will probably be made the subject of legislative enactment. There are extensive tracts of land in the States unsuitable for cultivation, but well adapted for grazing lands. Their value for grazing purposes has, however, been greatly diminished by claims being made for special spots suitable for watering cattle, and which are necessary for the utilisation of the adjoining land. Men make their fortunes by selecting such spots, and then charging a toll for the use of the water. Legislation in the States, as in other parts of the world, is a constant contest between the greed and selfishness of individuals and the public interest, but it must be admitted that brave, and generally successful, attempts have been made in the States to protect the interests of the public ; and no doubt some means will be devised to provide for an equitable use of the enormous districts of grazing land, the value of which has greatly increased since the export of meat has become possible.

I have before me rent and tax papers for farms in Wiltshire, and for farms in the Western States. On three farms in Wiltshire, consisting of 698 acres, the charges are as follow :—

	£	s.	d.
Rent	632	0	0
Tithe	156	9	5
Rates	88	2	6
	£876	11	11

In the Western States the rate of taxation varies greatly, but 1½ per cent. as the total amount to be paid would be a high estimate. Taking the value of 698 acres with buildings at four pounds per acre, the taxation would be £40 17s. 7d. per annum ; as an equivalent for rent in Wiltshire 10 per cent. should be charged on the value of the land, or £279 4s. 0d., so that the annual cost of rent and taxes in the Western States would be

U

	£	s.	d.
Taxes	40	17	7
Rent or Interest at 10 per cent. ...	279	4	0
	£320	1	7

as compared with £876 11s. 11d. in Wiltshire.

In addition to the landlord, the gentleman farmer, and uninterested labourers, an English farm has to support the church and the poor-house. It is not, however, the heavy charges on land in England which constitute the greatest drawback to our system, but that the farmers have only a temporary interest in the land, and the labourers are merely hirelings.

The great charm which attaches to farms in the States is that the land is occupied and cultivated by the owners thereof. Men work willingly when they labour for themselves, and bring to bear upon their undertakings a degree of intelligence and energy which under other conditions would be unattainable.

TAXATION AND EXPENDITURE.

In order to give a correct idea of taxation in the United States, it will be desirable to compare their taxation with that of the United Kingdom. Without such a comparison a long array of figures would convey but little notion of what American taxation really is, but with it we shall be enabled to obtain a very definite idea of the relative merits of the United States Government and our own, so far as the cost of each, and the work which they do in return for the taxes they obtain, will enable us to form an opinion.

The expenditure of the Federal Government, and of the several State Governments, must be taken together to make a comparison with our own general expenditure, while the expenditure of counties and municipalities in the States may be compared with our own local outlay.

THE UNITED STATES REVENUES FOR THE FISCAL YEAR ENDING JUNE 30TH, 1880, ESTIMATED ON EXISTING LAWS, WILL BE

FROM TAXATION.

From Customs	£26,600,000
„ Internal Revenue	23,000,000

Carried forward...£49,600,000

Brought forward...£49,600,000

FROM OTHER SOURCES.

From	Sales of Public Lands	200,000
„	Tax on circulation and deposits of National Banks	1,350,000
„	Repayment of Interest by Pacific Railway Companies	280,000
„	Customs' Fees, Fines, and Penalties...............	220,000
„	Fees, Letters Patent, and Lands..................	400,000
„	Sales of Government Property	20,000
„	Profits on Coinage....................................	320,000
„	Miscellaneous Sources	480,000

£52,870,000

EXPENDITURE OF THE UNITED STATES AS ESTIMATED FOR THE FISCAL YEAR ENDING JUNE 30TH, 1880 :—

Legislative		£596,621
Executive		2,629,219
Judicial.............		78,280
Foreign Intercourse..............................		235,723
Military Establishment		5,867,145
Naval Establishment		2,837,476
Indian Affairs		986,648
Pensions		5,923,200

PUBLIC WORKS.

Treasury Department	£849,589	
War Department	1,520,356	
Navy Department	75,000	
Interior Department	84,543	
Department of Justice..	3,600	
„ Agriculture	1,300	
		2,534,388
Postal Service		1,181,575
Miscellaneous .... ,...................		2,969,360

Carried forward...£25,829,635

Brought forward...£25,829,635

Interest on Public Debt 19,000,000
Refunding Customs, Internal Revenue, Lands, &c. ... 935,000
Collecting Revenue from Customs 1,160,000
Miscellaneous 332,240

£47,266,875

The taxation by State Legislatures for the general government of all the States was given in the census returns for 1870 as £13,610,259. I have not been able to obtain a detailed statement of the taxation of all the States for a later date than 1870, but since that period there has been generally a reduction. I have the particulars of taxation and expenditure in 1877 for a large number of the States separately, and, as compared with the expenditure of 1870, there is an average reduction of ten per cent. I, therefore, estimate the present expenditure for the Government of States and Territories at £12,500,000.

THE TOTAL EXPENDITURE FOR THE GENERAL GOVERNMENT OF THE UNITED STATES, AND EXCLUSIVE OF REDUCTION OF DEBT, IS, THEREFORE, AS FOLLOWS :—

Federal Government £47,266,875
States and Territories.................................... 12,500,000

Total £59,766,875

THE REVENUE OF THE UNITED KINGDOM FOR THE YEAR ENDING MARCH 31ST, 1880, IS ESTIMATED AS FOLLOWS :—

FROM TAXATION.

Customs	£20,000,000
Excise	27,270,000
Stamps	10,780,000
Land Tax and House Duty	2,700,000
Income Tax	9,250,800
	£70,000,000

FROM OTHER SOURCES.

Post Office	£6,250,000
Telegraph Service	1,340,000
Crown Lands	390,000
Interest on Advances for Local Works	1,175,000
Miscellaneous	3,900,000
	£83,055,000

THE ESTIMATED EXPENDITURE OF THE UNITED KINGDOM FOR THE YEAR ENDING MARCH 31ST, 1880, IS AS FOLLOWS, EXCLUSIVE OF REPAYMENT OF DEBT AND OF THE CHARGES FOR THE POST-OFFICE AND TELEGRAPH SERVICE, WHICH IS SELF-SUPPORTING :—

Interest and Charges on Debt (excluding £5,000,000 for Repayment of Debt)	£25,620,000
Army	15,645,700
Home Charges for Forces in India	1,100,000
Navy	10,586,894
Civil Service	15,084,851
Collection of Customs and Inland Revenue	2,865,383
	£70,902,828

It thus appears that the cost of the general government of the United States, with 3½ millions of square miles of territory and 47 millions of population, amounts to 59¾ millions, or 25s. 5d. per head ; while that of the United Kingdom, with 121 thousand square miles of territory and 33 millions of population, exceeds 70 millions, or 43s. per head.

It will be seen that the taxation of the United States Federal Government is nearly all obtained from Customs and Excise. Thus we have an instance of a Democratic community taxing consumption and industry, while property is left untaxed, so far as the Federal Government is concerned ; and the war debt, interest and principal, as well as the war pensions, are being paid exclusively by taxes on industry.

The various State Governments raise their taxation in such a multitude of forms that it would be impossible to ascertain precisely what proportion of the 12½ millions which they collect is taken from real property. I have analysed the taxation of several States, of which the details are before me, and I find that if we take somewhat less than half this amount, or six millions, as obtained from real estate, we shall be about right. The remaining 6½ millions are realised from taxes on personal property, licenses, and poll-tax.

The General Government of the United States is, therefore, supported by 58 millions of taxation upon consumption and industry, and six millions, or 10 per cent. on real property.

It will be interesting to see how this compares with British taxation.

IN THE UNITED KINGDOM THE GENERAL TAXATION ON REAL PROPERTY CONSISTS OF

Land Tax and House Duty......................................	£2,700,000
One Quarter of Stamps	2,695,000
Income Tax	3,400,000
	£8,795,000

or say 8½ millions on a total of 70 millions, or 12 per cent.

From Customs we raise 20 millions in duties upon an import of over 350 millions. The United States extract 26½ millions of duties upon an import of 87½ millions.

From Excise, or Inland Revenue, we obtain 27 millions, and the States 23 millions. Of this sum, eight millions have been realised from tobacco, which is there a matter of internal revenue, while with us it figures in the Customs. The revenue from alcoholic liquors in the States is much less than in this country, partly because their duties are lower, but chiefly on account of their smaller consumption.

So far as General Government is concerned the States are free of income tax, from which we derive over nine millions, and from stamps, which put us to so much inconvenience, and take over $10\frac{1}{2}$ millions from our pockets every year.

In the United Kingdom we derive a handsome profit of over two millions annually from the Post-Office by the carriage of letters at 1d., whereas in the States the carriage of letters at $1\frac{1}{2}$d. involves a loss to the revenue of over a million sterling—a difference which arises mainly from the large extent of territory as compared with population in the States.

After a comparison of taxation, we come naturally to a comparison of expenditure. In each country the largest item is the interest on debt, upon which we have to pay 25 millions annually, and the Americans 19 millions. The cost of their army and navy is about one-third of our own. The three chief items of expenditure, compared in a tabulated form from the most recent official estimates, are as follow :—

	UNITED KINGDOM.	UNITED STATES.
Interest and Charges on Debt	£25,000,000	£19,000,000
Army	15,645,700	5,867,145
Navy	10,586,894	2,837,476

The interest on the debt will be considerably reduced by the funding of large portions of the debt at a lower rate of interest, since the estimate of £19,000,000 was made by the Secretary to the Treasury.

Moderate as the expenditure for government in the United States appears to be when we remember that the territory governed is more than thirty times as large as that of the United Kingdom, and the population 40 per cent. greater than our own, the present cost is enormous when compared with the expenditure previous to the Civil War.

The Secretary to the Treasury publishes a very interesting statement in his annual report, showing the expenditure of the United States for each year since 1791.   At that time the nett expenditure, including interest on debt, amounted to the very modest sum of £620,000.   Twenty years later it had crept up to £1,635,000.   Twenty years later still, in 1831, we find an expenditure of £3,047,000, and in 1851 of £9,550,000.   The highest expenditure for any year before the war was in 1858, when the expenditure reached £14,756,000. It then rose with prompt rapidity—in 1862 to £93,913,000, in 1863 to £143,746,000, in 1864 to £172,893,000, and in 1865 to £259,363,000 ; from which it rapidly descended to the present amount, of about 50 millions per annum.   Of this, one-half is chargeable to the Civil War, viz.,

£19,000,000 interest on debt, and £6,000,000 in pensions, which shews that the expenditure not affected by the war has increased from 14 millions to 25 millions since 1858.

Although the Civil War commenced in 1861, we do not discover any indication of increased expenditure until the following year, and even then the total amount raised by taxation was under 10 millions, to meet an expenditure of 93 millions ; in 1863 the revenue was only 22 millions, in 1864 48 millions, in 1865 64 millions ; so that in four years an expenditure was incurred of 670 millions, of which only 144 millions were provided by taxation, the remainder being raised by loans. It was this fatal carelessness at the commencement of the war which led to its prolongation, and made the burden of debt so heavy. In 1866 the taxation exceeded 100 millions, and nearly equalled the expenditure. The Americans had so little experience of taxation that they were quite at a loss how to proceed. Previous to the war the Customs' duties provided for all their requirements, and sometimes brought in a greater revenue than they could tell what to do with. Their first thought at the outbreak of the war was to increase the Customs' duties, and these were raised from a total of 10 millions in 1862, until they reached 35 millions in 1866.

But Customs, although strained to the utmost, would not produce sufficient income, and it was necessary to establish an Internal Revenue Department; and this department, by means of duties, licenses, income tax, and a small property tax of $\frac{1}{8}$ per cent. on real and personal property, became for a time the chief source of American taxation, and from a moderate commencement at seven millions in 1863, the internal revenue rose to over sixty millions in 1866. By maintaining a moderate rate of taxation after the war, the debt which was so suddenly accumulated was rapidly reduced.

The Local Taxation by counties and municipalities in the United States is raised from taxation on property, both real and personal, and from various forms of licenses. The usual mode is to tax all property so much per cent. on its value, and the tax-gatherer expects the ratepayer to enumerate every article of property in his possession, and to pay on it in proportion to its value. The ingenuity of the revenue officers seems to have been greatly exercised in the imposition of license duties.

The following extracts from the tax laws of Virginia will give some idea of the variety of taxes to which the residents in this fine old State are subjected. The Taxes are :—

On Land, ½ per cent. on the value.

On every Male over 21, one dollar.

On Personal Estate, under which heading every conceivable article is mentioned, including pianos, bowie-knives, carriages, cattle, &c., ½ per cent.

The Probate on every will is ¹⁄₁₀ per cent.

On Deeds, ¹⁄₁₀ per cent.

On Suits, ¹⁄₁₀ per cent. of the amount claimed.

Insurance Companies' License Tax 200 dollars, and ½ per cent. on the value of their property.

Railroad Companies, ½ per cent. on the value of their property, and an Income Tax of one per cent. on their nett receipts.

Carrying Companies, ½ per cent. on the value of their property, and ½ per cent. on their gross earnings.

Telegraph Companies' License Tax of 250 dollars, and ½ per cent. on the value of their property.

Merchants, ½ per cent. on their sales up to 2,000 dollars, gradually reduced to ¹⁄₁₀ per cent. on sales over 100,000 dollars.

Liquor Merchants, for wholesale and retail license, 250 dollars, and a graduated tax on the sales from one per cent. to ¹⁄₁₀ per cent. when the sale exceeds 50,000 dollars.

Commisson Merchants' License 50 dollars, and one per cent. on sales.

Sample Merchants, 100 dollars.

Pedlars, 50 dollars.

On the sale of a Patent Right, 25 dollars.

Land Agent, 50 dollars, and $\frac{1}{4}$ per cent. on sales.

Book Agents, 10 dollars.

Agents for the sale of articles manufactured in other States, 25 dollars.

General Auctioneer, 50 dollars, and $\frac{1}{4}$ per cent. on sales.

Real Estate Auctioneers, 50 dollars, and $\frac{1}{4}$ per cent. on sales.

Tobacco Auctioneers, 50 dollars.

Retailers of Tobacco, 5 dollars.

Common Criers, 10 dollars.

Ship Brokers, 25 dollars.

Stock Brokers, 250 dollars.

Commercial Brokers and Insurance Brokers, 250 dollars.

Private Banks, 50 dollars on a capital of 5,000 dollars or under; 250 dollars on a capital under 30,000 dollars; and 5 dollars per 1,000 on additional capital.

Pawnbrokers, 250 dollars.

Brewers mashing less than 100 bushels a day 250 dollars; other quantities in proportion.

On Private Entertainments, 5 dollars and a per centage on the rental.

Boarding Houses, 5 dollars and 1 per cent. on the rental.

Eating Houses, 25 dollars.

Bowling Saloons, 25 dollars.

Billiard Saloons, 50 dollars, and 25 dollars for each additional table over one.

Bagatelle Saloons, 10 dollars, and 5 dollars for each additional table over one.

Theatres, 3 dollars for each performance, 10 dollars for each week of such performance, and 1 per cent. on the gross receipts of each performance.

For Circuses 25 to 100 dollars per day, and 5 per cent. on the receipts.

Hobby Horses, 10 dollars.

Public Rooms, 20 dollars.

Attorneys-at-Law, 25 dollars.

Doctors and Dentists, 15 dollars.

Photographers, 20 dollars.

Stallions or Jackasses, 10 dollars.

House Agents, 30 dollars.

Labour Agents, 25 dollars.

Livery Stable Keepers, 15 dollars, and $\frac{1}{2}$ dollar for each stall.

And many other taxes too numerous to mention.

The principle of taxing land and all other property on the value, and not upon the rental, appears to be universally maintained. This course would naturally be adopted in a country where nearly all the land is owned by the cultivators, and rents almost unknown. In the States it is regarded as a cardinal principle that for all land which is owned taxes according to its value must be paid, whether the land is occupied or not. But for this system speculators might purchase and hold land until the value had been increased by the activity of surrounding residents, and thus participate in an "unearned increment" without even contributing to the public exchequer. The natural man in America has as much horror as John Stuart Mill of capitalists enyoying an unearned increment, and the public take the liberty of stirring up in various ways the sleeping landlords who seek to benefit by the industry of others. They will pass a law for the destruction of weeds or for the construction of fences, and such laws, with the constant pressure of rates, soon bring the idle landlord to account, and he quickly finds his land claimed by local officers and sold for public liabilities to some one who will be a better steward. In all parts of the States the people like to see progress, and they have no notion of taxing the industrious landlord and letting the idle go free, so that if a man does not improve an estate, they say that he ought to improve it, and tax him accordingly.

The tax upon agricultural land is, however, remarkably light, partly because the value per acre is so small as compared with land in this country, and partly because municipalities are usually called upon to contribute to the county expenditure. In English boroughs the taxpayers are not required to pay for the county expenditure, but in the States the municipalities usually pay all their own charges, and the same proportion of county expenditure as if they lived outside the municipal boundary.

Although the following table has a dry appearance, it will interest those who wish to investigate the subject of taxation. It shows the kinds of property subjected to taxation, and the number and value of each in the State to which it refers :—

STATE OF ILLINOIS.
Recapitulation of Assessment, 1875.

Personal Property.	Number.	Average Value.	Assessed Value.
Horses of all ages	923,468	£8 3 11	£7 562 741
Cattle of all ages	1,985 155	2 17 1½	5,064,790
Mules and asses of all ages...............	116,373	9 3 1½	1,069,339
Sheep of all ages	928 056	0 6 0¼	279,879
Hogs of all ages	2,809,969	0 11 7	1,631,425
Steam engines, including boilers	2,729	100 17 1	275,280
Fire or burglar-proof safes..............	4,449	15 7 4	68,562
Billiard, pigeon-hole, bagatelle, or other similar tables	2,021	13 2 3	26,500
Carriages and waggons of whatsoever kind	349 575	5 11 0	1,937,994
Watches and clocks	283 301	1 0 2½	286,238
Sewing and knitting machines	41,850	4 6 8	611,583
Pianofortes	15,037	20 10 3½	308,464
Melodeons and organs	18,621	9 8 11	175,875
Franchises	62	272 7 4½	16,886
Annuities and royalties	49	335 17 8	16,458
Patent rights	84	29 10 2	2,478
Steamboats, sailing vessels, wharf boats, barges or other water craft	706	302 17 1½	213,916
Total assessed value of enumerated property	....	....	£20,148,208

W

Assessed Value carried forward		£20,148,208

	Amount of Unenumerated Property.	
Merchandise..	£6,178,575 12 0	
Material and manufactured articles	771,409 4 0	
Manufacturers' tools, implements, and machinery	459,184 16 0	
Agricultural tools, implements, and machinery	1,343,767 16 0	
Gold and silver plate and plated ware...........	24,450 0 0	
Diamonds and jewellery	11,309 0 0	
Moneys of banks, bankers, brokers, &c	751,512 12 0	
Credits of banks, bankers, brokers, &c.	390,614 12 0	
Moneys of other than bankers, &c	3,049,679 16 0	
Credits of other than bankers, &c.	4,808 647 8 0	
Bonds and stocks	329,018 16 0	
Shares of capital stock of companies, not of this State ..	61,703 12 0	
Pawnbrokers' property..............................	3,535 12 0	
Property of corporations not before enumerated........	68,331 8 0	
Property of saloons and eating houses	86,109 0 0	
Household and office property	3,189,851 16 0	
Investments in real estates and improvements thereon..	93,254 4 0	
Shares of stock, state, and national banks	2,142,071 16 0	
All other personal property	3,919,163 4 0	
Total assessed value of unenumerated property	£27,672,223 4 0	27,672,233
Total assessed value of personal property	....	£47,820,441

Railroad Property Assessed in Counties.	Av'ge Val.	Assessed Val.
Class C Personal property	....	£245,730 8 0
Class D Lands	....	351,611 0 0
Class D – Lots	....	502,390 8 0
Total value of railroad property assessed in counties		1,099,731

Real Estate – Lands.	Number of Acres.	Av'ge Value per Acre	Assessed Value.
Improved lands	25,110.708	£3 17 9½	£98,150,425 12 0*
Unimproved lands	8,947,325	1 7 5	12,252,152 4 0
Total....................	34,058.033	£3 4 7½	110,402,577 16 0*
Total assessed value of land			110,402,577

Real Estate—Town and City Lots.	No. of Lots.	Average Value per Lot	Assessed Val.
Improved town and city lots	372,262	£101 0 6½	£37,608,181 0
Unimproved town and city lots ..	464,697	17 10 10½	8,154,729 8
Total	836,959	£54 13 7	£45,762,910 8
Total assessed value of town and city lots			45,762,910
Total value of all taxable property assessed in counties			£205,085,659

* Total includes £120,000 assessment of east end of bridge across the Mississippi River, in Henderson county, and £330,000 of east end of St. Louis Bridge, in St. Clair county—not included in determining the average value per acre.

The following table shows the number of acres in cultivation in the State of Illinois in 1875 :—

Acres in cultivation—wheat			2,433,050
,,	,,	corn	7,797,851
,,	,,	oats	2,226,744
,,	,,	meadows	2,331,518
,,	,,	other field products	841,874
Acres in enclosed pasture			4,325,948
,,	orchard		755,462
,,	woodland		7,103,816

THE AMOUNT OF REVENUE REQUIRED FOR THE STATE OF ILLINOIS FOR THE YEAR 1875 WAS, FOR

General State Purposes £360,000

State School Purposes.................................... 200,000

£560,000

To provide for this amount a rate was imposed of three-tenths per cent., or three farthings in the £, on the value of the property. As the value of the "improved lands" is taken at £3 18s. per acre, it follows that the taxation for State purposes would be about threepence per acre.

The details of the expenditure of the Federal Government afford a good indication of the nature of the work which they undertake, and these can be compared with the details of the expenditure of the United Kingdom; but to make a complete comparison of the general government of the two countries we must see what is the work done by the State Governments, Counties, and Municipalities.

The following details of the revenue and expenditure of the State of Georgia will give some idea of the nature of a State Government, and the work which it performs for the public.

The disbursements especially will repay a perusal, as showing the mode in which the public money is expended, and the advantages which the people obtain for the expenditure :—

STATE OF GEORGIA.

Estimates of Probable Receipts and Disbursements at the Treasury for and during the Fiscal Year ending December 31st, 1877.

RECEIPTS FROM TAXES.

From General Tax of 1877, at 5 mills. (½ per cent.)	£175.000
From General Tax of 1876	45.000
From Insurance Tax of 1877	4,000
From Railroad Tax of 1877	2,000
From Taxes of former years	1,000
	£227,000

RECEIPTS FROM OTHER SOURCES.

From Rental of Western and Atlantic Railroad	£60,000
From Dividends	500
From Hire of Convicts	2,000
From all other sources	2,000
	£291,500

DISBURSEMENTS.

To Civil Establishment	£20,000
To Legislative Pay Roll	20,000
To Lunatic Asylum—Support of	20,000
To Lunatic Asylum, pay of Chaplain and Trustees	500
To Deaf and Dumb Asylum—Support of	2,600
To Academy for the Blind—Support of	2,200
To University of Georgia	1,600
Carried forward	£66,900

Brought forward	£66,900
To University of Atlan.a	1.600
To Printing Fund	4,000
To Contingent Fund	4.000
To Public Buildings	3,000
To Officers Executive Department	1.400
To Superintendent Public Works	320
To Clerk Wild Land Offic ·	320
To State Agent for Vaccination	60
To Educational Fund	30.000
To School Commissioner and Clerk	740
To Department State Geologist	2.000
To Department Commissioner of Agriculture......	2.0˜0
To Supreme Court Reports	700
To Solicitor-General's cost, Supreme Court.........	400
To Old Debts Western and Atlantic Railroad......	5.000
To Old Change BillsWestern and Atlantic Railroad	1.000
To Public Debt and Balance Due in 1877............	141,402
To Special Appropriations	25.000
Balance..	1.658
	£291,500

In many of the States a charge appears for the militia, which is probably covered in Georgia by the " Special Appropriations," and often a considerable sum is put down for "Artificial Limbs" for soldiers wounded in the war.

The State of Georgia extends over 58,000 square miles, with a population of about 1,200,000. It will be seen that the actual expenditure from taxation amounts to £227,000 per annum, and from other sources to £64,500. About £100,000 is required for interest on debt, and provision was made for reducing the principal by £20,000. The total expenditure of the Government, irrespective of interest on debt, is about £100,000 per annum, the greater part of which is directly effective. The expenditure on Asylums is £25,000, and for Education £33,000, while the State Geologist and Commissioner of Agriculture take £4,000.

The salaries of officers in Georgia are as follow :—

Governor	£800
Secretary of State	400
Comptroller-General	400
Treasurer	400
Attorney-General	400
Commissioner of Agriculture	400
Geologist	600
School Commissioner	500
Judges Supreme Court	700
Judges Superior Court	500
Solicitor-General	50
Reporter Supreme Court	200
Principal Keeper Penitentiary	400
Resident Physician Lunatic Asylum	500
Governor's Secretaries (two)	360
Clerks in Departments (each)	320

The local taxation of the United States is not like that of the United Kingdom, raised chiefly from rates upon real property. When property is taxed in the States the term usually includes all kinds of possessions, from houses and lands to pianos and pigs, but local taxation is by no means confined to property, whether real or personal ; it branches out into poll taxes and licenses in manifold forms. No State, county, or municipality can impose customs duties, or tax imports, either from abroad or from other States ; but there seems to be no limit to the exercise of their ingenuity in other directions, and some of the tax laws are very interesting documents, which show that necessity is the mother of invention, and that remarkable devices can be adopted in a country which has had the awakening experience of a civil war. One of the latest inventions is a tax upon the sale of every glass of beer, wine, or spirits which passes over the counter ; for the collection of this tax an apparatus is provided for registering the number of glasses sold, much in the same manner as the punch used by conductors registers the number of tickets perforated. Three sorts of enumerators are provided, and it is the duty of the barman to ticket the one which represents the kind of drink he has just supplied. This kind of taxation seems to be rather popular ; the publican has to pay precisely in proportion to the amount of business he transacts, and the larger the sum he pays to the collector the more profit he makes for himself.

No man seems to get tired of paying for his pleasures, and the satisfaction of having the throat tickled by alcohol is evidently so great that those who indulge in the habit appear to be almost glad of the privilege of offering a farthing to the Government as a thankoffering for each tipple. As the Federal Government tax the import and manufacture of alcoholic liquors it was a bright notion of local Chancellors of Exchequer to adopt the device of taxing the sale, which was the only course open to them.

Americans undoubtedly work too hard, and it is perhaps to check this tendency to over exertion that in some places a tax is imposed upon every man who attempts to do anything. I have before me " An ordinance to establish the rate of licenses for professions, callings, and other business for the year, 1877," in the City of New Orleans. It must be a most unfortunate thing for any man to have a calling under such circumstances, for, in whatever direction duty may prompt him, he must not obey his conscience until he has paid a heavy fine to the State. The lowest charge seems to be five dollars, which would be imposed on a man if he sold split wood or charcoal by retail, or if he were guilty of shoeing a horse or dyeing a coat; if he draws a tooth, or acts as counsellor, or attorney, or physician, he is taxed to the extent of 20 dollars. Every member of a company keeping a flying horse or skating rink, 25 dollars; every lottery agent, 50 dollars; every lottery company, 2,500 dollars; every stevedore, 50 dollars; a keeper of a cockpit, 75 dollars; an undertaker, 100 dollars; and so on through a list, fixing a tax upon almost every imaginable form of occupation, varying from 5 to 2,500 dollars. If these taxes on lottery-tickets and cockpits are held to involve a license it is a curious question as to how the subject of compensation would be dealt with in the event of the public conscience becoming enlightened on these points. If a man does more than one thing he must pay the full tax for everything he does, and every partner in a business is taxed separately. The ordinance seems to have had the effect of lessening that excessive activity which is generally manifested in the States, but is conspicuous by its absence in New Orleans.

It would be difficult to make a detailed analysis of local taxation in America, as the modes by which it is raised are so various. Poll tax and licenses do not produce large sums, and the great bulk of the revenues is raised from direct taxation on property, real and personal. Where all property is included real property usually amounts to about two-thirds of the whole; it is, therefore, probable that one-half of the local taxation in the States is raised from real property, and the remainder from personal property, licenses, and poll tax.

In the Eastern States the owners of property have received an "unearned increment" by the aggregation of population, very much in the same manner as in the United Kingdom, and it would seem right that persons whose property has thus increased in value through no merits of their own should be called upon to share this unearned increment with the State by becoming the subjects of special taxation. In the Western States the circumstances are essentially different; land is still abundant, almost everybody owns it, and it is of the utmost importance that every inducement should be offered to settlers to come and give a value to what, in its natural condition, is valueless. So far as the improvement in land is the result of industry, it is clearly desirable that the application of such improving industry should not be checked by burdensome taxation; but in a country which is rapidly advancing in population, certain districts which become the centres of business suddenly attain a value for which the fortunate owners can claim no credit, and some means should be adopted for securing to the State a portion of this unearned increment. In newly developed districts large expenditure is necessary for public purposes, and part of the means could be obtained by claiming for the State a share in the increased value of all land which rises above an agricultural price through the necessities of an increasing population. For instance, a man buys a piece of land for a small sum, and in five or six years his land becomes the centre of a township and worth many thousands of pounds ; under such circumstances, his property having been increased in value by the action of others, it would involve no injustice or restriction if the Government participated largely in the improved value, and claimed a ground rent, which would represent a portion of the unearned increment.

The necessity for such legislation is less felt in the Western States, where nearly all the people are landowners, than it is in the older and more settled States, or in this country, where the land is held by a few persons ; but in any case the principle would be equitable and convenient, though it would be more easily adopted in a new country than in an old one.

The total county expenditure in the United States for 1870 was £15,549,223, and since that date this expenditure has been diminished by the extension of municipalities, and by the general practice of economy. The present cost of County Government may, therefore, be taken at £12,500,000.

The municipal expenditure in 1870, for all the towns and cities in the United States, amounted to £22,958,821, but this sum has been increased since that date, and at the present time it is probable that it amounts to £30,000,000.

THE TOTAL EXPENDITURE FOR GOVERNMENT IN THE UNITED STATES IS AS FOLLOWS :—

Federal Government	£47,266,875
State Governments	12,500,000
County Governments	12,500,000
Municipal Governments	30,000,000
Total	£102,266,875

or 44s. 4d. per head.

Assuming that one-half of the county and municipal expenditure in the United States is raised from real property, this taxation would amount for local purposes to £16,225,000. We have seen that real property for general government is taxed to the extent of £6,000,000, so that of the total expenditure of the United States, £22,225,000, or 22 per cent., is raised from taxes on real property.

THE TOTAL EXPENDITURE FOR GOVERNMENT IN THE UNITED KINGDOM IS AS FOLLOWS :—

For General Government	£70,902,828
„ Local Government, year 1875-6 (less £2,404,675 supplied by Government contribution)	40,941,516
	£111,844,344

or 67s. 10d. per head.

It will thus be seen that the cost of Government in this country is 52 per cent. greater than in the United States in proportion to the population.

The proportion of local expenditure which is provided for by taxation on real property is £24,322,069, and, as previously stated, the amount so raised from imperial taxation is £8,495,000, making together a sum of £32,817,069, or rather more than 29 per cent. of the whole.

In the expenditure of the United Kingdom I have included a sum of about £4,000,000 spent on harbours, lights, and pilotage, but as similar items occur in the expenditure of the United States this sum is justly included.

Of the local expenditure, we are raising about eight millions annually on loans, and, therefore, our present taxation is thereby lessened; and a proportionate amount is expended for buildings and permanent improvements, but in the States these are often made or erected out of current income, and at the present time their local debts are being paid off quite as rapidly as new loans are raised. I believe, therefore, that the statement, as it stands, affords a just comparison.

It would be misleading to compare the cost of the two Governments without considering their respective efficiency, and, although it would be difficult to make a complete comparison in this respect, there are some leading points which may be advantageously compared.

No one can have travelled in both countries without being struck with the great difference in the state of the roads. The advantage which the United Kingdom possesses in this respect it would be difficult to over-estimate, and it is one which we obtain at a cost altogether inconsiderable as compared with the great benefit which we receive. The evil of bad roads in the States is mitigated in some degree by the extension of tramways, which are almost universal, but they are not in all respects a substitute for good roads, the absence of which often makes transport and locomotion both costly and disagreeable. A very large extension of county and municipal expenditure in the States would be amply repaid if good roads could be obtained thereby.

For some reason which is not very apparent to me, I have always compared the bad roads in the United States with the obstructive nature of officialism in this country. In the States you may have much difficulty in getting to a public office, but when there you are sure to receive prompt attention and ample assistance; here it may be easy to reach the place, but when there the ruggedness begins; and upon the whole I would rather have to encounter a rough road than careless and contemptuous officials.

In the repression of violence the advantage is on the side of the United Kingdom, but not so decidedly as some persons might be inclined to imagine. We read of railway strikes and serious conflicts with revenue officers in the States; but these circumstances are exceptional and rare. Although we are more prepared for the repression of violence, yet, in the main, order is better preserved in the States than in this country, and life and property are there at least equally secure.

Upon education the expenditure in the United States, from taxation and State grants, is about double that of the United Kingdom. There education is free—here we still rely in no small degree upon the school-pence ; it must, therefore, be admitted that in this respect the Government of the United States do more than our own.

In the States the Government undertake the registration of land, and thus the cost involved in the transfer or mortgage of a farm amounts to a few shillings only. Emigration Offices, Geological Institutions, with Bureaus of Agriculture, Mining, and Commerce afford facilities at the cost of the Government. The arrangements in public offices are so simplified, and the attention given by officials is so prompt, that transactions with these departments can be carried on without difficulty, and there is seldom any need for legal assistance; whereas, in this country no civilian would go to a public office unless he was too poor to obtain legal help, or felt some sense of amusement in that peculiar style of snubbing which is so freely administered to all visitors.

The Government in the States is always willing to assist, or take in hand, institutions which have been established for the public benefit; even public amusements are promoted, and the "drill halls" are often utilised for public entertainments, while enormous sums are cheerfully spent on public parks.

It must be remembered that the cost of the Government, as well as that of all other business in the States, is greatly increased by the enormous extent of territory which is occupied by the States; and, taking this into account, it is surprising that the people can have so much good government, and such substantial assistance on every hand, for the comparatively small expenditure which is incurred. We are in the habit of attributing our excessive expenditure to the army and navy, but if we abolished our army and navy our expenditure would still be much greater per head than that of the United States. For war debts and war purposes we expend 51 millions per annum, the United States

$33\frac{1}{2}$ millions. The difference between the two does not account for more than $16\frac{1}{2}$ millions, whereas our excess of expenditure over that of the States, when compared with population, is over 40 millions. What becomes of our excessive expenditure, and what do we get for it?

With a more compact population, and a Government longer established, it should be less costly. As everything else is cheaper, why is government so dear? The explanation is probably to be found in the systematic waste and extravagance of Government departments of which we get occasional glimpses, such as the expenditure of £1,700 on oil for the Houses of Parliament. No one could visit Somerset House, our dockyards, or other public establishments, without being struck with the waste of time which occurs in public offices; and when time is wasted it is not likely that other matters are economised.

Under much more difficult circumstances the United States are more thoroughly and efficiently governed at less than two-thirds of the expenditure which we incur. The subject is one which might repay the fullest investigation.

X

PUBLIC DEBTS.

A comparison of the respective indebtedness of the two countries will be scarcely less interesting than a comparison of taxation. Our shoulders have long been accustomed to debt, and some of our people regard it almost as a national blessing, seeing that it provides a safe investment for those who wish to keep money without using it. Perhaps those sanguine persons do not reflect that a safe investment at three per cent. is nearly equal to tying up a talent in a napkin, which, in the Gospel, we are taught to regard as objectionable. Such a mode of investment certainly fails to represent the natural connection between the possession of capital and the exercise of judgment and industry. The subject, moreover, concerns future generations, and if they could be consulted they might prefer being without the debt; and our right to impose it upon them, with scarcely an effort towards its reduction, may well be called in question.

An essential difference should be recognised in the circumstances of a new country and an old one. A new country requires a large outlay of capital and usually affords excellent opportunities for its investment. It is obviously reasonable that the unemployed capital in the old should be used in the subjugation of the new world. With regard to this country it may be fairly contended that we have approached the zenith of our prosperity, and it is clear that we are exhausting our resources. During the last thirty years we have enjoyed leaps and bounds of prosperity which are perhaps without parallel in the history of any nation ; we could have spared ten millions annually for the reduction of debt almost without feeling it, and this would have swept away two-thirds of our indebtedness, and given us a better outlook for the future.

During this prosperous period we have not reduced our debt in any appreciable degree, and there has been no reduction whatever if we set off the increased amount of local indebtedness against the slight diminution of national indebtedness.

Taking the last financial statement of the Chancellor of the Exchequer, it appears that

THE AMOUNT OF THE NATIONAL DEBT OF THE UNITED KINGDOM ON THE 31ST MARCH, 1879, WAS

Funded Debt	£709,402,000
Value of Annuities	42,776,000
Unfunded Debt	25,870,000
Total	£778,048,000

The amount of the National Debt in 1837 was £787,529,114, so that in 41 years the actual reduction of debt has been less than ten millions. We have, however, spent something for telegraphs, bought the Suez Canal, and made advances on local loans, so that we may take the credit of having reduced our debt, or made payments on capital account, to the extent of £50,000,000, or about a million and a quarter per annum. We might have shewn a better result if we had not indulged in a Russian war ; but we cannot claim much credit on that account.

Our local indebtedness amounts to £120,000,000, and it increases at the rate of about eight millions annually. This increase is undoubtedly expended on various local purchases or improvements, and most of the money is borrowed under fixed arrangements for repayment in 30, 50, or 80 years. The expenditure on local improvements is a healthy effort when it is wisely made, but the limit of repayment should not exceed 30 years or one generation.

THE TOTAL NATIONAL INDEBTEDNESS OF THE UNITED KINGDOM IS

Government National Debt £778,048,000
Local Indebtedness 120,000,000

Carried forward.................... £898,048,000

Brought forward	£898,048,000
Less amount of Government Advances to local bodies	23,017,000
Nett total indebtedness	£875,031,000

At the close of the Civil War the Federal Government of the United States found itself with a debt, funded and unfunded, of £600,000,000, the annual interest of which amounted to £30,195,539. The feeling throughout the States was that the National Debt should be paid off in a generation, and a law was passed declaring that the debt should be reduced at the rate of one per cent. per annum ; and considerably more than this has been accomplished.

In a recent speech, Mr. Hayes, the President of the United States, made a statement respecting the United States Debt which puts the subject in so clear and complete a manner that I cannot do better than reproduce his observations. Speaking at St. Paul's on September 5th, 1878, he said that " the ascertained debt reached its highest point soon after the close of the war, in August, 1865, and amounted to £551,537,914. In addition to this, it was estimated that there were enough unadjusted claims against the Government of unquestioned validity to swell the total debt to £600,000,000. How to deal with this great burden was one of the gravest

questions which pressed for decision as a result of
the war. It will be remembered that in important
speeches and in the public press the opinion was
confidently declared that the debt could never be
paid ; that great nations never did pay their war
debts ; that our debt would be like that of England,
permanent and a burden upon ourselves and our
posterity for all time. Some advocated and many
feared repudiation. There were those also who
thought a National Debt was a national blessing.
Fortunately, however, the eminent gentleman at the
head of the Treasury, Mr. Hugh McCulloch, did not
hold these views. He believed, and the people
believed, that the debt was not a blessing, but a
burden, and that it ought to be paid and could be
honestly paid. The policy adopted was to reduce
the debt, and thereby strengthen the public credit,
so as to refund the debt at a lower rate of interest.
And now I give you the results. The debt has been
reduced, until now it is only £407,116,064. This is
a reduction, as compared with the ascertained debt
thirteen years ago, of £144,421,849. More than
one-fourth of the debt has been paid off in thirteen
years. If we compare the present debt with the
actual debt thirteen years ago, placing the actual
debt at £600,000,000, the reduction amounts to
about £200,000,000, or one-third of the total debt."

The American people may well be proud of financial efforts which enable their President to make such a satisfactory statement.

In addition to the debt of the Federal Government, public indebtedness in the United States arises under three heads, viz., State Governments, Counties, and Municipalities. The census tables of the United States gave the State indebtedness in 1870 as £70,573,339, the county indebtedness £37,259,508, and the municipal indebtedness £65,125,256. I am assured that the State and County indebtedness have been somewhat diminished since that time, but the municipal indebtedness has largely increased.

The Hon. James G. Blaine, Speaker of the Lower House of Congress, states that the municipal indebtedness in 1874 was £114,000,000, and since that time it probably has not increased, as after that date severer economy was generally practised.

THE TOTAL PUBLIC INDEBTEDNESS OF THE UNITED STATES IN 1879 WAS, THEREFORE—

Federal, as per Treasurer's statement, May, 1879	£405,426,043
State	70,573,339
County	37,259,508
Municipal	114,000,000
	£627,426,890

The indebtedness of the United Kingdom is £875,031,000, or £23 10s. per head of the population. The indebtedness of the United States shows £13 6s. 11d. per head.

The Americans are reaping the reward of their energetic honesty. Ten years ago their five per cent. bonds were selling on the London Stock Exchange at 73, thus paying investors within a small fraction of seven per cent ; at the time of writing, May, 1879, the United States four per cents. are worth 104, showing that we are willing to lend to them at £3 16s. 11d. per cent., or at a lower rate than we lend to any other nation except ourselves. The French five per cents. are worth 114, which shows £4 7s. 6d. per cent. interest. Russian four-and-a-half per cents. sell at 80, giving £5 12s. 6d., and Italian five per cents. at 78 afford £6 8s. per cent. interest. The credits of borrowing nations, therefore, stand as under, the amount per cent. showing the rate of interest which satisfies investors :—

	£	s.	d.	
United Kingdom	3	1	0	per cent.
United States	3	16	11	,,
France	4	7	6	,,
Russia	5	12	6	,,
Italy	6	8	0	,,

These figures will be eloquent to those who are interested in the subject, and to other readers nothing which I can add would make them interesting.

IMPORTS AND EXPORTS.

Whether it is more blessed to give than to receive is a question which of late has greatly agitated the public mind. Some persons insist upon it that the test of our advancement is to be found in the amount of our exports ; and others declare that our imports afford the real test by which we must measure our prosperity. Some difficulty arises in this case from the air of certainty assumed on both sides, which has made assertion more common than argument ; but the fact is that neither exports nor imports can be regarded as evidence of prosperity, without taking into account the causes from which they originate. The Irish cotter may export his pig because he has been so successful and prosperous that he has more bacon than he requires, or he may sell the animal because he cannot afford to keep it ; in one case the export would be a sign of prosperity, in the other of adversity. So with imports :—A family may receive a large quantity of goods, because they are prosperous and can well afford to pay for them, or for the reason that they are reckless and are going into debt. With nations precisely the same considerations operate as with individuals and families; the cause of increased exports may be successful industry or extending poverty, and the cause of increased imports may be either prosperity or extravagance.

As a rule exports represent successful industry, and imports indicate the possession of wealth. A decline in exports would indicate either that other nations had become poorer, or that we had become less capable of supplying their requirements, and a decline in imports would indicate that we had become poorer and less capable of purchasing; but these general deductions are subject to various modifications, according to circumstances, and it is to be regretted that so many writers on this subject attempt to square all facts to theories, instead of recognising the numerous contingencies by which trade is influenced. International trade is exceedingly sensitive, and capable of great extension or repression.

An American wants clothes, and he has to determine what he will do to obtain them. He may grow corn, and send the corn to Liverpool or Hull in exchange for cloth or calico, or he may spin the wool or cotton in his own country, in which case he will have less time for growing corn; it is simply a question as to the best mode of employing labour. On such points individuals are very good judges of their own interest, and if left free to choose they will produce what suits their capacities, and purchase what best supplies their wants. It is strange that it should have occurred to any one to interfere with the natural course of trade, or to suppose that nations can be made more prosperous by preventing individuals from buying and selling as they please. Those who buy and sell are benefited thereby, as without an advantage they would not act; why therefore, should they be prevented from obtaining those benefits? If there is any danger of excess, that danger attaches more to exports than to imports. A man or a nation may be compelled by poverty to sell, and thus to part with property under cost price, which occasions a loss to the seller and a profit to the purchaser; but it is difficult to imagine any reason by which an individual can be obliged to purchase; buying is always a voluntary operation, and, therefore, there is but little ground for viewing an increase of imports with alarm. As a rule, an increase of either imports or exports is an indication of prosperity, as they are usually the result of voluntary and beneficial actions.

An increase of imports does not involve a diminution of home industry. This statement may be tested by a reference to the circumstance that about 20 years ago discoveries of petroleum oil were made in the United States, and large quantities have been sent to the United Kingdom ; by this means thousands of British homes have been made more cheerful. Light is life, and it affords the means of industry. If the Americans had made us a present of this oil it would have been an unmixed blessing, and as they have required payment for it we are none the worse; British industry has been stimulated by the necessity for producing something in payment for the oil, and the oil itself has afforded the means of exercising industry by giving improved light and comfort. Would the interest of either nation be advanced by imposing restrictions on this trade?

Take another case. We have recently discovered improved methods of making steel rails, which are now being supplied to our railway companies at less than £5 per ton. To the Americans, railways are one of the most important means of national development; but they shut out our rails by a heavy Customs' duty, upon the plea that native industries must be encouraged and educated by Protection. Are their ironmasters likely to adopt new modes of manufacture so long as they are protected from competition? If they felt that British steel would be poured into their country unless they promptly adopted the same improved process they would set about the change at once; but under Protection it will probably be years before they will move, and in the meantime American industry will be hampered by dear and inferior iron.

Our trade with the United States is shown in the following table:—

	IMPORTS.	EXPORTS.
1863	£19,572,010	£19,696,785
1864	17,923,678	20,183,566
1865	21,624,125	25,170,787
1866	46,854,218	31,843,836
1867	41,045,957	24,119,630
1868	43,062,299	23,801,851
1869	42,572,933	26,787,731
1870	49,894,681	31,306,089
1871	61,134,463	38,692,837
1872	54,663,948	45,907,998
1873	71,471,493	36,698,426
1874	73,897,400	32,238,321
1875	69,590,054	25,062,226
1876	75,899,008	20,226,627
1877	77,825,973	19,885,893

It will be seen by this table that our exports to the United States rose from 19 millions in 1863 to 45 millions in 1872, and that they have since fallen to their original level of 19 millions. On the other hand, the imports from the United States, which commenced at 19 millions in 1863, have continuously risen until they reached 77 millions in 1877. Of course these figures, like all our statistics of imports and exports, give an exaggerated view of the case. Freight, merchants' profits, and interest have usually to be added to both sides in favour of Britain before we arrive at the final balance. In the American account of imports and exports to the United States we find, under the head of Great Britain and Ireland, that they give us credit for sending to them exports to the value of 25 millions instead of 19 millions, and their exports to us they estimate at 68 millions instead of 77 millions, making the difference 43 millions instead of 58 millions; but still the amount shows an enormous balance against us. It is certain that the Americans do not make us a present of the difference, and that in some way or other they receive payment.

There is one mode by which a large portion of the balance is adjusted, to which I think sufficient importance has not been attached. During the war and the few excited years that followed the United States borrowed from us large sums. The total amount of these loans cannot be ascertained, but probably it was not under four hundred millions for national and railway purposes; and, in addition to this, enormous sums were advanced as private loans. Now, it must be carefully noted that where these loans were made in currency the lender was credited with seven, eight, ten, and, in some cases, twelve or fourteen dollars for every English sovereign. These loans are now being repaid after an appreciation of the States currency has taken place, which makes five dollars equal to a sovereign ; our lenders are getting their money back with an addition of 50, 100, or 150 per cent. The return of these loans with those additions will account for all the excess of imports which has hitherto taken place, and for a good deal more to come, and such a state of affairs is not one of which we need complain. There are, however, other reasons for the great change in the course of trade, and the chief of these is the extreme depression which has occurred in the States since 1872. We have known something of depression here, but our depression is slight compared with what has taken place in the States. It is customary to attribute the falling off in the imports to the development of native manufactures, but it mainly arises from a far less satisfactory cause—*i.e.*, from the failure of the consuming power of the people in the States. As a test of this statement we may refer to their imports of articles which they cannot produce, and it will be seen that the falling off has been as great in these articles as in those which they can supply for themselves. The Americans have not yet discovered tin or been able to grow tea, and if any decrease has taken place in the import of these articles it must arise from the decrease in the consumption, and not from an increased production at home.

The United States imports of tin in 1873 amounted to £3,671,330, but in 1878 these had fallen to £2,442,506 ; and the imports of tea, which were 24,446,180lbs. in 1873, fell to 15,660,168lbs. in 1878. During the same period the consumption of nearly all articles in use by the working classes in the United Kingdom greatly increased. Thus we find that the quantities imported or retained for home consumption per head of the total population were, in

		1872.	1877.
Bacon	lbs.	5·44	8·04
Butter	,,	3·90	5·34
Cheese	,,	3·65	5·37
Eggs	number	16	22
Sugar	lbs.	47	64
Tea	,,	4	4½

These figures show that although the upper and middle classes have suffered from depression of trade, the great bulk of the people have been able to increase their consumption of nearly all the necessaries of life.

But the question of chief importance in connection with this subject is how far the people of the United States have developed their exports of

manufactures.   It is there that they enter into
competition with us ; and, as the markets of the
world are equally open to them and to ourselves,
we can make a fair comparison as to the respective
position of each country in this important respect.
The export of articles of British and Irish produce
during the year 1877, after deducting such as were
not manufactures, was £186,578,065.   The exportation of manufactured articles from the United States
during the year ended June 30th, 1878, was
£7,450,175.   The result, therefore, of a century of
Protection in the United States, for the purpose of
educating their people to develop manufactures, is
that their export trade is less than one twenty-
fourth of our own.

Take another test.   In ship building the
Americans have enjoyed an important natural
advantage over ourselves in the low price of
timber ; but how does their shipping compare with
that of the United Kingdom?   This is shown by
the following return :—

TONNAGE OF VESSELS FROM FOREIGN COUNTRIES,
WHICH ENTERED UNITED STATES PORTS DURING THE
YEAR ENDED JUNE, 1878 :—

American Vessels .... 3,642,417 tons.
Foreign Vessels 10,821,387   „

Y

TONNAGE OF VESSELS FROM FOREIGN COUNTRIES, WHICH ENTERED PORTS OF THE UNITED KINGDOM DURING THE YEAR ENDED DECEMBER, 1877 :—

British Vessels ....17,281,334 tons.
Foreign Vessels............................... 8,330,839 ,,

and, by a comparison with previous years, we find that the proportion of American tonnage as compared with Foreign is decreasing, and that the proportion of British as compared with Foreign is increasing. Whichever way we turn we find that one hundred years of protection has failed to develop manufactures and commerce in the States; while 30 years of free trade has given to the United Kingdom the greatest extension of trade ever known within a similar period.

Of course the Americans can, if they please, exclude foreigners like the Chinese, and thus produce their own manufactures, or do without them. But such a system, while subjecting their own population to very serious privations, entirely precludes them from becoming active competitors with ourselves in the markets of the world. If we are anxious to avoid this competition, we cannot hope for anything better than that the Americans should preserve their system of exclusion; under which the markets of the world are left open to ourselves.

It is pleasant to turn to the other side of the picture, and refer for a moment to the substantial prosperity which the States have obtained through the development of agriculture. Nature asserts herself in spite of human folly, and although the American agriculturists are seriously prejudiced by the Protective policy of the States, they continue to prosper, and their exports show an enormous extension during the last ten years, as will be seen by the following table :—

AGRICULTURAL EXPORTS FROM THE UNITED STATES :—

	YEARS ENDED JUNE 30TH,	
	1868.	1878.
Live Animals	£146,678	£1,168,930
Bread and Breadstuffs	13,796,199	36,354,901
Fruit	974,210	2,287,125
Provisions	6,055,650	24,709,997

The nation ought to be prosperous which can show such a remarkable progress. There can be little room to doubt that the agricultural advancement of the States will rapidly bring about a return of general prosperity, in which we shall in some degree participate, and, if the Custom House barriers were broken down, the prosperity of both nations would be secured.

It is satisfactory to notice that the export of meat continues to increase with great rapidity. By the latest returns it appears that the importations of fresh beef from the United States for the months

of January and February in 1877 were 67,853 cwts.;
in 1878, 78,916 cwts.; and in 1879, 118,346 cwts.
It is pleasant to know that we are likely to obtain
abundant supplies of this important article of
consumption from the American prairies, without
subjecting living animals to the suffering involved
in transport across the Atlantic.

THINGS IN GENERAL.

A worthy Mayor of a provincial city, after making a long speech, in which he had referred in detail to subjects of special interest to the Council, alarmed and amused his audience by observing that, as he had touched upon all topics in particular, he would say a few words on things in general. I never expected to follow the example of that worthy chief citizen, but I now find it convenient to do so. A reference to topics separately cannot give that general view of life which is obtained from combination, and much would remain unexplained unless we comprehend the relation of various topics to each other.

The present condition of the United States arises from a variety of causes which have converged to a common centre, each contributing its quota to the general outcome. War, with its feverish excitement, inflated currency, and wild speculation, produced fraud on a gigantic scale. This fraud has been manifested in Tammany Rings, Whisky Rings, Credit Mobiliers, and Political Jugglery, in which judges and statesmen were corrupted, investors robbed, and the nation deceived and paralysed.

It is scarcely possible to conceive the extent of demoralisation produced by the sudden outbreak of a civil war such as occurred in the States. In older and more settled countries the circumstances attending war are in some measure provided for, and subjected to rules for the prevention of fraud, but even in such countries war is always accompanied with an enormous amount of jobbery and corruption. In the States a life and death struggle was suddenly commenced without any previous preparation. The great majority of the nation entered into the contest with deep convictions and patriotic intentions ; but just as pickpockets have their eyes on an eager crowd, so did shrewd and unscrupulous persons turn this great struggle to their own advantage ; and their rapid success led to an extension of demoralisation. How deep and base this demoralisation was may be gathered from a single instance. Towards the close of the war a firm of contractors engaged to make a large number of waggons for the Northern army. Just as these waggons were completed, and about to be delivered, there appeared a prospect of peace, which would have destroyed the chance of a repetition of the contract. The contractors were determined to do what lay in their little power to prevent such a happy consummation, and in order to encourage the

South to prolonged resistance they caused these waggons to be carried beyond the lines of the Northern army, so that they could be captured by the Southerners, of course taking care to give their fraud the appearance of an error on the part of seemingly innocent parties.

Feverish excitement is often mistaken for strength, and when the United States were borrowing from Europe at a more rapid rate than any nation ever borrowed before, they supposed that they were growing rich instead of becoming poor. I venture to affirm—and I hope to give some substantial reasons for the assertion—that extensive fraud has been possible in the States mainly from the general straightforward honesty of the American people. It is notorious that an old poacher makes the best gamekeeper, and if there had been more rogues among the people in the United States, it would have been far more difficult to rob them. At Chicago I was much amused at seeing large placards posted up at the railway stations,

Don't lend your Money to Strangers.

I inquired if the people were so much in the habit of lending money to strangers that such a notice was necessary, and in reply I was informed that nothing was more common than for a farmer to sell his produce at Chicago, and, on returning by rail, place the proceeds in the hands of some plausible stranger, who, having spoken of an advantageous investment, obtained and departed with the cash.

We occasionally hear of the confidence trick being practised upon some unfortunate Zany in London, but the victim is always from the agricultural districts. In the States farmers are much more isolated and solitary than in the country districts of Britain, and they are, therefore, more liable to be imposed upon when they enter a town. The railway frauds would have been impossible in some countries where honesty is less general than in the States, and where it would be understood that special precautions had to be taken against fraud. During a prolonged tour in the States I came in contact with professional thieves, but in the ordinary walks of life straightforward honesty is stamped upon the features and conduct of the people. No one ever tried to give short change, and although I am not a very careful traveller not a single article did I lose.

Tradesmen in the States may be blunt and unaccommodating, but, in my experience, no one ever failed to do fully what he promised to do. I am aware that none of these statements are conclusive, and they will not convince those who believe that fraud is indigenous in America, but, in addition to such personal arguments, reference may be made to the fact that no country has repaid their national debt so rapidly as the Americans, and that vigorous efforts have been made to uphold the national credit.

There are, and always will be, a number of persons interested in schemes which involve national discredit, but, if I may judge from the tone of the persons with whom I came in contact in the States, there is an overwhelming preponderance of opinion in favour of maintaining the national credit in the most substantial manner. Vigorous efforts were made to circulate silver as a national currency. At street corners in the evening I constantly came upon groups listening to some excited orator, and the theme almost invariably was the silver question, the rubbish poured forth on such occasions being of the most lamentable character. I heard over and again that England was on the brink of ruin, and that Germany was in a most distressed condition, because in these countries the capitalists prevented the coinage of silver in order to swell the value of the debts owing to them, and thus the poor were deprived of work, and small capitalists were over-whelmed by men who had got rich by defrauding the public. These meetings were not noticed by the leading newspapers, but the nonsense seems to have taken more effect upon the public mind than political leaders imagined; for at the ensuing meeting of Congress it became apparent that the silver party were actually in a majority, and it was only by making some concessions that the question could be met. The hard money men, however, had hard heads, and they adroitly agreed to coin silver to the extent of two million dollars a month, and put it in circulation if it was asked for, in exchange for gold or notes at par. By this arrangement no one but the Government could profit by putting silver into circulation, and as few persons took the trouble to call for the cumbersome coins most of the silver dollars remain in the treasury.

The producers of silver are a wealthy and powerful class in the States, but although they have used their influence in a most unscrupulous manner to raise the value of their produce at the national expense, it must not be supposed that they were the sole agents in promoting the silver agitation. I met with many working men who evidently believed that they were being prejudiced by the contraction of the currency, and undoubtedly they were, in common with all other classes, subjected to great inconvenience in consequence. We have so long enjoyed the advantages of a fixed currency that we do not realise the great injury and disturbance caused by fluctuations which disturb every contract and custom upon which industry is based.

At Niagara I met with an amusing instance of
the manner in which cute Yankees endeavour to
" do " their visitors. I was walking in the streets
in the evening, when a small man asked me if I
could tell him the way to ——. I said that I did
not know the way, as I was a stranger. " Are you
a stranger? So am I—never from home before,—
live in Indianopolis—son of Senator Morton. You
have heard of Senator Morton? On my way to New
York—feel kind of lonely. One of your countrymen
has been staying with father—Dr. Playfair, who was
your Postmaster-General. He is now gone to
Harrisburgh. Hope to see him again." By this
time I had reached my hotel, and wished him good
evening. Two hours later he again found me in
the streets. " Oh, good evening, how odd
that we should have met again. Just heard a
piece of good news. Hotel-keeper tells me that I
have won a lottery ticket—going to see how much
I have to take up. Will you come along with me?"
It then dawned upon me that a trap was being
laid, and I determined to see what sort of a trap it
was. I had but little money and no valuables
about me, and as I knew that clever rogues would
not want my brains I felt that I could safely follow
him. He went upstairs to a large room on the first
floor, where was a graver looking man sitting behind a

counter. My companion, addressing this man, said,
"I am told that my lottery ticket has won a prize ; is it
so?" The ticket was produced and carefully examined.
" Yes, you have won a prize of 165 dollars," which
amount was handed to him. The young man asked
eagerly, " Do you sell lottery tickets here ? " " No,"
was the response, " we do not sell lottery tickets ;
we only pay the prizes." " But," said the innocent,
" you have a system which I see by the notice on
the walls you promise to explain to any one who
wishes to know. What is your system?" " Our
system," said the solemn man, "is this. We have a
board with numbers and sums stated under each
number. You pay a dollar, and then draw two
cards ; if the numbers on these cards make any of
the numbers on the board you receive the sum
stated under it." " Oh," said the young man,
" Here is a dollar ; give me the cards." He drew
two, and they came to a number under which was
written 120 dollars, and these were handed to him.
" Now," said he, " turning to me, " I have had such
good luck, you must allow me to put down a dollar
for you as well as for myself." I protested, but he
put down two dollars, and drew two cards making
a number under which 165 dollars were written.
The solemn man counted out a packet of notes and
handed them to the young man, and a similar packet

to me, but before they could be taken up he said, "Stay! This is a conditional prize. You see the word 'conditional' written under the figures, which means that before you can receive this prize, each person must put down twenty dollars of his own money for future trials." The young man promptly put down twenty dollars, and was about to take up the one hundred and sixty-five dollars. "Stop!" said the solemn man, "you put in for yourself and friend, and before you can take up the stakes each must put down the twenty dollars as required by the conditions." Turning to me, the young man said, "You will, of course, do that, as you have only to put down twenty dollars and take up one hundred and sixty-five dollars." I declined. Then said he, "I will put down the twenty dollars for you." "No," said the solemn man, "your friend must do that for himself, or both prizes revert to me." The young man then became pathetic, and urged me to put down the twenty dollars, in order that he might take up his prize, which he must otherwise lose. I replied, "Thank you, gentlemen, for showing me a very interesting game," and walked out of the room.

On returning to the International Hotel I related what had occurred, and the proprietor told me that the previous week one of his guests lost one thousand five hundred dollars at the same place, and that

visitors were constantly ruined by these gambling
tricks. He said, "The authorities tried all they could
to stop them, but were unsuccessful, as the
attendants at the rooms are changed every day,
the concern being managed by a large gang of
sharpers who work together in all parts of the
country." I afterwards found repeated instances of
men having lost all they had with them by the
action of these fellows. One simple-minded visitor,
at Niagara, asked a man in the street where he
could find a bank to change a letter of credit.
"Oh," said the stranger, "I will take you to my
bank." On entering an office the visitor handed
over a letter of credit, and the stranger coolly walked
into the next room, desiring the visitor to wait a
moment. He waited, the stranger did not return.
He timidly opened the door—no one was there.
Neither the stranger nor the circular note were seen
again ; but fortunately a telegraphic message
stopped the payment of the note.

It is not, however, by such vulgar means as
these that the American people are chiefly robbed.
The arch robbers become directors of railways, chairmen of banks, or officials in municipal institutions.
During the last five years the American people have
been awaking to the extent of the robberies
practised upon them, and the press is by no means

reticent on the subject. As to railway robberies, a contributor to the *Bankers' Magazine* (New York) for December, 1878, writes that " In railway calculations an element interposes itself which cannot be reduced to the form of an accurate account, and that is the element of stealing ; where men of the stamp of James Fisk have had an unchecked control it becomes a case for the imagination." He adds, " One of the best paying roads in the country, that from New York to New Haven, besides declaring ten per cent. dividends, has been carrying for generations the load of an extra million made out of the construction, and of two millions stolen by ———." In the magazine the blank is filled up, but it is unnecessary to do so here.

Every visitor to New York obtains practical experience of the doings of the Tweed ring, who received enormous funds for municipal purposes and left the streets in such a wretched state that in many parts no vehicle can travel above a walking pace ; the money which should have been paid to paviours was spent in bribing judges, and filling the pockets of officials and contractors.

In spite of the frauds practiced during the last 15 years, which in extent and enormity exceed everything previously known, I maintain that the great bulk of the public and private business of the nation is carried on with scrupulous honesty and good faith. No one can travel in America without feeling that he is amongst honest and honourable people. The frauds have resulted mainly from the demoralisation caused by the war, which completely undermined the honesty of many individuals, who found in the wealth and confidence of the people a field well suited for their operations. No other country has possessed anything like the same amount of wealth amongst a population so widely scattered, and where people dwell alone they are always more open to imposition.

Free institutions are no check upon personal frauds; on the contrary, they may be almost said to be favourable to them. A despotic Government usually seeks and obtains ample powers, which may be used with advantage against those who attempt dishonest practices ; and despotic rulers are almost sure to be surrounded by able and un-scrupulous men, whose personal experience gives them a keen sense of fraud. Popular Governments are not usually allowed the use of powers which would be useful in suppressing fraud, but which may be employed to limit the freedom of the people ; and the officers of Constitutional Govern-ments are not always persons who are experienced in fraud, and the most capable of its detection and suppression. We attach vast importance to a free press, and it undoubtedly cures and prevents many evils, but it is almost powerless against personal frauds. Libel laws make it impossible to warn the public respecting attempts to defraud. The proceedings of public men may be criticised, and severe language respecting them will be allowed to pass ; but against private persons and companies nothing must be said. Newspaper proprietors are often compelled to be silent under the knowledge of fraud, because they have no such legal proof as would protect them against an action for libel. Thus it arises that dishonest men find the amplest scope for their energies in countries which are free as well as wealthy ; and for this very reason England is, next to the United States, probably the place where fraud flourishes in the greatest degree.

Robbery is so easy in America that it requires but little ability to succeed in that line, and yet great robbers are generally regarded as heroes. They are interviewed by enterprising reporters, who publish harrowing accounts of the temptations by which they were surrounded, and the noble intentions of the thief, if he had but succeeded in his investments, so as to enable him to carry out his honest desire to pay back what he had stolen. If,

z

as rarely happens, he is sent to prison, the reporter
follows him, and brings tears to the eyes of his
readers by describing his meek and condescending
demeanour. About a year ago one of these robbers
who, it was estimated, had ruined more widows
and orphans than any other scoundrel in New York,
was sentenced to five years' imprisonment. The
Judge was so affected on passing sentence that he
blubbered profusely, and the whole Court wept. It
was altogether a touching scene, and it was made
more touching and ridiculous by the reporter who
followed the man to jail, as a spectator only, and
told his readers how bravely the villain bore the
treatment to which he was subjected. In the course
of his duties the robber had to walk in a line with
minor criminals, and it was the rule for each
prisoner to place his hands upon the shoulders of
the man who preceded him. The prisoner who
preceded this despoiler of the widow and orphan
was a coloured person, and the reporter
gravely notes, as a striking instance of his
hero's humility, that he did not shrink from
touching a coloured man!! I wonder if the coloured
man winced when he felt the fingers of the arch
criminal upon his shoulders. The absurd degree
of tenderness manifested towards criminals in the
States is the most serious feature in connection

with the subject of fraud. If men are allowed to steal with impunity, stealing will go on until the community becomes so impregnated with fraud that honest people will have no chance.

Frauds on the revenue have been enormous and systematic. During General Grant's administration whisky rings, and other associations for defrauding the Government, were in a most flourishing condition. The scattered state of the population makes it difficult to suppress fraud, and it is no doubt much easier to connive at robbery than it is to oppose it. Since the advent of Mr. Hayes' administration vigorous efforts have been made to put down illicit distillation, and in the latest report issued by the Treasury of the United States a graphic account is given of the means which have been adopted. The Commissioner of Internal Revenue, who writes on November 25, 1878, says :—

" Great difficulties have been, and still are, encountered in many of the Southern States in the enforcement of the laws. In the mountain regions of West Virginia, Virginia, Kentucky, Tennessee, Georgia, and Alabama, and in some portions of Missouri, Arkansas, and Texas, the illicit manufacture of spirits has been carried on for a number of years, and I am satisfied that the annual loss to the Government from this source has been very nearly, if not quite, equal to the annual appropriation for the collection of the internal revenue tax throughout the whole country. In the regions of the country named there are known to exist about five thousand copper stills, and a large portion of these stills have been, and are, used in the illicit manufacture of spirits. This nefarious business has been carried on, as a rule, by a determined set of men, who in their various neighbourhoods league together for defence against the officers of the law, and at a given signal are ready to come together with arms in their hands to drive the officers of internal revenue out of the country.

"As illustrating the extraordinary resistance which the officers have had on some occasions to encounter, I refer to occurrences in Overton, County Tennessee, in August last, when a posse of eleven internal revenue officers, who had stopped at a farmer's house for the night, were attacked by a band of armed illicit distillers, who kept up a constant fusilade during the whole night, and whose force was augmented during the following day till it numbered nearly two hundred men. The officers took shelter in a log house, which served them as a fort, returning the fire as best they could, and were there besieged for forty-two hours, three of the party being shot—one through the body, one through the arm, and one in the face. I directed a strong force to go to their relief, but in the meantime, through the intervention of citizens, the besieged officers were permitted to retire, taking their wounded with them, without surrendering their arms.

"So formidable has been the resistance to the enforcements of the laws that I have found it necessary to supply collectors with breech-loading carbines. I regret to have to record the fact that when the officers of the United States have been shot down from ambuscade, in cold blood, as a rule no efforts have been made on the part of the State officers to arrest the murderers; but, in cases where the officers of the United States have been engaged in the enforcement of the laws, and have unfortunately come in conflict with the violators of the law, and homicides have occurred, active steps have been at once taken for the arrest of such officers, and nothing has been left undone by the State authorities to bring them to trial and punishment.'

Cases in point are then given, and the Commissioner proceeds :—

"Much of the opposition to the enforcement of the internal revenue laws is properly attributable to a latent feeling of hostility to the government and laws of the United States still prevailing in the breasts of a portion of the people of these districts; and in consequence of this condition of things the officers of the United States have often been treated very much as though they were emissaries from some foreign country quartered upon the people for the collection of tribute.

" The operations against illicit distillers for the seizure of their distilleries and the arrest of their persons are extremely hazardous, and, in fact, an officer who goes upon a mission of this kind feels that he carries his life in his hand. For this desperate work it has not been found practicable to obtain the services of the most educated and refined citizens, especially in view of the fact that the service is temporary and the pay not large.

" The usual force of deputies heretofore allowed collectors for the collection of the revenue in the districts where illicit distillery has mostly prevailed has been found totally inadequate for the suppression of frauds, and, with your approval, I have adopted the plan of giving collectors authority to employ, from time to time, a suitable number of special deputies to aid in making seizures. To meet the extraordinary expenses thus incurred, I have found it necessary to cut down the salaries of officers throughout the country.

" I am of opinion that if active measures can be kept up against illicit distillers for twelve months more the business will be substantially broken up, and that violations of internal revenue laws in the districts named will be scarcely more frequent than in other portions of the country."

By a return which is appended to this report it appears that during the year ended June 30th, 1878, 1,020 stills were seized, and 1,974 persons arrested, and in doing this work 5 officers and guides were killed and 13 wounded.

One of the most unfavourable symptoms of American politics is the movement which is being made to bring about the nomination of General Grant as the Republican candidate for the Presidency. This movement has been originated, and is now chiefly stimulated, by those who benefited through the frauds which were so rampant during his term of office. It is impossible to say what will be the result of such a nomination, as a vast amount of energy may be expended by those who expect personal profit from such an election, but his selection would be a most unfortunate event for the United States. At the time of my visit to America his nomination was not generally spoken of, and therefore the expressions of opinion which reached me were probably unbiassed by party prejudice. I heard a good deal of him, as at that time Grant was in Europe, and an almost universal feeling of regret was expressed in America that the States should be represented in England by a person so little calculated to give a favourable idea of the national character.

Next to the enormous extension of fraud, the very general use of tobacco is perhaps the most demoralising influence in operation in the United States, and judging from the tenacity with which social habits are retained, we may fear that tobacco chewing will be the most permanent evil. It would be impossible to convey to English readers any idea of the extent to which the chewing of tobacco and the filthy habits to which it gives rise are prevalent in the States. The first day that I spent at New York I called upon a gentleman whose name is known throughout Europe as a railway magnate of the first magnitude. A chair was placed for me about three feet from his own, and I noticed that between us was a handsome china vase. As my friend asked permission to finish a note, I contemplated this vase from the outside, and became doubtful whether this was the American substitute for a waste-paper basket, or whether the owner was a lover of old china and always kept a handsome specimen by his side. On the note being finished, he turned, as I thought, to speak; but before doing so he poured a cascade of brown fluid from his

mouth into the vase, followed by the remains
of an enormous quid, and it was not until
after this operation had been completed that the
gentleman was able to proceed to conversation.

But my experiences at New York were mild
compared with what I found further West. At
Chicago the floor of the Exchange was entirely
covered, and quite slippery, with discharged mucous
and saliva, mixed with chewed tobacco leaves. On
a raised platform stood a number of the leading
members engaged in making bids. They appeared
to be as close together as they could stand; but
this did not prevent them from discharging streams
of saliva from their mouths, which poured down
quite close to the coats of their neighbours. The
Corn Exchange at Kansas City is not crowded like
the Exchange at Chicago, and I was admitted to it
just after the conclusion of a sale. Seats had been
placed for the purchasers, and it was easy to discover exactly how many seats had been occupied
by the pool of saliva discharged by each visitor
during the short time he was present. At
public meetings I constantly found a stream
of saliva pouring down close to my coat from the
lips of a bystander, and if a pause occurred in the
discourse, instead of the traditional pin, you heard
saliva pattering on the floor.

This is by far the greatest scourge of American life. In travelling it is impossible to escape from it, and, although it is not perhaps so constantly seen in private houses, I found some cases in which men did not hesitate to expectorate upon their own, or other people's, carpets. The loss of national health and strength resulting from this practice must be enormous, and probably the money value of the waste of saliva in the States is greater than the annual interest of all the national debts in Europe.

It would hardly be supposed that in any part of the States there was a surplus population, but in the course of a recent speech President Hayes made the following observations on the Eastern emigration to the West. He said :—" There is another interesting subject that is worth giving attention to, and I think it is encouraging and full of hope. The surplus populations of the Atlantic slope of States are finding their way, as they never have done before, to the beautiful States and Territories of the West. (Applause.) And what does that mean? It means relief to the East. The surplus population that goes off gives a better opportunity for employment of labour and industry there, and here in the new States they are making their homes, and they are furnishing them a market for their supplies from the old States. But it has more than a double

advantage. There are three advantages. It
relieves the States, it furnishes a market to the old
States, and with their products in the new States
they help to swell the tide of exports to the old
countries."

It is not a little singular that with the comparatively thin population of the Eastern States,
emigration is spoken of in the same terms as are
applicable to old and densely populated countries.
The tide of Western emigration has materially
reduced the value of property in the Eastern States,
and left openings for emigrants from Europe to
settle in them, instead of going to the extreme West.
An English agriculturist would undoubtedly feel
more at home in the Eastern States than in the
Western, and possibly this gradual and dual system
of emigration may be the best.

The rapid adaptation of American energy to
new inventions is seen in the fact that the telephone
was in active operation in most of the leading cities
of the States within a few weeks of its discovery.
In September, 1877, I found a central office in
Boston to which about 100 telephones had been
introduced, connecting it with various establishments in the city, and by this means either of the
hundred offices could be put in communication with
any other. Eighteen months later there is scarcely
a telephone in operation in England.

In America every facility is afforded for the
erection of telegraphic wires. No householder
would raise an objection to the fixing of a wire rest
on the top of his house, and thus private enterprise
in the matter of telegraphs is not checked as it has
been here by the difficulty of arranging with
owners of property.

The people in the States have a habit of adopt-
ing English inventions, and bringing them into use,
before we can tell whether we like them or not.
In addition to the telephone, they have beaten us in
the manufacture of watches by applying to their
manufacture those principles of measurement which
Sir Joseph Witworth has brought to great perfection. A few years since England and Switzerland
supplied America with watches; now the States
supply England, and they do this not because they
have any natural advantages, but by the practical
application of our own inventions.

Mr. Arthur Granville Bradley, writing for
Macmillan in November, gives " A Peep at the
Southern Negro," from his own experience ; and
although the picture he presents is by no means
flattering he endorses the opinion which I have
expressed, that the people of the Southern States,
with all their existing trials and difficulties, admit
that freedom is better than slavery. He illustrates
this view by the following graphic sketch :—

" I met the ' ole massa,' who, with his son, did all the work on a poor and worked-out farm. He pointed, with a finger black with tobacco stripping, to the ruins of what had once been slave cabins, but were then but a row of brick chimneys rising out of a heap of tangled briars, and volunteered the remark that ' poor as he was he would not go back to the times when them cabins were standing. No sir, they'd like to have eaten me out of house and home.' It is by no means uncommon to hear the generally accepted ideas of the outer world reversed like this ; and the same opinions, in a more modified form and more mildly expressed, prevail largely."

I have often felt suprised that merchants and manufacturers in the States appear to have been so little affected by the numerous failures which have taken place of late years. Exporters from this country seem to have lost very little in bad debts, although so many American failures have occurred. I believe the explanation of this circumstance is to be found in the peculair mode of discounting acceptances which prevails in the United States, and which throws the losses occasioned by bad debts upon the discount houses and not upon the traders. When a manufacturer sells his goods, and takes a bill at three, four, or six months, he sells his customer's bill to a banker or a discount house, and his *responsibility ceases.* Should his customer make default, the seller of the bill hears no more of it—at least, he is in no way responsible for the payment of the bill which he has sold, and for which a discount has been allowed to cover the risk of failure, as well as the interest of the money. The business of the merchant or manufacturer is thus greatly simplified. He is not called upon to investigate the responsibility of the purchaser. He knows the state of his customer's credit by the rate at which his acceptances can be discounted ; if the rate is higher than usual he adds to the price of his goods. There are many advantages in this system, one being that it places the risk of bad debts upon the bill-broker, whose special business it is to take such risks, and prosecute the inquiries which will reduce them to a minimum.

It is just as inconvenient to a struggling manufacturer to lose two thousand pounds in a bad debt as it would be to lose the same amount by a fire, and it is as well to guard against one risk as against another. The plan adopted is an assurance against making bad debts, which, being a financial risk, is properly taken by those who make it their business to estimate the value of the risks which are brought under their notice. Another advantage of the system is that each buyer at once feels the state of his own credit, and is made to pay for any unusual risk that may attach to it; the rate at which his bills can be discounted is known to the seller, and he makes his price accordingly.

With that directness which is a striking characteristic of Americans, inquiry officers are allowed to demand from every man carrying on business a distinct statement of his affairs for the guidance of the office in answering applications respecting him. Of course no man is bound to supply this information, but if he did not supply it when required his credit would receive a serious blow, and if he gave a wrong statement it would be regarded as a fraud, and in the event of his failure, he would be liable to severe punishment. The openness which prevails in American life is astonishing to an Englishman. It seems to be the duty of every man to tell his neighbours all that he knows about himself, and it is their business to learn all they can. In many cases this is done officially, and certain companies are called upon to make periodical returns to the officials of their State, and these statements are published in detail. You see in the report published by the State Treasurer at Alabama, for instance, that the Liverpool, London, and Globe Insurance Company, amongst others, has submitted a detailed statement

of its affairs, which is published at the expense of
the State, but to which, however, the Company has
to pay a heavy tax.

I do not know that all these precautions have
lessened the number of failures, but they have the
effect of placing the losses on shoulders better able
to bear the burden than those of young merchants
or striving manufacturers ; many of these in our
own country are nipped in the bud by a bad debt,
although it would be scarcely felt by a discount
company, receiving suitable premiums to provide
against such losses.

In every public office that I entered in America
I not only received the most active and polite
attention, but I saw the same civility manifested to
each applicant—rich or poor. The highest official is
always accessible if you can only wait a few minutes
until he has disposed of the earlier arrivals, with
whom he is in conversation. You are expected to
stand at the coat tails of your immediate pre-
decessor, and hear all that passes. The sub-
ordinates, or rather the co-officials, will put in a
word if they have occasion without the slightest
hesitation, but without any disrespect. I could
never tell by the manner of men which were
highest in rank.

How different in London ! In one week it was
my ill fortune to pay four visits to public depart-

ments. On the first occasion the clerk was combing his hair, and after giving me a stare he proceeded with the operation. Some minutes elapsed, when, without turning his head, he said "You're too late for to-day." On the second visit I took care to be there before three o'clock. Several clerks were present, apparently with nothing to do; and I was passed on from one to another with a series of small sneers until I got to the last, who had no excuse for putting off the work to his neighbour. At another office I cannot say that I did not get prompt attention, for the clerks were able to supply my wants without for a moment interrupting the loud conversation they were carrying on with each other, on topics which were no doubt interesting, as they had nothing to do with official work.

At the fourth visit, after wasting about half-an-hour because the chief, whom I had to see, was at lunch, I was ushered into his august and pompous presence. Here I saw another side to the vulgar indifference which the clerks manifested in the outer office. Their servility was positively painful, and, as they cowered under the dogmatic manner in which they were addressed by the chief, I thought that it might be better for them, as well as for the public, if they recognised, and were under, the sovereignty of the people.

A 2

American newspapers are conducted with an energy at least equal to that which is manifested in the United Kingdom. The daily papers published in New York, Chicago, and San Francisco occupy a Metropolitan position, and may be compared with newspapers published in London, Dublin, and Edinburgh. Their telegraphic news is wonderfully comprehensive, their local news very lively and somewhat personal, their leading articles always interesting. It seems to be a standing instruction to all connected with American papers that they must on no account be dull; if the facts to be given are not exciting, the imagination must be drawn upon. Every inch of the paper, including the money article, must be lively. They advocate with sparkling energy the views and objects to which they are devoted; but, with one or two exceptions, they are not patterns of consistency.

In the places named most of the papers are personal property, and under personal management; but in smaller towns newspapers are often published as party organs and sustained for party purposes. Almost every town in the States has its daily paper, and many of these could not be carried on but for caucus support. Sunday is the great day for American newspapers; the most racy articles and the most lively descriptions are given on that day, which is also the great day for advertisements. Nearly all daily papers appear on Sunday, but some are not published on Monday mornings; the papers published on Mondays often devote a page to sermons.

In the States the number of newspapers published daily is 749 ; tri-weekly, 60 ; semi-weekly, 112 ; weekly, 6,272 ; total, 7,193. The comparison of these numbers with the number of newspapers published in this country shows how far we are behindhand in point of numbers. In the United Kingdom we have—daily papers, 160 ; tri-weekly, 27 ; semi-weekly, 120 ; and weekly, 1,467 ; total, 1,774 ; against 7,193 in the States.

In point of size our penny papers compare favourably with the newspapers of the States, which are charged from 1½d. to 2½d. per copy ; but as to style and value there will, of course, be a difference of opinion. Americans think our papers unmistakably dull, and wonder why we give so many words for so little news, and they loudly complain that they cannot obtain in the English papers information of what takes place in the States. This complaint is well-founded, and it is the more striking from the fact that the English traveller in the States is kept well posted with what is passing in his own country Not only in the Eastern, but also in the Western,

States I found each morning a synopsis of everything important that had been said or done in the
United Kingdom.

In the *Nineteenth Century* Mr. Dale has
published a valuable series of papers, entitled
" Impressions of America."   I have read these
papers with that intense interest usually felt in a
subject to which one's attention has been specially
directed ; and I am not a little pleased to find
that Mr. Dale confirms, in many respects, my own
observations.   This is especially the case in
reference to the quiet and orderly demeanour of
the American people.   But in two important particulars my experience differed so much from
Mr. Dale's that I venture to make some comments
upon these topics.

Writing of the Conservative feeling which
prevails in a population of farmers owning their
own land, Mr. Dale says, " If a couple of millions
of American voters were suddenly transferred to
English constituencies, the Conservative reaction
would probably receive a great accession of
vigour. Of course the Church would be dis-
established within a few months after the first
general election."

What effect the suggested importation of
American voters would have upon the Conser-

vative reaction I do not propose to discuss, but
the statement that it would, "of course, lead to
the disestablishment of the English Church," or
have any tendency in that direction, involves a
view of American opinion entirely opposed to
anything which I was able to discover. Before
I visited America, I had been constantly told
that I should find there such a liberal voluntary
support of religious teaching and services as
would at once prove the non-necessity for any
State aid for religious purposes. I did find
throughout the States—in the North, the West,
and the South—remarkable illustrations of vigorous
and liberal voluntary support; but I also discovered that personal voluntary efforts were constantly assisted by State aid in the shape of
grants, the aggregate value of which is enormous.
I was unable to discover the slightest indisposition
on the part of any persons to give or accept State
aid for the support of religious or benevolent
institutions ; on the contrary, it seemed to be
regarded as the most natural thing that the State
should assist institutions which were found to
be of public advantage.

     It was not an uncommon circumstance for the
State to vote supplies for the support of Schools or
Asylums which had been established by voluntary

efforts, and in which religious teaching was an essential part of the scheme. In doing so, the management was usually allowed to remain in the hands of the promoters, and it appeared to be generally considered that the State was doing a good thing in availing itself of the assistance of philanthropic and experienced gentlemen, while the promoters welcomed the assistance of the State as calculated to give permanence and stability to their conceptions. A good understanding and kindly feeling between the State and the people form one of the most pleasing and advantageous features of American life. It does not seem to occur to anyone to look upon the State as antagonistic, and as to its being irreligious, why, is it not a part of themselves? This friendly feeling all round towards the State may lead to concurrent endowment, and in fact it has tended to this, but as to disestablishment it would not be thought of as a principle. If an institution supported by the State become useless or corrupt it must be reformed or given up, but it would appear to an American quite natural that the State should continue to support an institution, provided that it continued to be worthy of support.

If an American had to consider the question of disestablishment in England he would look at the subject from a practical point of view ; he would make himself acquainted with what the Church was doing, how far her work was useful, and what it cost the State. It would not occur to him that the existence of an Established Church was of itself a standing injustice to Catholics or Dissenters ; for as a Quaker is aggrieved by the existence of an army, so may a Catholic or Dissenter be aggrieved by the existence of a State Church ; but in each case the Government are bound to regard the safety and welfare of the community from their own point, of view, and it would be upon a balance of advantages to the community that an American would decide for or against disestablishment.

Mr. Dale says that in America " The respect for the rights of property is positively super-stitious. 'Mr. Cross's Artisans' Dwelling Act,' and the proceedings of the Charity Commissioners appear to many Americans perfectly revolutionary." Here again my experience differed entirely from Mr. Dale's. It appears to me that in the States public interests are regarded as being of far more importance than the rights of property or private rights of any kind. The owners of property, so far as I could judge, scarcely assume those absolute and uncompromising rights of which we know so much. The owner of a house would not seek to prevent the use of his roof for the fixing of a telegraph pole—he would be looked upon as a perfect bear if he did so. The owner of a field would not expect the public to go round if it were more convenient to walk or drive across it. It seems to be admitted that property must be held subject to the least possible interference with natural rights ; whereas, in England it appears to be taken for granted that all natural rights have long since ceased. A landowner on this side of the Atlantic thinks it a great hardship that he has to give the public a narrow right of way in lieu of the unlimited freedom they once enjoyed, but in the States a landowner would be delighted if he could get the public to keep to a definite road instead of wandering where they please.

When an American comes to this country he feels acutely the limitations which law and custom have placed upon individual action. He admits that we have good horses, but he adds there is "nowhere to ride to." If he feels inclined to be industrious, he can't get a bit of land to cultivate ; if he could buy a cow there is no place upon which she could be grazed. His road is limited to fixed and narrow paths, and his labour to be successful must be confined in like manner. If he offered himself as a man who could do anything he would get no employment, as it is understood that a man who can do anything is one who can do nothing well; whereas, in the States, a man who could not, or would not, do anything is regarded as wanting in will and capacity.

Life in the States, both by law and custom, is far more free and open than it is in this country, and yet the Americans justly pride themselves in being a law abiding people. In fact, they combine order and freedom in perhaps a greater degree than is to be found in any other country.

It is greatly to be regretted that the United States census of 1870 was very imperfectly taken. Several causes contributed to this unfortunate result; instead of making the enumeration on one day, as is done in this country, one hundred days were allowed, during any part of which time the enumerator might do his work. This introduced a serious element of uncertainty, for, although in theory the duplication arising from change of residence during the hundred days would be precisely the same as the tendency to omission, in practice there existed a practical resistance to duplication, for the head of a family previously enumerated objects to be taken again, whereas a family not taken at all does not make any effort to get on the register. The greatest failure in

reference to the census was occasioned by the insufficient payment made to the enumerators, who
soon discovered that the work to be done was more
than they expected, and that the payment for it
was inadequate.   More than two thousand of them
threw up the work, but were compelled to continue it
under the provisions of the Census Act.   These
unwilling officers were not likely to do their work
carefully.

The census showed some startling results.   It
was found that the population was three millions
short of what it would have been but for the war,
for, although the direct loss by wounds and
disease was 850,000—viz., 500,000 among the
Union Army, and 350,000 in the Confederate—yet
the check on births and immigration and other causes
made a total difference of three millions.   It was
found that there had been a great retardation of
increase in the coloured population.   The pro-
portional gain amongst them in ten years should
have been about one million ; the actual increase
was only 438,178.

The Chief Enumerator, Mr. Superintendent
Walker, in a very significant paragraph on
the subject, writes—" A fifth cause may be
alluded to, namely, the notorious growth of
habits of life in many sections of the country

which tend strongly to reduce the rate of the national increase, and which, if persisted in, will make the showing of another census hardly as satisfactory as the present, even without a devastating war to account for the loss of hundreds of thousands in the hospital or battle field. No one can be familiar with life in the Eastern and Middle States generally, and in the Western cities, and not be aware that children are not born to American parents as they were in the early days of the country. Luxury, fashion, and the vice of ' boarding ' combine to limit the increase of families to a degree that in some sections even threatens the perpetuation of our native stock. This tendency is not one that requires to be brought out by statistical comparisons. It is patent, palpable, and needs no proof."

It is a pity that Mr. Superintendent Walker did not condescend to particulars. Statisticians are apt to doubt assertions " which do not require proof." It is therefore fortunate that Dr. Edwin Snow, the Chief Superintendent of the Census in Rhode Island, has supplied some statistics which corroborate in a remarkable manner Mr. Walker's statement.

THE FOLLOWING TABLE SHOWS THE AGES AND NATIVITY OF MARRIED WOMEN IN THE CITY OF

PROVIDENCE, AND NUMBER OF CHILDREN IN 1875 :—

Birth-places of the Mothers.	Married Women, 15 to 50.	Children born in 1875.	Ratio, Women to 1 Child.	Children to each 100 Women.
United States	9,159	1,227	7·46	13·39
Ireland	4,335	948	4 57	21·86
England, Scotland, and Wales......	1,330	243	5 47	18·27
Germany...........................	298	63	4 73	21 14
British America	524	116	4 51	22·13
Portugal and Western Island	93	24	3 87	25·80
Sweden and Norway	31	11	2 82	35 50
France............................	27	4	6 75	14·81
Switzerland	17	1	17·00	5 83
Italy.............................	16	12	1·33	75·00
Other foreign countries...........	49	15	3 26	30·61
Total foreign	6,720	1,437	4·67	21·38
Total American and foreign	15,879	2,665	5 95	16 77

Dr. Snow writes :—" This table shows that, during the year 1875, the American married women in Providence in the usual child-bearing period of life, bore a very greatly less percentage of children than the foreign married women in the same period of life. Each hundred of the women born in Ireland had 8·47 more children, on an average, in 1875, than the same number of women born in the United States. The 6,720 women in the table who were born in foreign countries had in that year 210 more children than the 9,159 women who were born in the United States. If the women of American birth had borne the same proportion of children in 1875 as the women of foreign birth there would have been in that year 1,958 children of American parentage, instead of

1,227, the actual number, or an increase of 731 over the number reported."

It would have been better to have omitted from this table the instances where fewer than 100 mothers were enumerated, as a smaller number cannot give a reliable average, but if the reader will examine the cases where larger numbers are dealt with he will discover most important results. The census of 1880 will probably throw further light upon this and many other topics of great interest.

Tables have been compiled showing the number of deaths from various diseases in the States, but it is difficult to know whether any great reliance can be placed on them, as there is no efficient system of registration in the States. The census enumerators were required to ascertain all the deaths that had taken place in families from June 1st, 1869, to May 31st, 1870, which is evidently a very uncertain mode of getting at the facts; and so imperfect did it prove to be that only 59 per cent. of the total number of deaths known to have taken place were returned.

The following statistics are extremely interesting, although it is doubtful how far American statements are strictly accurate.

PROPORTIONS BORN AND SURVIVING AT CERTAIN
AGES, AND EXPECTATION OF LIFE :—

Age.	Survivors. United States Census, 1870. Elliott.	Survivors. England and Wales, 1838 to 1854. Farr.	Expectation of Life.	
			United States.	England and Wales.
0	10,000	10,000	39·25	40·9
10	6,986	7,025	45 3	47·4
20	6,568	6,628	38·2	39 9
30	5,774	6,037	32·5	33·3
40	5,049	5,386	26·4	26·7
50	4,261	4,643	20·4	20·1
60	3,316	3,698	14·7	13·9
70	2,159	2,380	9·8	8·7
80	954	901	6·0	5·1
90	183	115	3·4	2·9
100	5.8	2	2·5	2·2

According to these tables, the expectation of
life is greatly in favour of England until about the
age of 45, when it turns in favour of the States.
At 50 and every subsequent decade the balance is
decidedly in their favour. At the age of 100 the
proportion of Americans living out of 10,000 is 5·8
and in England only 2 ; although at ten years of
age the expectation of life is 5 per cent. better in
England than in the States.

The next census of the United States is looked
for with great interest, and it is to be hoped that no
pains or cost will be spared to make it as perfect as
possible. The States have a wider and more varied
field of inquiry into vital and social statistics than
any other nation, and it would be difficult to over-
estimate the importance to themselves and to the
world of making a good use of their opportunities.

To discover the conditions of human life and the influence of human actions is one of the noblest studies. Such excellent results have followed the attention which the subject has received—in the prolongation of life and the diminution of disease—that every encouragement is given to persevere in a course from which so much may be anticipated. In the States these investigations are of the utmost importance. The statistics given show that the deaths from specified diseases, which diminished between 1850 and 1860, increased between 1860 and 1870, this increase being probably due to the fact that the war diverted attention from social and sanitary questions. It will be interesting to learn whether the subsequent ten years of peace have renewed attention to these subjects.

Perhaps the most obvious and important difference in the social life of England and America is the position occupied by women. In an English family, as a rule, the greatest consideration is shown to the boys ; their amusement and education must be first regarded. If one member of the family is to be sent to college, who would think of sending a girl? It must be a boy, of course. What is the use of assisting a girl, who cannot carry the family name down to posterity? or, if it is a question of

profit and loss, what is the advantage of teaching
girls, who can seldom earn money under any
circumstances? Things are viewed differently in
the States. There the wishes of the girls would be
first listened to, and their education would be first
provided for. It seems to be taken for granted
that the boys must make their own way; from
sixteen upwards they have no difficulty in earning
their own living. They are expected to do it, and
moreover, they like to do it. An American boy is as
eager to start life on his own account as is a grey-
hound to rush after the hare.

In the matter of early independence both sexes
are equal; it seems to be a principle of American
education to impress upon the smallest children a
sense of responsibility and independence. Neither
in home life nor at school are children dictated to
as they are in this country. An American mother
will appeal to, and reason with, or ridicule, the
smallest child, treating it at once as if it were a
reasonable and responsible being. At a very early
age girls are expected to manage their own affairs
in the matter of dress and expenses, for which,
frequently, property will be given, upon the annual
proceeds of which the girl meets her expenses. A
little later in life she receives visitors of both sexes
on her own account, and when a young gentleman

or a lady calls on Miss ——— neither the father nor the mother is expected to appear. In ordinary business engagements women are constantly found. I seldom went into any office where I did not see women engaged. It is not an uncommon thing for a man in business to engage a woman as his short-hand clerk, who takes down his letters from dictation, and acts as his secretary.

This state of things has been brought about largely by the war; when men were demanded for the army their places were in many instances taken by women, and thus they were extensively introduced into business life. The great respect universally paid to women is obvious under all circumstances. At hotels a special entrance is provided for them, and at the post offices, railway stations, and other public establishments, separate places are arranged for their applications. In travelling, a woman is universally treated with consideration, and it is the pride of Americans that a woman, unaccompanied, can travel from one end of their country to the other without being subjected to any unpleasantness or to a vestige of impertinence. This course is made the more easy as disreputable women are not allowed to appear in public. They are not openly seen in streets, parks, or places of amusement, either by day or by night. Nothing disgusts

B 2

Americans and other foreigners so much as the
freedom allowed to abandoned women in our
streets, parks, and railway stations, the counterpart
of which can be found in no other country in the
world.

Women might emigrate to the United States
and settle in any locality without the slightest
difficulty. If three or four women left England and
established themselves in almost any part of the
States they would find the work of life freely open
to them, and they might enter upon any ordinary
calling without reproach or suspicion. The laws
respecting women vary in different States, but,
generally speaking, they are very similar to our
own, and, although they are in many respects
unjust, but little is heard about women's rights in
the States, because custom usually gives woman
more than her rights.

No one, I think, will hesitate to admit that
the superior position assigned to women in the
States has had an excellent effect upon their own
characters and upon the general tone of society.
To some extent women may owe their position in
the States to the fact of being in a minority, as
there are about 103 men to every 100 women ; but
I do not think this is the real cause of their
advancement. It arises, in my opinion, from the

universal principle, or tone, which pervades American society, attributing to every one personal rights and responsibilities as an individual ; and this universal recognition of personal rights is favourable to the development of those qualities in which women can excel.

One of the problems which the progress of the United States is likely to solve is the results of amalgamation of races. Not only are the German and French, the Scotch and Irish, and all other varieties of Europeans intermarrying, but the Negro and Chinese elements have come into the account more completely than some persons are disposed to admit. Both these races are becoming amalgamated with the other races in a manner which it is impossible to distinguish ; and the process, once commenced, proceeds with accelerated rapidity as it becomes more and more impossible to trace the ancestry. No one can look at the children in the schools for coloured persons without seeing that the negro race is rapidly losing its complexion. The Chinese are more easily rendered undiscoverable, and it is not an unknown thing for white girls to marry Chinamen, who, it is said, make very docile and domestic husbands.

What the effect will be of this amalgamation of all the races in the world no one seems able to

predict. We may feel some confidence in the fact
that it takes place in accordance with a strong
natural tendency which presumably is given
for the advancement of the human race. The
inclination to marry in those who differ in character
and temperament is perhaps one of the most effective means of human advancement; and if that
inclination overleaps the bonds of race we may
still hope that it will serve some good purpose, and
promote the survival of the fittest.

The men who are now at the head of the Federal
Government are worthy of the important position
which they occupy. Although the salaries of the
President and all his Ministers amount to less than
half the sum settled upon the King of Greece, no one
can complain that the business of the country is in
idle or inefficient hands. We hear less of Cabinet
Ministers in America than of those occupying a
similar position in this country, because the
Ministers are not members of Congress, and thus
their sayings and doings obtain less publicity than
with us.

The actual administrative business of the
Federal Government is conducted by seven heads
of departments, who form the Cabinet.

Mr. Hayes named as his Secretary of State for
Foreign Affairs William Evarts, a prominent New
York lawyer. He was for a short time United States

Attorney-General—from July 15th, 1868, to March 4th, 1869—when Mr. Andrew Johnson was President. Mr. Evarts represented the United States at the Geneva Arbitration of the Alabama Claims in 1872. He has never belonged to the office-seeking class of politicians, and has not hitherto been regarded as a strict partisan. Originally an old-line Whig, then a Republican during the period of the civil war, he afterwards affiliated with the "Liberals," and took part in the "Greely movement," or the political combination of Republicans and Democrats who sought to elect Horace Greely President. Mr. Evarts' fame as a lawyer extends throughout the States, and although he is never an impassioned advocate, no more persistent or painstaking counsel ever laboured to carry a client's cause to a successful issue. He was employed to conduct Mr. Hayes' case before the Electoral Commission, and it is universally conceded that he managed it as he did the defence of the Rev. Henry Ward Beecher—with singular adroitness and marvellous grasp of legal points. Mr. Evarts defended Mr. Johnson when the latter was impeached, and it was said that to his success on that occasion he owed his appointment as United States Attorney-General.

Mr. Hayes chose as his Secretary of the Treasury Mr. John Sherman, brother of the

celebrated General Sherman.   As Mr. Sherman
was suspected of favouring the " Ohio idea " of an
unlimited paper currency, and a bi-metallic standard
which included the free coinage of silver, his appointment was not very favourably received at first by the
moneyed interests in the Eastern and Middle States.
Like all the other members of the Cabinet, with the
exception of the Secretary of the Interior, Mr.
Sherman is by profession a lawyer.   Mr. Sherman
has always been regarded as a strict Republican.
He represented Ohio, his native State, in the House
of Representatives, and in 1861 was elected to the
United States Senate, in which body he remained
until his elevation to the Secretaryship.

The appointment of Mr. George W. Mc.Crary,
of Iowa, as Secretary of War, was a disappointment
to the leaders of the Republican party, but it is now
generally admitted that he has made an excellent
Cabinet officer.

Mr. Richard W. Thompson, the Secretary of
the Navy, who was born in Virginia, may be
looked upon as partly representing the South, its
views and claims, which Mr. Hayes promised
should not be ignored in his Cabinet.   His appointment was another surprise to the strict
Republican politicians, as he had never been
identified as the follower of any of the great leaders

of the party. It is affirmed that he has lived West most of his life, and has seen but little of ships.

Mr. Carl Schurz, a well-known German Democrat, who participated in the insurrection at Baden in 1848-9, and afterwards fled to America, was chosen to fill the post of Secretary of the Interior. Mr. Schurz settled in the State of Missouri, and followed the profession of journalism. When the Civil War broke out he joined the Federals, and rose to the rank of Brigadier-General of Volunteers. In 1869 he was elected as United States Senator from Missouri, and in conjunction with Mr. Evarts he warmly espoused the cause of Mr. Greely, being, in fact, one of the prime leaders of the Liberal Republican movement. Mr. Schurz gave as his chief reason for supporting Mr. Hayes that the great need of the country was Civil Service reform, and that Mr. Hayes had un-reservedly promised to bring it about. The appointment of Mr. Schurz was generally well received, as his abilities and eminence were widely recognised.

The acknowledged Southern representative in the Cabinet is the Postmaster-General, Mr. David McKey, of Tennessee, of which place he is a native. Mr. Mc.Key is a Democrat, and is supposed to have had in his earlier years leanings to the Whig

party. During the Civil War he was Lieut.-Colonel of
the 43rd Tennessee Infantry of the Confederate States.
He was elected United States Senator from his own
State in 1875, and when overtures were opened
with the Southern members by Mr. Hayes to induce
one of them to take a place in the Cabinet, Mr.
Mc.Key, after some delay, received this appointment.

The remaining member of the Cabinet is the
Attorney-General, Mr. Charles Devens, of Massachusetts. Mr. Devens was a conspicuous citizen of
his section, and was an Associate Justice of the
Supreme Court of Massachusetts during 1873-77. In
politics he is a Republican, but not of the extreme
school.

The President, Mr. Hayes, was a lawyer
in Ohio, greatly esteemed in his own State, but
elsewhere he was not so well known. His
election, as we have seen, was the result of a
compromise, and was probably one of the most
fortunate circumstances which have occurred for the
United States. Had an extreme partisan been
nominated by the Republicans, and elected President, the conflict between the North and South
might have assumed a very serious character. Mr.
Hayes promised conciliation to the South, and
reformation of the Civil Service. In both respects
he has achieved a large amount of success, not-

withstanding the strenuous opposition of extreme politicians in his own party. The tone of official and social life in Washington has been completely changed since his election. He has been ably supported in this social reformation by Mrs. Hayes, who presides at the White House with an intelligent dignity which has won universal respect.

In bringing these pages to a close, it is pleasant to be able to record the advent of renewed prosperity in the States ; recent advices speak of depression passing away, and industry reviving. If forecasts in human affairs possess any value, we may feel every confidence that the immediate future of the United States will be marked by prosperity even more substantial than that which they have enjoyed in any period of their history.

UNITED STATES.

Statement, showing the Areas, Families, and Dwellings, 1870.

STATES AND TERRITORIES.	AREAS.		FAMILIES.		DWELLINGS.	
	Square Miles.	Number of Persons to a Square Mile.	Number of Families.	Number of Persons to a Family.	Number of Dwellings.	Number of Persons to a Dwelling.
Alabama.............	50,722	19·66	102,7(4	4·92	196,3_7	5·03
Arkansas.............	52,198	9·30	96,1g5	5·04	93,195	5·20
California	188,981	2·29	128,752	4·35	126,307	4·44
Connecticut	4,750	113·15	1 4.981	4·67	96.880	5·55
Delaware	2,1:0	58·97	: 2·900	5·46	22.577	5·54
Florida	59,268	3·19	39,394	4·77	41,017	4·57
Georgia	58,800	20·42	237,85y	4·98	236,436	5·01
Illinois...............	55,410	45·84	474,533	5·35	464,1.5	5·47
Indiana	33,809	39·71	320,160	5·25	318,409	5·48
Iowa.................	55,045	21·69	222,430	5·37	219·846	5·44
Kansas..............	81,310	4·48	72·493	5·03	71,671	5·13
Kentucky	37,680	35·33	232,797	5·67	224·969	5·87
Louisiana	41,346	17·58	158,099	4·60	150,427	4·83
Maine	35,000	17·41	131,071	4·78	12r,953	5·14
Maryland	11,124	70·20	140.078	5·57	129,620	6·02
Massachusetts	7,800	186·81	3 5.534	4·77	236,473	6·16
Michigan........	56,451	20.90	241,006	4·91	237,(3 i	5·t0
Minnesota	83,531	5·26	82,471	5·33	81.1(0	5·42
Mississippi	47,000	17·56	164,828	4·96	164·150	6·04
Missouri	50,704	26·34	316,917	6·13	292.796	5·87
Nebraska	75,995	1·69	25,075	4·91	25,144	4·89
Nevada	104,125	0·41	9,880	4·30	12,990	3·27
New Hampshire	9 280	34·30	72,144	4·11	67,043	4·75
New Jersey	8,320	108·91	183,(4 ;	·95	155,936	5·81
New York	47,000	93·25	898.772	4·88	688·559	6·37
North Carolina.......	50,704	21·13	205.970	5·20	202,769	5·29
Ohio	39,964	66·69	521.981	5·11	495,(67	5·38
Oregon.............	95,274	0·95	18.504	4·9)	19,372	4·69
Pennsylvania.........	46,000	76·56	675.498	5· 1	635,680	5·54
Rhode Island........	1,306	166·43	46,133	4·71	34,·28	6·24
South Carolina.......	34,000	20·75	15r,105	4·67	143,485	4·92
Tennessee	45,600	27·60	231,3·5	5·44	224·816	5·60
Texas	274,356	2·98	154,483	5·30	141,685	5·73
Vermont.............	10,312	32·37	76,062	4·t9	66,145	5·00
Virginia	38,348	31·95	231,574	5·29	224,947	4·45
West Virginia	23,000	19·22	78,474	5·63	7·,854	5·61
Wisconsin	53,924	13·56	300,155	5·27	1r7,·98	5·35
THE STATES	1,'81,467	19·11	7,431,607	5·09	6,941,603	5·49
Alaska (unorganised)..	577,390	—	—	—	—	—
Arizona	113,916	0·08	2,299	4·22	2,822	3·42
Colorado	104,800	0·38	9.358	4·23	10,009	3·98
Dakota	150,932	0·90	3.090	4·59	3,231	4·39
District of Columbia ..	64	2057·81	25.272	5·21	23·308	5·65
Idaho	86,294	0·17	4,104	3·(5	4,632	3·25
Indian (country)	68,991	—	—	—	—	—
Montana.............	143,776	0·14	7,053	2·9:	9.450	2·18
New Mexico	121,201	0·76	21,4·9	4·28	21,053	4·36
Utah................	84,476	1·03	17.210	5·04	18·290	4·75
Washington	69,994	0·34	5,673	4·22	6.066	3·95
Wyoming	97,883	0·09	2,248	4·06	2,379	3·83
THE TERRITORIES..	1,619,417	0·27	97,756	4·48	101,230	4·37
TOTAL— THE UNITED STATES	3,6 3,88	10·39	7,579·363	5·00	7,(42·833	5·47
1860.	3,026,494	10·39	5 210·934	5·28	4.969·6·2	5·53
1850.	2,980,950	7·78	2 598·240	5·5	3 36·,o37	5·4

STATEMENT, *showing the aggregate Population at each Census.*

STATES AND TERRITORIES.	1790.	1810.	18?0.	1840.	1850.	1860.	1870.
NUMBER OF STATES:	**17.**	**24.**	**27.**	**29.**	**33.**	**36.**	**37.**
Virginia............	747,61*	974,600	1,211,405	1,239,797	1,421,661	1,596 318	1.225,163
Pennsylvania	434,373	810,091	1 348,233	1,724,033	2,311.782	2,9 6,215	3,521.951
North Carolina	393 751	555,500	737,987	753,419	869,039	992,622	1,071,361
Massachusetts	378,787	472,040	610,408	737,699	994,514	1,231.066	1 457.351
New York..........	310,120	959 040	1,918,608	2,423 921	3,097,394	3,880.735	4,382,759
Maryland	319,728	380 546	447,040	470,019	583,034	687,049	780.894
South Carolina	249 073	415,115	581,185	594,398	668,507	703,708	705,606
Connecticut	237,946	261,942	297,675	309,978	370,792	460,147	537,454
New Jersey	184,139	245 562	320,823	373,306	489,555	672,035	906,096
New Hampshire	141,885	214,460	269,328	284,574	317,976	326,073	318 300
Maine.............	96,540	228,705	399,453	501,793	583 169	628 279	626.915
Vermont	85,425	21 .895	280,652	291,948	314,120	315,098	330,551
Georgia ....:	82,548	252 433	516,823	691,392	906.185	1 057 286	1,184,109
Kentucky	73,677	406,511	687,917	779 828	982,405	1,155 684	1,321.011
Rhode Island	68,825	76,931	97,199	108 830	147.545	174 620	217,353
Delaware	59,096	72 674	76 748	78,085	91,532	112 216	125.015
Tennessee	35,691	261.727	681,904	829 210	1,002.717	1,109 801	1 258,520
Ohio		230,760	937,903	1,519,467	1.980,329	2,339,511	2,665,260
Mississippi		40,352	136,621	375,651	606,526	791 305	827.922
Indiana		24 520	343 031	685,866	988,416	1,360,428	1,680,637
Louisiana		76 556	215,739	352,411	517.762	608,002	726,915
Missouri..........		20,845	140,455	383,702	682,044	1,182 012	1,721,295
Illinois		12,282	157.447	476,183	851,470	1,711 951	2,539,891
Michigan		4,762	31,639	212,267	397,654	749 113	1,184.059
Alabama			309,527	590,756	771,623	964,201	996 992
Arkansas			30,388	97,574	209,897	435,450	484,471
Florida			34,730	54,477	87,445	140,424	187,748
Iowa				43,112	192,214	674,913	1,194,020
Wisconsin.........				30,915	305,391	775,881	1,054 670
California					92,597	379 994	560,347
Minnesota					6,077	172,023	439,706
Oregon					13,294	52,465	90,923
Texas					212,592	604,215	818,579
Kansas						107,203	364,399
Nebraska						28,841	122,993
Nevada						6,857	42,491
West Virginia							442,014
TOTAL— THE STATES	3,929,214	7,215.858	12,820,868	17,019,641	23,167,262	31,183.744	38,115,641
Arizona							9,658
Colorado						34.277	39,864
Dakota						4 837	14 181
District of Columbia		24,023	39,834	43,712	51.687	75,080	131,700
Idaho							14,999
Montana							20,595
New Mexico.......					61,547	93,516	91,874
Utah					11,380	40,273	86.786
Washington						11,504	23.955
Wyoming							9,118
TOTAL— THE TERRITORIES..		24,023	39,834	43,712	124,614	259,057	442,730
GRAND TOTAL— THE UNITED STATES.	3,929,214	7,239,881	12 866,002	17,069,453	23,291,876	31,443,821	38,558,371

STATEMENT, *showing the Number of Schools, All Classes, Teachers, Pupils and Income from all Sources.*

1870. SCHOOLS.	Number of Schools.	TEACHERS.		PUPILS.		INCOME YEAR ENDING 1st JUNE, 1870.			
		Male.	Female.	Male.	Female.	From Endowment.	From Taxation and Public Funds.	From other Sources, including Tuition.	Total.
						£	£	£	£
PUBLIC SCHOOLS	125,059	74,174	109,624	3,120,052	3,108,008	28,966	11,771,101	1,006,126	12,806,134
NOT PUBLIC — Classical, Professional, and Scientific	2,545	7,776	5,001	148,810	106,380	671,200	464,050	2,399,980	3,535,181
NOT PUBLIC — Others than Classical, Professional, and Scientific	14,025	11,389	13,688	353,134	373,554	32,649	114,056	2,592,523	2,739,229
TOTAL	141,629	93,329	127,713	3,621,436	3,587,942	732,757	12,349,207	5,998,580	19,080,545

SUMMARY.

Year.	Number of Schools.	Number of Teachers.	Number of Pupils.	INCOME YEAR ENDING 1st JUNE.			
				From Endowment.	From Taxation and Public Funds.	From other Sources, including Tuition.	Total.
				£	£	£	£
1870	141,629	221,042	7,209,938	732,757	12,349,207	5,998,580	19,080,545
1866	115,224	160,241	5,477,037	439,926	3,983,907	2,517,788	6,943,622
1850	87,257	105,853	3,642,694	184,752	1,518,023	1,529,624	3,232,400

Foreign Travelers in America
1810–1935

AN ARNO PRESS COLLECTION

Hardy, Mary (McDowell) Duffus. **Through Cities and Prairie Lands:** Sketches of an American Tour. 1881.

Holmes, Isaac. **An Account of the United States of America,** Derived from Actual Observation, During a Residence of Four Years in That République, Including Original Communications. [1823].

Ilf, Ilya and Eugene Petrov. **Little Golden America:** Two Famous Soviet Humorists Survey These United States. Translated by Charles Malamuth. 1937.

Kerr, Lennox. **Back Door Guest.** 1930.

Kipling, Rudyard. **American Notes.** 1899.

Leng, John. **America in 1876:** Pencillings During a Tour in the Centennial Year, With a Chapter on the Aspects of American Life. 1877.

Longworth, Maria Theresa (Yelverton). **Teresina in America.** 1875. 2 volumes in one.

Low, A[lfred] Maurice. **America at Home.** [1908].

Marshall, W[alter] G[ore]. **Through America:** Or, Nine Months in the United States. 1881.

Mitchell, Ronald Elwy. **America:** A Practical Handbook. 1935.

Moehring, Eugene P. **Urban America and the Foreign Traveler, 1815-1855.** With Selected Documents on 19th-Century American Cities. 1974.

Muir, Ramsay. **America the Golden:** An Englishman's Notes and Comparisons. 1927.

Price, M[organ] Philips. **America After Sixty Years:** The Travel Diaries of Two Generations of Englishmen. 1936.

Sala, George Augustus. **America Revisited:** From the Bay of New York to the Gulf of Mexico and from Lake Michigan to the Pacific. 1883. 3rd edition. 2 volumes in one.

Saunders, William. **Through the Light Continent;** Or, the United States in 1877-8. 1879. 2nd edition.

Smith, Frederick [Edwin] (Lord Birkenhead). **My American Visit.** 1918.

Stuart, James. **Three Years in North America.** 1833. 2 volumes in one.

Teeling, William. **American Stew.** 1933.

Vivian, H. Hussey. **Notes of a Tour in America from August 7th to November 17th, 1877.** 1878.

Wagner, Charles. **My Impressions of America.** Translated by Mary Louise Hendee. 1906.

Wells, H. G. **The Future in America:** A Search After Realities. 1906.